Sean O'Faolain

❧ A Critical Introduction

By Maurice Harmon

WOLFHOUND PRESS

Published 1984 Wolfhound Press, 68 Mountjoy Square, Dublin 1.

© Maurice Harmon 1967. New material 1984

First edition by the University of Notre Dame Press,
Notre Dame, Indiana

This is a revised, updated edition

We acknowledge the permission of the University of Notre Dame
for typographical reproduction.

British Library Cataloguing in Publication Data

  Harmon, Maurice
    Sean O'Faolain; a critical introduction
    1. O'Faolain, Sean - Criticism and Interpretation
    I. Title
    823'.91Z. PR6029. F3Z/

    ISBN 0-86327-020-4
    ISBN 0-86327-019-0 Pbk

Cover photo courtesy the *Irish Press*
Typesetting by Redsetter Ltd., Dublin.
Printed and bound by Billings & Sons Ltd.

For Maura

Acknowledgments

Acknowledgments and thanks are due to the following publishers who gave me permission to quote from books by Sean O'Faolain:

The Viking Press, Inc., for permission to quote from *A Nest of Simple Folk* and *Come Back to Erin*.

Jonathan Cape, Ltd., for permission to quote from *Constance Markievicz, Bird Alone,* and *Teresa*.

Thomas Nelson and Sons, Ltd., for permission to quote from *The Autobiography of Theobald Wolfe Tone* and *King of the Beggars*.

Penguin Books for permission to quote from *De Valera* and *The Irish*.

Duell, Sloan & Pearce for permission to quote from *The Great O'Neill*.

William Collins Sons & Co. for permission to quote from *The Short Story* and *South to Sicily*.

Eyre and Spottiswoode, Ltd., for permission to quote from *The Vanishing Hero, Studies in Novelists of the Twenties*.

Little, Brown and Company for permission to quote from *The Finest Stories of Sean O'Faolain; Vive Moi!; The Heat of the Sun; Short Stories, A Study in Pleasure;* and *I Remember! I Remember!*

I also want to thank the publishers who have allowed me to quote the following works:

Lionel Trilling. *The Liberal Imagination, Essays on Literature and Society*. Doubleday and Co., New York, 1954.

Daniel Corkery. *Synge and Anglo-Irish Literature*. Cork University Press, 1931.

Michael Tierney, ed. *Daniel O'Connell, Nine Centenary Essays*. Browne & Nolan, Ltd., Dublin, 1949.

Rev. W. D. Killen. *History of Congregations of the Presbyterian Church in Ireland.* James Clerland, Belfast, 1886.

Seamus Pender, ed. *Feilscribhinn Torna.* Clo Ollscoile Chorcai, 1949.

James A. Reynolds. *The Catholic Emancipation Crisis in Ireland, 1823–1829.* Yale University Press, 1954.

Charles Neider, ed. *The Stature of Thomas Mann.* New Directions Pub. Corp., New York, 1947.

Donal O'Sullivan. *The Irish Free State and Its Senate.* Faber and Faber, Ltd., London, 1950.

S. F. Kenny. *Sources for the Early History of Ireland.* Columbia University Press, New York, 1929.

S. L. Goldberg. *James Joyce.* Grove Press, Inc., New York, 1962.

I also wish to acknowledge the kind permission of the Controller, Stationery Office, Dublin 4, to reprint extracts from the Irish Constitution and Dail Debates.

I am grateful to the *Irish Times* for allowing me to use material first printed in their pages.

I am particularly indebted to Mr. Sean O'Faolain himself, who has generously allowed me to quote from all his writings, including his editorials in *The Bell* and his many articles.

Various scholars and friends have helped me in preparing the book. I am happy to acknowledge the courteous criticism offered by President Jeremiah J. Hogan of University College, Dublin. Professor Roger McHugh, Chairman of the Department of English at that university, read the manuscript and made many helpful observations and suggestions. Dr. Kevin Nowlan of the Department of History helped with the chapter on Daniel O'Connell.

In America I had the good fortune to receive advice and encouragement from Professor John V. Kelleher. Others who offered criticism on various sections were Robert Burns, John Edward Hardy, Francis Murphy, James H. O'Brien, and Maurice O'Connell.

These friends did much to ensure the completion of a study that was pursued amid many journeys to and from America and back and forth across that wide, hospitable continent.

Contents

Introduction
The Man From Half Moon Street   xi

Part I The National Mind

1. *King of the Beggars*   3
2. *The Great O'Neill*   19
3. *De Valera*   32
4. A Dreary Eden   44

Part II Imagination and Faith: The Short Stories

5. Introduction   61
6. Reluctant Rebels   64
7. A Broken World   69
8. Admiring the Scenery: Theory and Practice   81
9. The Silence of the Valley   93
10. A Design for Confusion   107
11. Lovers of the Lake: A Penitential Journey   115
12. Some Bright Destination   129

Part III Revolution and Dislocation

13. The Misfit Hero   139
14. Character and Personality   164
15. Man's Most Ingenious Invention   179
16. The Growth of a Writer   190
    Epilogue   198

    Appendix   200
    Notes   204
    Bibliography   214
    Index   233

The Man From Half Moon Street

Sean O'Faolain was affected by so many of the political, social, and cultural currents of Irish life during the first three decades of this century that his biography reveals not only his own growth to maturity but the progress of his country from colonial dependency to independence. Most Irish writers of his generation were involved with national issues at an impressionable age, but none responded so fervently to so many and such varied attractions.

He was born on February 22, 1900, in Cork, the youngest of a family of three boys. The parents had both come from the country, part of that general drift from farm to town that was characteristic of Irish society at the turn of the century. They lived at No. 5, Half Moon Street, romantic, perhaps, in name and to some degree in O'Faolain's memories of it, but anything but romantic in its day-to-day conditions. His accounts of home stress the dull quality of life that resulted from parental ambitions for their children, from their excessive emphasis on frugality, prayer, hard work, and respectability.

His father, a police constable in the Royal Irish Constabulary, embodied the "law." He was devotedly loyal to the British Empire and its hierarchy of officials, including the local representatives. The boys, consequently, were enjoined to behave properly at all times lest some Cork dignitary or official might be watching them. Their mother, equally devoted to the idea of respectability, urged them to rise in the world, to improve themselves socially. She was a sorrowfully pious, self-driving woman, burdened with anxieties. She took in lodgers to supplement her husband's small salary, roused the boys daily for early Mass, sent them on monotonous walks—up Wellington Road and down Saint Luke's—and dinned into them the need to study hard so that they might get good jobs after they finished school.

It is some measure of the success of the parents' ambitions, although it tells little of the emotional cost for the children, that the eldest son became a priest, the second a revenue inspector in the British Civil Service, and the third a graduate of University College, Cork. Between them they made life almost unbearable for the children. It was a life of poverty and parsimony, a frugal, restrictive existence. Summing it up in his autobiography, *Vive Moi!* (1964), O'Faolain wrote:

> We were shabby-genteels at the lowest possible social level, always living on the edge of false shames and stupid affections, caught between honorable ambitions and pathetic fears, between painful strugglings and gallant strivings, never where we were or where we hoped to be, Janus-faced, throwing glances of desire and ambition upwards and ahead, glances of hatred or contempt downwards and behind.[1]

O'Faolain began his education at the Lancastrian National School. Run by simple brothers, it had a shabby, unprogressive air. There he was happy, lost in its uncomplicated, thoughtless simplicity, attending school for the simple and satisfying reason that he enjoyed it. Later, in 1914, when he went to the Presentation Brothers Secondary School, a "useful cramming factory"[2] for children of the lower middle class, he was unhappy. Education had become something merely practical. He remained there for four years, spurred on by punishment from the teachers and by the "loving blackmail" of the parents, who frequently reminded him that his "wonderful education was costing them great hardship and that for their sake as well as my own, I must profit by it."[3]

Not all his memories of those years are painful. There were compensations for the frugal, restrictive life. One was the possibility of visits to the Cork Opera House, across from his own front door. There his imaginative world was enlarged. Many of the artists stayed at his house. Simon Legree helped him with his homework, as did Long John Silver. Mrs. Wiggs of *Mrs. Wiggs and the Cabbage Patch* drank tea in the kitchen with his mother. The ghost of Hamlet's father chatted with his own father. Through the tall arched stage door he saw men and women passing, "a robed king with a crown, a pirate with a cutlass, ladies and gentlemen in rich robes, beautiful girls . . . soldiers . . . cowboys, a Negro in chains, or a tattered beggar."[4] The Cork Butter Exchange Bank took part in the Battle of Waterloo and played the "Marseillaise." In bewildered and fascinated astonishment, he saw "the here constantly become the elsewhere, the solid dissolve, the familiar become unfamiliar, things and people become most persuasively whatever they were only when they were least whatever they had been so persuasively before and would, just as persuasively, become again a few hours hence."[5] He went to the theater constantly, savoring the romantic delights of *Eliza Comes to Stay, A Girl in a Taxi, The Sorrows of Satan,* and many more.

Annual vacations with relatives in the country also brought release from the respectable regimen of home life. He went, alternately, to his mother's sister in Rathkeale, County Limerick, and to his father's sister in County Dublin or County Kildare. Of the two places, Rathkeale left the strongest impression:

I was where nothing ever changes, where everything recurs. . . . Everything was as solid as the fields, common as a cow, yet timeless and tenuous. . . . Habit and custom ruled here. It was a place breathing its own essence. Nothing was imposed, nothing made, everything grew as softly as the morning light through the blind. Here there was no up W. Road and Down Saint L., no watch-your-step, no for-God's-sake-mind-who-is-behind-you, nothing except Nothing—the lake, a road, a path, a spring-well tasting of iron, the swish of a scythe, a rock to lie on, a hillock to stand on. . . .[6]

It was all holy ground to him. He formed an attachment to it that remained forever, an ineradicable memory of boyhood pleasures. His first novel, *A Nest of Simple Folk* (1934), and a very recent collection of stories, *I Remember! I Remember!* (1961), pay tender and poetic tribute to the seemingly timeless world of Rathkeale.

These rural vacations made him aware of the disadvantages of his urban world, but it was only toward the end of his boyhood that he found compelling reasons for rebelling against its humiliations and restrictions. The effects of such curtailment of freedom is apparent in many places in his writings that are mainly concerned with the struggle of individuals to achieve dignity as human beings within a society that tends to be excessively paternalistic and restrictive. But it is in Book Three of that first novel that O'Faolain's particular situation receives most careful treatment. That final section is a moving account of the boy, Denis Hussey's, homelife, its small pleasures, its poverty, its cruel demands on youth, its piety, its utilitarian view of education. Like most heroes in O'Faolain's novels, his escape to personal freedom is inextricably bound up with the cause of national liberty. Strangely enough, in O'Faolain's own case, it was at school, under an educational system designed to prevent its happening, that he began to hear of his country's heritage of oppression. In a word or a phrase from a teacher, an intonation in his voice, an account of the bravery of Irish soldiers, in numerous little ways, he learnt of the ancient and bitter memories of his race. It was a slow, unconscious process that "burst in a fountaining image of the courage of man"[7] in his response to the Easter Rising of 1916.

His initial reaction to that event was predictably in keeping with the loyalties of his home. Seeing some Irish Volunteers drilling near Half Moon Street, his blood "curled against them, they were so shabby, so absurd, so awkward, so unheroic-looking."[8] The Rising, he felt, was a betrayal of England. But, as the men held out in the burning capitol, as they surrendered with dignity, and as their leaders were shot "in ones, and twos, and threes, everybody and everything I had believed in began to tumble about me."[9] It was the turning point of his early life, leading him away from what his parents believed in and valued, away from their practical, class-conscious ambitions for him, to a romantic identi-

fication with the oppressed people of Ireland and with the sur-
viving relics of native culture and traditions in the Irish-speaking
sections of the West.

He had already begun to learn the native language. By 1917 he
spoke it fluently. By 1918 he no longer went to Rathkeale but to
Irish-speaking Gougane Barra, in West Cork. His symbols now
were a rocky promontory on the Atlantic, a ruined chapel, an
old graveyard, a few small fields—"transfigured by my longing for
that liberty from the body in a nobly patterned world which I
now equated with remoteness, hardness, age, and a traditional life
whose pieties they rounded."[10] That summer he attended school
to learn Irish.

It was a wholly voluntary pursuit; the language represented
personal and national freedoms to be achieved. On vacation in
the West he met men and women similarly affected by the rising
spirit of nationalism. All were "reborn of the Rising and all that
led to it, so that the language acted both as a matrix to the tissues
of our political faith and as its sign and password."[11] Attending
that first summer school also introduced him to Eileen Gould,
the girl he would marry ten years later. Already filled with the
national spirit, she too vacationed in the West. Together they
went to Gougane Barra, so that for O'Faolain everything came
together at once. Youth and love and nationalism were inextricably and wonderfully joined. He enjoyed the release from his
stuffy urban home, discovered the ancestral heritage through his
contact with the language, its literature, and its native speakers,
and rapidly identified with the cause of national oppression.

When he entered the University in 1918, his involvement with
national passion became even more intense. A student by day and
a revolutionary by night, he had at last found what his friendless
childhood and dismal adolescence in Cork's "damp, dark, miasmic
valley"[12] lacked—the love of his fellow men. The Irish Volunteers, preparing to strike Ireland's final blow for freedom, were
bound together in friendship and in dedication to a common,
ennobling cause.

It was a supreme experience to know that you may not only admire
your fellow men, or respect them, or even like them, but that you can
love them so much that they have no faults, no weaknesses, so that

you will never distrust them even for a second and will forgive them every slightest minor fault or flaw, as they will yours. This extraordinary heartlifting revelation, this gaiety, this liberation of the spirit, was to stay with us all through the exciting years to come.[13]

He was a revolutionary for six years, first in the Volunteers and then, during the Civil War (1922–23), in the Irish Republican Army. But he was not cut out to be a soldier. As one of the rank-and-file, he was given the undemanding, necessary jobs: carrying dispatches, doing police work, scouting. The Anglo-Irish War (1919–21), euphemistically known as The Troubles, was mainly guerilla, and in common with most of his countrymen O'Faolain experienced the effects of its war of nerves—the early curfew, incessant and inventive terrorism, frequent and not always necessary raids and arrests, casual killings, torture, and all the other familiar terrors of such a warfare. His real battle began with the Civil War, and it was primarily internal.

Although he had not seen much of the fighting during The Troubles, he had been deeply attached to the cause of freedom. He had, he knew, been part of a widespread and deepening Irish response to the idea of independence. Civil war came, therefore, as a shock. As the promise of freedom, so ripe in the idealistic and romantic years after the Easter Rising, was shattered by civil dissension, the country experienced a sense of dismay. His own particular reaction was complicated by personal factors. The fact that he had become a rebel had meant a break with his father's proud patriotism of Empire, the stuff on which his own youth had been fed. 'Joining with the poor and oppressed had meant, or would seem to have meant, a rejection of his parents' hopes for his social advancement along clearly established lines. Finally, when the Bishop of Cork condemned Republicans in his diocese for killing or trying to kill their fellow-countrymen during the Civil War, O'Faolain had to put political faith before obedience to his Church. He had, in other words, to deny the authority revered by his mother. The effects of that decision, its spiritual and intellectual questionings of the role and function of the Church, were long lasting.

In the Civil War, he was successively a bomb-maker, a hunted guerilla, a director of propaganda for the First Southern Division of the I.R.A., and finally for eight months in Dublin, Director of Publicity, at the age of twenty-three, for the whole Republican movement. Bomb-making was monotonous, inglorious work, and when the Free State forces suddenly landed troops behind Cork the Republicans took to the hills. The bomb-makers went first to Macroom and then, as pursuit continued, further west to Ballyvourney. That retreat from Cork was a sign of Republican weakness. Defeat was in the air, and like most of his companions O'Faolain was hunted through the wintry mountains, increasingly weary and demoralized. For part of that winter he was back in Cork, directing publicity for his Division from the secrecy of his room, with Eileen Gould and some of her friends as his couriers. Then, when the actual fighting was over, he was called to Dublin to be Director of Publicity. There he cabled all across the world protesting the Republican defeat, an embittered idealist who could not accept the reality of the treaty with England and could not bring himself to withdraw from what he no longer believed in. But his moment of greatest disillusionment was at hand. It was when he saw that the Republicans lacked a worthwhile social and political program that he finally began to face the reality of his situation: "I had enough gumption to see . . . that if what we all knew between us about society or politics in any intellectual sense, were printed consecutively it would not cover a threepenny bit. . . . In that year I woke up."[14] The country had been motivated by purely emotional impulses. When the time came for negotiation with England as to what kind of association the two countries might have, internal dissension led to civil strife. The Republicans had wanted "a completely autonomous, all-Ireland, Republican parliament completely cut off from that source of evil, the British Empire."[15] It was an impossible ideal.

But worse was yet to follow. Looking about him in 1924, trying to understand what had happened, O'Faolain detected "a strong sense of moral decay."[16] The old Anglo-Irish aristocracy and middle class was replaced by a native bourgeois class in the course of the revolution. The loss of aristocratic leadership in matters of politics, culture, and taste was not compensated for by the rise of the Catholic Church to great influence, since, in Ireland, it had little cultural ancestry. His impression then was "that this combination of an acquisitive middle class and a vigorous and uncultivated Church meant that the fight for a republic as I now understand it—that is, a republic in the shape of France or the United States—had ended in total defeat."[17]

In that mood he went back to Cork in February 1924. For the next few years he tried to find a purpose in life. Returning to the University, he took an M.A. in Irish. For a year he taught school in Ennis, County Clare, an experience that only confirmed his belief that he did not want to live in any of Ireland's dull, provincial towns. Eileen Gould's similar experiences in Ballinasloe made her equally determined to escape to imaginative variety and riches. Almost in desperation he went back yet again to academic life, this time to get an M.A. in English, but with the hope that it might lead to a better job. His successful application for a Commonwealth Fellowship gave him the time he so badly needed to recover from his bitterness and put his life in some sort of perspective. He would, in fact, spend almost forty years in a search for understanding of and detachment from the forces that had implicated him so deeply.

He left for America in September 1926 and stayed for three years. At first he enjoyed the ascetic life of the Harvard graduate student, enduring the dry rigors of American-Germanic scholarship under George Lyman Kittredge and F. N. Robinson. But the fascination faded within a year, as his interest and success in creative writing grew. He sent for Eileen to tide him over his last year at Harvard. They got married in 1928, just as his money ran out, and went on a honeymoon trip by automobile across the United States. On their return they both worked in Boston for a year, he as an instructor in Anglo-Irish literature at Boston College. But already they had made their decision. As they camped with the Rio Grande at their feet and the Rockies facing them, they decided to go back to Ireland: "We belonged to an old, small, intimate and much-trodden country, where every field, every path, every ruin had its memories, where every last corner had its story."[18]

It would be five years before they could make that simple dream a reality. But even in 1929, as he saw the familiar scene again, O'Faolain knew what he wanted. "So far as I knew there was only one change in me. I now knew for certain what I wanted to do with my life. I wanted to write about this sleeping country, these sleeping fields, those sleeping villages, before my eyes under the summer moon."[19] Since Ireland offered no desirable means of support, they went to London, partly because of Edward Garnett's encouragement. O'Faolain got a job teaching in Strawberry Hill and worked steadily at his first book of stories, *Midsummer Night Madness* (1932), hoping all the time that opportunity would come back in Ireland. Finally, in June 1933, with a small subsidy from Jonathan Cape and a large determination to live by his pen, he returned to his own country. He had been away seven years. Now he would discover the kind of society that had emerged from the disturbed revolutionary period. Within six years he would describe his homeland as a "dreary Eden."

PART I
The National Mind

Chapter 1

King of the Beggars

King of the Beggars, a Life of Daniel O'Connell, the Irish Liberator, in *A Study of the Rise of Modern Irish Democracy, 1775–1847* (1938), supports the basic assertion that the Ireland of the present may best be understood in terms of Daniel O'Connell and his period. Anchored firmly to the supposition that the content of Irish life is the content of Irish character, it finds in him the fullest available evidence on which to build a comprehensive image of that character. "In body and soul, origin and life, in his ways and his words, he was," O'Faolain declares, "the epitome of all their pride, passion, surge, and hope—their very essence."[1]

This method of concentrating on a particular person as a way of illuminating a time in history characterizes all of his historical biographies. Each is an attempt at understanding how a great figure emerges from his background, at calculating to what degree he is a personification of the people's instinctive or explicit needs, and at determining the extent and nature of the heritage he created for subsequent Irishmen. As such, the biographies, as Professor John V. Kelleher has observed, are "successive backward projections of ascertainable continuity with the hope of calculating the present hidden directions of Irish life."[2] "No history," O'Faolain believes, "is a history unless it moves towards an end. It must extract from confusion the emergent order."[3]

From the literary or technical point of view the study of historical figures has advantages over the analysis of fictional characters in the contemporary world. For both Daniel O'Connell and Hugh O'Neill there are clearly defined environmental factors to be established, geographical conditions and their psychological effects, mental growth within an established educational or philosophical milieu, psychological characteristics embedded in historical records of actual statements or behavior, and spiritual and moral qualities implicit in the records. To the attractive complexity of character is added the dramatic flux of great events. But in addition there is the important fact that both men are pivotal figures living at moments of great change in which the course of Irish history was significantly altered and their part in that period of unusual change was central. These men are of heroic stature; they exercise free will in the face of circumstance, override the limitations of any deterministic elements within their environment, and personify a synthesis of the tradition of the naturalistic novel and the Yeatsian aesthetic of personality.[4]

There are, however, a number of possible approaches to the writing of a biography. In a critique of M. J. MacManus's *Eamon De Valera,* O'Faolain has made some general observations on the different interests that may engage a biographer. He may discuss the personality of the subject; he may analyze his character, or he may act as his apologist. He may simply relate the events of his life and make no effort at a critical assessment of character. Alternatively, he may be motivated by the same conception of biography as O'Faolain, who believes in considering men as types.

In the largest possible ways public men serve as models for the whole nation. They can disseminate a general philosophy of living, popularize certain attitudes of mind, set standards, and create values, apart altogether from what they can do for the lesser graces of living.[5]

In Daniel O'Connell O'Faolain presents what he regards as the epitome of the typical Irish mind, which he sees as a serpentining entity, full of qualification, subterfuge, and niceties of behavior. It is a central idea in his subsequent biographical studies and can be seen in various ways in his fiction. Nowhere does it receive as complete analysis and exposition as here, where the treatment revolves around four major factors: the formation of O'Connell's mind through childhood in Kerry and education abroad; a consideration of the effect of this kind of mentality upon the private conscience; a more general presentation of the advantages and disadvantages of such a mind; and, an apologia for its existence.

The permanent features of O'Connell's mind in O'Faolain's estimation were shrewdness, hardness, ambiguity, and self-protection, and these are explained as being largely the result of the conditions of his life in Derrynane; they are evident in letters written to his uncle from London when he was there as a law student[6] and also in entries in a diary that he kept at that time.[7] The way of life of his own family was characteristic of local feeling about the individual's responsibilities toward the law of the land. They combined smuggling from the Continent with aiding or seeking protection from the law when occasion demanded or made convenient. O'Faolain sees here a distinctly Irish definition of law as a blending of charity and necessity, an imaginative codification of the Catholic belief that there is no justice where there is no charity with which to temper it. Historically this ambiguous moral attitude was a defensive mechanism by which the people escaped from the injustices adhering to the rigid formalism of English law as practiced in Ireland. Other communal elements inherited by O'Connell were prudence, forethought, tortuosity, resourcefulness, doggedness, secrecy, and the gift of silence. A product of a particular time and place he is seen as a recomposition of the diverse elements of his race and this to a much greater degree than any other Irishman.[8] He had, too, the resilience and endurance of a people who had suffered and survived. But the most important of the inherited qualities, from O'Faolain's point of view, is that moral ambiguity which characterized him for most of his life and presents this biographer with the difficult problem of determining how much of a man's private convictions are revealed in his public behavior.

In presenting the intellectual ideas he formed in France and

London, O'Faolain argues that they are no more than the articulation of his instinctive ideas, born of a growing mental association between his own problems and the needs of his people. His training as an eighteenth-century rationalist, his absorption of the teaching of Benthamite utilitarianism, his devotion to deistic principles, his libertarian tenets are not solely responsible for his response to the needs of his people. Their effects, however, are readily evident in his abandonment of the Gaelic past, his non-sectarianism and his liberalism in the Church-state conflict. What O'Faolain seeks to establish is the influence of both his inherited qualities and his acquired attitudes upon his private conscience. That he was politically shrewd and embarrassingly evasive is evident from a cursory reading of his life. What is less apparent but more interesting, particularly if he is to be seen as typical of the Irish mind, is the sincerity or insincerity of his religious convictions, since from 1800 on he behaved as though he were a Catholic, defending Catholic doctrine from Protestant attacks and identifying his cause with clerical interests.

The problem, then, of the Irish mind as it affects the private conscience is considered first of all in relation to the evidence of his political behavior. In that sphere the duality of his nature appears "in the *double entendre,* the mental reservation, the limiting clause, the disingenuous qualification and proviso."[9] O'Faolain finds it difficult to believe that his religious life was not founded on the same pattern, but even after summarizing the progress of his beliefs no definite conclusion can be stated. From being a Tory in France, frightened by the Revolution, to becoming a Radical in London then almost becoming an atheist but recovering as a deist, he ended "not quite as a Catholic, but as an Irish Catholic."[10] Although O'Faolain is reluctant to arrive at any absolute position as regards the man's private conscience, he feels that after political and religious beliefs had been aligned O'Connell entered "the normal condition of most Irishmen," that is, "piously Catholic in practice, indeed, vociferously Catholic, while retaining at bottom a strong reservation of independence, some smothered scepticism, the widest tolerance of other religions, and great elasticity in action."[11] O'Connell's statement that sins against faith are worse than sins against morality probably means that morality was for him, as for his people, an elastic law. Certainly this was true in the political sphere. But it is doubtful of O'Faolain's sweeping statement about the nature of the Irish Catholic is true. It certainly cannot be logically supported or refuted. What is evident is that he finds reflections of his own position on religious matters in O'Connell. The main point he establishes out of a long consideration of the coexistence of deism and Catholicism in O'Connell for some indefinite time is that, no matter by what private complications, he succeeded in establishing for the emergent Ireland the right of the individual to his own conscience. "In whatever way he brought tolerance into Irish life, he kept the religion of the simple democracy he was fashioning from consolidating for forty years, into any form of bitter Low-Churchism."[12]

The advantages and disadvantages of the Irish mind are discussed in various sections of the biography. The former are mainly practical and may be conveniently examined in the later treatment of O'Faolain's position as apologist. The disadvantages are mainly personal and relate closely to the idea of the heritage left by this man. His adept qualification and scholastic definition almost betrayed his conscience and toward the end of his life, O'Faolain argues, disintegrated all sense of reality.[13] The fatal weakness in his character and his technique of living is revealed by a letter he wrote at the age of fifty-four.[14] It was a period of his life in which there was no great cause to which he was fully dedicated. Ambiguity and duality, O'Faolain notes, are excellent modes in time of stress, when the mind is always conscious of an ulterior and greater motive behind the surface evasions, the cantings and recantings, but at times of calm and natural indecision their power is weakened and their potential danger to the individual is strengthened. O'Faolain wonders if in his final years O'Connell was at the mercy of his own ambiguity and not in control of it. In examining a portrait of the old O'Connell, he sees the genius of the leader's country in his face, where the mobility of the mouth is matched by the cold secrecy of the right eye.

For Minotaur and Sphinx lie in ambush in his countenance, where, as in that of most men, there is the differentiation of his double nature in the play of his looks; always the right eye held the secret calculation; always the left had been a challenge and a doubt. One corner of the lip is likewise turned upward in a half-smile; the other is gripped downward with a horrible suggestion of latent ruthlessness and brutality.[15]

The heritage of such a man is dangerous for lesser men. For him ambition, Ireland and, finally, religion held him in perseverance to a cause that by being greater than he magnified him. Lesser men, less dedicated, less capable of creative vision, less restrained by natural powers of resilience, self-reliance and endurance, would inherit from him more evil than good. O'Faolain sees in him perpetuation of that type of Irish nature "where truth is always in hiding and where the very soul ends in being in hiding from itself."[16]

Part of the greatness of this work is the broad-minded point of view that controls the writer. Feeling dissatisfied with the image of O'Connell that emerged from a centenary collection of essays[17] because it portrayed him without that diversity that can be found in *King of the Beggars,* he remarked that heroism is the conquering of a man's interior enemies first of all. "The greatest injustice we can do to any hero is to deprive him of his weaknesses."[18] O'Faolain has been careful to include all aspects, even those that frighten or disgust. But the acceptance of the failures, of the disadvantages of the sphinx-like mentality, of the inescapable vulgarity of the uncultured personality, and so forth, is constantly related to understandable and excusing conditions that produced them. Thus the technique of evasion is presented as an inevitable inheritance. In the first place it was absorbed as a boyhood lesson from his Kerry environment, where it had been produced by the exigencies of a particular mode of existence. There are historical reasons, too, for the elastic conscience. Apparent acquiescence was the lesson derived by an oppressed people for whom open avowal was dangerous. And behind a technique of self-protection lay a repressed scepticism. To his credit, O'Connell shunned the cringing attitude and gave the people the example of his open defiance. That the duality persisted in him was inevitable, since a hundred years had gone into its creation. O'Faolain's emphasis on his hero's ability to establish a pattern and a destination for his people leads him to the opinion that O'Connell made use of this inherited approach with the far-sighted vision of a condition and a time when his people would not be obliged to retain such a duality. But this seems most unlikely. O'Connell was first and foremost a practical politician. Long-range objectives and abstract conceptions of the future were not part of his nature, and it is doubtful that he recognized his own duality and deliberately used it.

In historical factors and environmental conditions O'Faolain finds defenses by which to act as O'Connell's apologist. The heritage of justice tempered by charity aided O'Connell in his fight against the injustice of a legal system in which the letter of the law was weighted against the people. The elasticity of conscience became an unguent against the literal-mindedness of the law; "it introduced a warm, kind, human note into life."[19] O'Faolain rightly insists on O'Connell's achievement: by accepting the limitations and disadvantages of the Ireland of his time, he succeeded in turning the infirmities and hardships into virtues and advantages.[20] He thus incarnated a whole people. He was above all in O'Faolain's estimation, "the greatest of all Irish realists, who knew that if he could but once define, he could thereby create. He did define, and he did create. He thought a democracy and it rose. He defined himself and his people became him. He imagined a future and the road appeared."[21] And it was hard work.

O'Faolain constantly emphasizes the industry and energy of O'Connell. The evidence abounds: his diary records his daily schedule from 4 A.M. to 10 P.M.; as a struggling young barrister on the Munster Circuit he travelled continually in all kinds of weather; as a political agitator he spent countless hours in committees, many of them fruitless, repetitious, and frustrating. One cannot read any of his biographers without recognizing his seemingly limitless energy and his willingness to drive himself. He had, in addition, enormous boldness and courage, as O'Faolain also stresses. Indeed his whole career is a tribute to his persistence and courage. In particular, there is the evidence of his behavior in the corrupt courts where a Catholic barrister was a rarity and a figure of contempt. There his exploits were legendary. O'Faolain cites at length the examples of his attack on the whole system of English law as administered in Ireland during his defense of the journalist Magee on the charge of libel.[22] Indeed, the creativity that characterizes his career and is so attractive to this biographer could not have brought such revolutionary effects to Irish life had it not been accompanied by these virtues of industry, energy, boldness, and courage.

Apart from these considerations of O'Connell's character, there is one other aspect of his behavior that ought to be mentioned, since O'Faolain's judgment of the quality of the man in the face of this crisis reveals his own mental outlook at the time of writing. This concerns O'Connell's decision not to hold the Monster Meeting at Clontarf when British military force threatened to disband it. The question for O'Connell rested on the possible advantages of repercussion had he not backed down and people had been slaughtered. O'Faolain avoids any discussion of the possible effects of an alternative decision, but is definite in his assessment of this event insofar as it affects the memory and overall picture of the man. Had O'Connell led or sanctioned a rebellion, he would, he says, be remembered for an even greater man than he is now estimated to be. He would have satisfied the natural human desire for the magnificent ending, would have rounded out his life either on the scaffold or in jail, would, therefore, have become part of the tradition of romantic Ireland, united by the wasteful virtues with the patriotic dead such as Wolfe Tone.

O'Faolain's wish that "he had added the fire of the gambler to the caution of the politician"[23] is explainable in part by the natural instinct of the novelist for the dramatic. His final comment is that because O'Connell failed to provide this great moment our sympathy turns from him to his more ardent followers, the Young Irelanders. Such a preference for the patriotic irrationality of the rebel contradicts the basic approach of the biography, which has been characterized by its objective and realistic view of the subject. The study has been motivated by the determination to understand O'Connell, to stress his most significant characteristics and principles and to analyze their relevance as part of the man's heritage to modern Ireland. But the fundamentally romantic nature of the author has led to the contradition that closes the study, causing him to withdraw full sympathy from the old leader in preference for the more colorful Young Irelanders.

In creating this complex characterization O'Faolain has found satisfying reflections of his own psychological state. In depicting O'Connell's loyalty to his people he is presenting his own; by showing O'Connell's establishment of a pattern of political revolution and social reform he is expressing his own reforming instincts. His fictional heroes are frustrated reformers. All tend to be perplexed by the conditions of their time. None are equipped with sufficient imagination or intelligence to define and thereby create. None has the personal dynamism by which a people can be led. All reflect O'Faolain's own insecurity and lack of an intellectual perception of an emergent order. Their frustration is his; their isolation and disbelief, their recurrent, useless martyrdom is his. It is no accident that the first story in *Purse of Coppers* (1937), "A Broken World," ends in a prayer for a resurrection and a better life. Daniel O'Connell is such a redeemer, a man who took the broken world of Irish life in the eighteenth century and formed a new and fruitful synthesis. In him O'Faolain's deepest needs and desires both as a person and as an artist are exemplified. It is understandable that in considering the man's political career he should be guilty of some overemphasis.

Two major considerations are involved in Sean O'Faolain's study of the career of Daniel O'Connell: his inclusive, nonsectarian attitude to democracy and his definition of the relationship between Church and state. All are principles by which the biographer intends to measure the Ireland of his own time, and historical biography becomes less of an objective analysis of the past as seen in the behavior of leading figures than a means of advancing personal opinions about the present state of Ireland. The result of such a propagandist purpose is a simplification of past events, due to the subjective reaction of the writer, who is not only influenced by his critical attitude to the issues of his own time but also is inclined to stress those aspects of the past that illustrate the validity of that attitude to the issues of his own time. Thus. although he is deliberately trying to evade the romantic tradition of late nineteenth- and twentieth-century historians, influenced by the prevailing nationalistic point of view, he succumbs to his own instinctive romanticism by searching in history for heroes with whom he can identify, whose actions give proof of an outlook similar to his own, and from whose behavior he can draw satisfying support for his own opinions about the new Ireland.

The pattern of using history to buttress critical opinions relating to the new Ireland is seen in O'Faolain's account of O'Connell as the liberal layman—inclusive and nonsectarian in his concept of society and sensitive and wise in his thinking about the kind of relationship within which Church and state could exist with mutual benefits in a predominantly Catholic country. Writing in the *Yale Review* in 1936 he had commented on the pervasive influence of the Church in Irish life and had observed the emergence of a one-class society.[24] In his first biography of De Valera (1933) he had noted that the Republican separatist idea had caused the image of a Gaelic Christian state with an extreme isolationist outlook to become the desirable goal of national life. He was not only opposed to the impractical ideal of a Gaelic state but was considerably agitated by the predominance of clerical influence and the absence of an intellectual liberal group within the new society. *King of the Beggars* has the fundamental aim of holding up the image of O'Connell as a corrective to the twentieth-century notion of democracy.

O'Connell represents the still warm and human idea of a hierarchical society. It is being lost in Ireland where the modern *bourgeois* is an imitation of his English prototype, and where the Church is, in its Jansenistic aridity, without the Jansenistic elevation of soul, or intellectual strength, severing itself from the people, by severing itself from their natural gaiety, and so losing the authority that should be based on love.[25]

The almost inevitable result of such a pedagogical approach to history is the tendency to simplify the complexity of the conditions within which O'Connell had to work and their restraining effects on his liberalism, in order to project a clearly visible, positive, somewhat idealized figure.

There is little doubt that O'Connell's formulation of the principle of nonsectarianism is significant in Irish history and that it is one of his major principles. Speaking against the Act of Union, he regretted that he had to speak as a Catholic rather than as an Irishman, because his coreligionists had been accused of abandoning their country in the hope of gaining religious toleration. He asserted that he would rather trust to the justice of the Protestants of Ireland than lay his country at the feet of foreigners. "I know that the Catholics of Ireland still remember they have a country and that they would never accept any advantages as a sect that could destroy them as a people."[26] Although the idea of nonsectarian, inclusive approach to Irish life had been previously supported by Wolfe Tone and the United Irishmen and by Grattan and the Patriot Party in the 1790's, this was the first time it had been advocated by a man of the people. O'Connell boldly and generously rose above the traditional racial and religious antagonisms, which a long history of conquest, oppression, and discrimination had fostered among the people, and postulated the oneness of Ireland and the creation of a new nation founded on the principle of nonsectarianism.

O'Connell's speech against the Act of Union does represent his general position, which was later illustrated by his response to the veto question, that is, to the idea that the British government should have a negative control over Catholic episcopal appointments. O'Faolain is correct in estimating the effect of O'Connell's opposition to the idea of a veto in stimulating a resistance among the bishops. But he fails to recognize clearly enough that O'Connell himself was to a large extent responsible for the subsequent break in Irish society. Mr. Kennedy F. Roche has pointed out that he precipitated dissension between the Catholic gentry and his own democratic supporters by his outspoken attitude to the Quarantotti Letter (1814) and created division later, by his mode of conducting the Repeal agitation, between the people and the upper classes, driving the latter into Unionism and eventually losing them their place in Irish life.[27] Instead of trusting to peaceful evolution he forced issues and created dissension, being more of a politician than a statesman. In extenuation, it has to be said that the inevitability of a beneficent evolutionary process in Irish affairs was by no means certain. O'Faolain's statement stresses one side of the issue: "He would have embraced all elements in Irish life, on terms, and it is not his fault, but the fault of the old Protestant vested interests, that his policy had to give way in the end to radicalism."[28] It was not merely the vested interests that caused difficulty. The widespread effect of the evangelical movement in the hands of such able men as Dr. Henry Cooke tended to replace the tolerance of the eighteenth century by sectarianism.[29]

O'Connell, in fact, cannot be seen as a consistent nonsectarian. There are two clear instances of an unpleasantly sectarian nature in his later career. One is his opposition to the Colleges Bill of 1845, under which provincial colleges were to be established on strictly undenominational lines. Without waiting for the bishops' more conservative opinion, O'Connell denounced the proposal as godless and favored a denominational system instead.[30] O'Faolain views this incident with understandable distaste. The discussion over the Colleges Bill caused the second incident in which O'Connell showed himself willing to use religion to beat an opponent, Davis, who welcomed the opportunities provided by nonsectarian education.[31] His preference to lose the support of Davis and the Young Irelanders in the Repeal Association in order to secure an ascendancy that a virtual Catholic organization would guarantee him shows a surprising degree of sectarianism.[32]

It is also incorrect to present him as a consistent antivetoist, since in 1813 he was trying with the help of a leading Dublin priest, Dr. Michael Blake, to evolve a compromise.[33] His attitude was not determined completely by a desire to make the bishops less subservient to the state and to keep politics out of their control, as O'Faolain says.[34] He was at least prepared to work within the existing view. The submission of episcopal appointments to the state for approval was and is the usual course in Catholic countries, where a *modus vivendi* between Church and state is desirable, if only on practical considerations. O'Faolain, motivated by his opposition to a pervasive clerical influence in his own time, tends to ignore the necessity of O'Connell's working within the ambience of contemporary thinking. Thus he regards the fact that the bishops had secretly agreed to a proposal identical to Grattan's (1808) as tantamount to a conspiracy between the Irish Church and the English state.[35] He does not mention that the power to nominate or to exclude Irish bishops when exercised by the British government raised the question of the independence of the priesthood from state pay and of the hierarchy from state control as essential symbols of national life, possibly as important to O'Connell as any liberal considerations. Had Ireland succeeded in gaining independence in which to set up her own parliament it is reasonable to assume that O'Connell would have been ready to recognize the need for some mutual tolerance and collaboration between Church and state in the question of episcopal appointments.

The role of O'Connell as the liberal Catholic layman creating a useful definition of the relationship that should exist between Church and state in Ireland is very important to this biographer. It is best illustrated by his reaction to Grattan's Relief Bill (1813), which gave all the rights that passed into law in 1829 with Catholic emancipation but contained a very elaborate oath of allegiance to be taken by all Catholics, which was intolerably sectarian and thoroughly objectionable from a democratic, libertarian point of view.[36] O'Connell strongly denounced the idea of suborning the clergy under the oath and voiced the opinion that O'Faolain uses most frequently to justify his own concern with Church-state relationships in the new Ireland. "Does any man imagine that this Catholic religion will prosper in Ireland if our prelates, instead of being what they are at present, shall become the tools of the administration? They would lose all respect for themselves, all respectability in the eyes of others."[37] The responsibility of the liberal Catholic layman lies in his role as mediator between Church and state. He can help define the proper balance of power within which they function.

O'Faolain's definition of that relationship was most clearly expressed in his response to the Noel Browne controversy in 1951. It was then, he felt, that the true nature of the kind of relationship between Church and state in Ireland became clear. In 1948 the government had decided to introduce a medical service, without a means test, to provide maternity treatment for mothers and their children up to the age of sixteen. In April 1951 public discussion over the merits and demerits of the scheme was suddenly overshadowed by disclosures of opposition to its proposals by the Catholic Church and by the Cabinet. On April 11 Dr. Noel Browne, Minister for Health and originator of the scheme, resigned in protest. On April 12 he released the relevant correspondence between Mr. Costello, the leader of the government, the hierarchy, and himself (Appendix A).

Sean O'Faolain's article in *The Bell,* entitled "The Dail and the Bishops," fully expresses his position on Church-state relationship in Ireland. He saw the controversy over the Mother and Child Scheme, the sudden demise of the bill, the dismissal of the Minister for Health, the assertive letters of the bishop, the weak compliancy of the leader of the government, and the secrecy behind which the representatives of the Church and the state had acted as highly illustrative of the true nature of modern Irish democracy. The basic factor is the nature of the authority exercised by the Church. For, as O'Faolain rightly argued, it is not merely a question of the right of a representative body to comment on government action, it is not merely the question of the Church's right to enunciate an official point of view. In practise the Catholic Church commands. Only the Catholic Church exercises the weapon of the sacraments. "The Dail," O'Faolain stated cogently, "proposes; Maynooth disposes."[38] The Catholic member of Parliament has no alternative but to obey the Church.

Because of this curious relationship, in which the Church has enormous power but very little social responsibility and the Parliament has all the responsibility but only a limited power, O'Faolain reiterated his wise and humane belief that the "relation of Church and State is, must be, and should be one of constant tussle."[39]

The relationship between Church and State always has been, and always must be, a healthy struggle, in which the Church will properly, *but always prudently* fight for power, and the State will always try to restrain that power within due limits.[40]

He used the Browne case as an example of how this principle

could work in practice. Since Mr. Costello was faced with clerical opposition to a piece of legislation which he and his cabinet were proposing on behalf of the government and the people, he should have strongly and stubbornly resisted the bishops to the limit. He should have been scrupulous in avoiding secret meetings with the bishops behind the backs of the parliament. He should have kept the cabinet fully informed and should have asked the hierarchy to state their objections openly. In this way the minimal principle of democractic ideology would have been preserved. "No other procedure," O'Faolain declared, "would have reconciled the two loyalties in Irish life—the loyalty owed to the people's parliament by patriotic Irishmen and the loyalty owed to the Second Parliament by Catholics."[41]

O'Faolain felt the whole affair had been bad for the morale of the country. The Church had shown its distrust of the people. For had the Mother and Child Scheme been allowed to function, it would, in an overwhelming Catholic country, have been worked almost entirely by a Catholic government, Catholic doctors, Catholic civil servants, and the ordinary Catholic layman. Quoting Cardinal Newman's remark that it is the whole man that moves, O'Faolain expressed his concern for the effect of the Church's proven distrust of the people.

If you shatter a man's pride—by, for example, shattering his belief that he is worthy of trust—you shatter his personality as a Christian: for as a Christian he is a whole man or he is nothing. If people are treated as children, and all that is asked of them is that they go here, go there, do this, do that, and are never left to *act* as whole Christians, why, then, you are left with children and childish morale.[42]

And once again he pointed to the figure and the example of Daniel O'Connell, the liberal layman, ready to work with the Church but ready also to resist the Church when he thought it necessary.[43]

King of the Beggars has received high praise. Professor Daniel A. Binchy wrote: ". . . quite apart from its literary distinction, it represents one of the most solid contributions to the history of modern Ireland that have appeared in our time."[44] Professor Gerard Murphy regarded it as "at the same time a masterpiece of biography, a masterpiece of historical evocation of the past and a masterpiece of . . . concrete criticism of the past."[45] These estimations are still true. The biography has not been surpassed. Recent studies make it possible to evaluate and stress certain historical aspects in a different light, but its central statements remain acceptable. The characterization of Daniel O'Connell is a psychological *tour de force* of great value and complexity and the polemical aspects retain their integrity and challenge. In no other work is O'Faolain's personality so fully expressed. His warm and generous feelings for his own country, his keen social conscience, his intelligent regard for universal humane principles, and the force and vigor of his creative imagination are all evidence in this study of the man in Irish history for whom he has most regard.

O'Connell's example is visible in O'Faolain's work, particularly in his years as editor of *The Bell* and in his historical biographies. Above all he has wanted to accept the conditions of Irish life, not to evade them in romanticism or in historical fiction. The creative miracle, based as it was on hard work and a keen intelligence, that enabled O'Connell to turn Ireland's terrible conditions into advantages and virtues, is one he would like to help bring about again. Just as O'Connell insisted on the hard and unpleasant facts, so does O'Faolain. What he said about O'Connell's task of formulating the instinctive values of Irish life in the eighteenth century applies to the state of the racial genius in his own day. In both cases the "native instinct was wild and uncultivated, haphazard, fumbling, largely negative, denying clearly but not affirming clearly. . . . It could not affirm because it had no concrete way of affirming its genius, as free nations affirm their genius, in educational institutions, political institutions, great buildings, social behavior, art and literature. . . ."[46] If one wanted to state a central motif in O'Faolain's critical commentaries on Irish life, this would be it. *King of the Beggars* stands as a monument to his sense of public responsibility. It is his greatest contribution to the task of clarifying the directions of Irish life in his own time.

Chapter 2

The Great O'Neill

The biography of Hugh O'Neill, Earl of Tyrone (1550–1616), is not as directly or as comprehensively related to the Ireland of the twentieth century as the story of Daniel O'Connell. Therefore it avoids the political and social polemic of the earlier biography and is a much more objective record. In general outline, however, it is not altogether detached from the present. The figure and career of the aristocratic leader exemplify some primary qualities of individual behavior and some primary principles of national outlook. The emphasis on the European status of O'Neill and the analysis of the effect of his divided loyalty between a natural affinity with his own culture and his acquired appreciation for the Renaissance world are directed to O'Faolain's own time. They relate to his need to bring Irish life into contact with the outside world and to his personal predicament as a man who has tried to make the best of both worlds. Traditionally O'Neill had been seen as the typical patriot imbued with national fervor, eager to assault England. O'Faolain's thesis is that he is not representative of the old Gaelic world and had, at most, an ambiguous sympathy with what he subsequently defended. To glorify him as part of a romantic patriotic tradition is to soften his individuality and to deny him the true reason for his greatness. O'Faolain has tried to see the whole man. The patriotic myth played down or derided some of his so-called unpleasant qualities, such as his habit of making obeisances to Elizabeth I. O'Faolain realistically sees this as part of the man's technique of survival and builds up his portrait accordingly. O'Neill's greatness comes from his intelligent understanding of the issues at stake in the clash of Elizabethan invaders and Irish defenders and from his ability to transcend the local issues by seeing their place in the wider context of European conflicts. It is this achievement of a European perspective and a European fame that O'Faolain wants to emphasize.

The man's character is of particular importance in supporting this thesis, and it is here that the novelist had much to attract him. For in contrast with O'Connell, O'Neill was reticent and silently conspiratorial, so that no intimate details of his character have survived. An enigma even to his contemporaries he left to posterity only the evidence of his behavior. O'Faolain's reconstruction of his psychological attributes is an intelligent and sensitive performance. From the bare historical records he builds up a complex human figure and gives convincing support to his assertion that O'Neill was acclaimed in Europe not because he was an idealistic Irish patriot but because he was a realistic Irish general of remarkable courage and shrewdness. There is no way of affirming or denying the authenticity of the final picture, but from the artistic point of view the character of O'Neill is in no way contradicted by the evidence of the recorded behavior. As another example of the Irish mind this is a remarkably life-sized and credible portrait.

That O'Neill was able to rise above his time and become a figure of European significance is partly a result of circumstances but mainly of his own creative intelligence. He was able to understand what was happening in the Irish wars of the sixteenth century when Tudor imperialists pushed resolutely into the various dynasties of Ireland. On one side was the centralized patriotism of a people consolidated as a nation and self-consciously proud of the fact. The spirit of Ireland, on the other, was not articulated to the same degree. Opposed to the greater moral force of the nation was a people politically unformed, disparate, and individual. O'Neill was, O'Faolain says, "the first modern man who gave that people a form, by giving it a speech that it could understand and which made it realize itself intelligently."[1] He realized that by joining his struggle for independence with the whole European movement of the Counter-Reformation he could surmount the limitations of the racial mind by opposing to the idea of a nation welded by patriotic fervor "the idea of a People informed by something midway between religious idealism and the intellectual idea."[2] He could break through tribalism and establish a confederacy.[3]

It is the magnitude of this decision that O'Faolain rightly stresses. For it seems to have meant that this man was imaginatively capable of estimating the value of making himself into a symbol, a personification of the latent urges in his own people, and the focal point of the whole religious conflict. It meant that he could examine the social structure of his country, could judge its pastoral contentment to be stagnant and in need of reinvigoration by some philosophical idea. By thinking creatively and by being self-critical and aware of himself he gave his people the benefit of becoming self-critical and objective about themselves and the world about them. He recognized the fundamental principle that tradition needs to be continuously analyzed to be kept fructive; he therefore led his people into contact with the rich stream of European tradition where the principle of change and development was supreme.

Unfortunately he gave them a destiny that they could not appreciate. When the Irish Wars ended in his defeat at Kinsale it meant for his people the end of the old Gaelic order that they had loved; they were blind to the idea that transcended physical defeat, the idea of European contact. It is this inheritance that O'Faolain is most anxious to propound; he believes that it retains its validity:

As it is, by that transfusion, something has persisted, or more accurately may persist, out of the old Gaelic world—purified, chastened, re-enlightened—to form an attractive element in life wherever the

Irish nature has the courage to live, like Tyrone, through Ireland into Europe, out of this remote island into the ubiquitous and contemporaneous world of civilized mind.[4]

O'Neill is also of great interest to O'Faolain because he personified the conflict of a loyalty divided between the Gaelic and the Tudor, the old and the new, the medieval and the Renaissance. In this, O'Faolain argues, he is typical of any Irishman so divided "by the impact of a complex and sophisticated civilization on the quiet certainties of a simpler way of life."[5] On the one hand there was the ancient civilization of his people with all the powerful attractions that would pull at his heart forever. On the other, was the world of the Renaissance and Reformation he had experienced when educated at the home of Sir Henry Sidney. O'Faolain gives a brilliant description of the two civilizations, knowing that in the forced juncture of modernity and antiquity that resulted from England's decision to make Ireland her first real colony two cultures that hated each other at first sight were brought face to face and that O'Neill stood inescapably amid that clash of mighty opposites.

His own way of life in Ulster had been celebrated in Gaelic literature for centuries; it was a civilization as ancient and as honorable and as valid for him as the Tudor civilization was for his enemies. They regarded the Gaelic ways as antique, uncivilized, remote, savage, dirty, and fit only for extermination; their scorn and contempt underlines the mental obscurity from which they spoke and acted. For O'Neill the attractions of that patriarchal, pastoral world of the Gaelic aristocratic order that had remained unchanged in its isolation and comfortable seclusion would be a major obstacle to his reforming, modernized mind. In England he had been brought up in the new religion and must have been imbued with some of the ideals of the time, its adventurous spirit, its earnestness and ambition, its intrigue, its opportunism, its competition—all the diverse qualities to be found in a Sidney a Raleigh or a Bacon; as a result he came close to having the coldly pragmatical mind of the Renaissance. From his experiences in England, O'Faolain feels, he would realize the advantages of a country that had the benefits of Roman law and order, the hierarchy of officials and the sovereignty of the state; he would realize the advantages of the elaborations in life and thought, manners and customs that the Renaissance had brought. He would be logically and rationally influenced by the ideals of that civilization and at the same time drawn instinctively and proudly by the ties of his own distinctive traditions. When he does rebel in the manner of all the Irish chieftains persecuted by Tudor imperialism, the basic motivation is the regard for his own mode of life, "that which is his appetite, his motive, his passion, his unacknowledged law."[6]

At the same time he is objectively aware of the disadvantages inherent in his own civilization and tries to surmount them by a European contact. He emerges therefore in this biography as an example of the great tragic type, "the man who is driven to what his nature inexorably demands and his reason denies."[7] Where other Irish chieftains rebelled in blind anger and outraged pride, he alone took the tragic sense of the drama forced on him. It is part of this image of him that he should fail so drastically at Kinsale. In deciding to attack when the evidence pointed to the wisdom of holding out for a few days more to starve the English army into submission, he turned his whole critical opinion of Ireland upside down. By giving in to the urging of his allies he gave in to those elements in Irish society, the rashness and recklessness, improvidence and incogitancy, that it had been his aim to restrain; his strength had lain in his cultivation of the virtues of discipline, restraint, and patience; now he gambled rashly and lost. "He was the modern man who had tried to bear up the rotting edifice of antiquity, and had fallen under its weight."[8]

Something of the diversity, complexity, and greatness of the man is visible in his adoption of the principle of European alignment and his ability to balance between two civilizations. O'Faolain is also interested in his religious idealism and his conspiratorial Irish mind. An objective, ruthless man in most instances, calculating and cunning in all his dealings, unaccustomed to hasty action, at times he was capable of being overborne by his emotional nature—as at Kinsale—and in his response to the idea of a war fought in the name of religious beliefs he exposed this passionate, imaginative aspect to a force that his logical, rational mind could not hold in check. For, O'Faolain maintains, when the idea of a war partly in the name of religion first struck his imagination it is likely that his humanistic mind would have secularized it, made it fit into his general conception as one more symbol of the Gaelic mode; it is probable that he began by exploiting the idea dispassionately. Merely to regard him as a pious patriot is to simplify his character. He had fought on the side of the Tudors during the Desmond Rebellion in the south, in which the flame of the Counter-Reformation first reached the Irish scene; he had helped in the ruthless butchery and devastation, stood by when the whole south was treated to a deliberate policy of extermination, and behaved as if the events were happening in another, remote island.

But he could not have been unaware of the lessons involved: Spanish aid, a religious identification, unstable Irish followers, ruthless invaders, and the ultimate fate of any man who failed to balance adroitly between the two worlds. When his own turn came he would know the value of the twin symbols of faith and fatherland; but as the war went on he succumbed to religious idealism, consumed like the rest of the country by the greatness of the issues involved, forgetful of the cautious limitations he had tried to put on his rebellion. "The enlargement of the impulse," O'Faolain concludes, "had meant the enlargement of the man until, as always happens in the history of men and peoples like his, he became a symbol or personification of all the forces latent in him and them."[9] He had so far overstepped mere personal ambition and all local reasons for the war that he was unable to withdraw again into the carefully sustained balance between the two worlds. He became a personality as defined by Yeats: ". . . personality is what remains when the dress of outward things falls away in moments of great tragedy and personality burns with a pure adamantine flame."[10]

The evidence of O'Neill's behavior postulates a most conspiratorial Irish mind, despite the fact that he came close to having the cold, pragmatical mentality of the Renaissance and is, therefore, similar to Daniel O'Connell—another Renaissance figure in

O'Faolain's eyes—calculating, whorled with reservations, "a humming conch of *arrière-pensées*."[11] His whole relationship with the Tudors was one of deception and evasion by which he was able not only to protract the war for years but even before that to keep them in a constant uncertainty as to his real intentions. Dissimulations, mock obeisances, constant truces, and frequent pardons were with him a matter of deliberate policy, a personal technique by which he lived in that age of intrigue. For an intelligent man, led by a great cause to which he is committed completely, this kind of behavior may not sap the character, but as O'Faolain points out, for lesser men, less intelligent, less committed, less governed by a stern self-discipline, the policy can be disastrous. Small men very quickly become infected by even a pretence at surrender since the benefits that follow corrupt by the very facility with which they are gained. When they begin to play the game of dissimulation for themselves the result is putrefaction of the will.

Inevitably the comparison with Daniel O'Connell comes to mind. He too had the technique of evasion and dissimulation seen as "the fatal weakness in his character and his technique of living."[12] Both men were saved from the degenerative influence of their own natures by the restraining effect of a great cause, O'Neill by the religious idealism of the Counter-Reformation, O'Connell by the ennobling inspiration of his people, who regarded him as their savior. There are, indeed, many similarities in the characters of these men. Both were realists and intelligently creative; both learned the technique of opportunism in England; both were capable of rising to extremes of dedication; both could be ruthless, arrogant, ingratiating, and cunning. Of the two O'Connell is shown to have more human kindness, more tenderness—the evidence of letters and diaries. O'Neill stands far back in time, half-barbaric in his killings, his elopement with Mabel Bagenal, his mistresses, his pride in the patriarchal society of which he is a product. O'Connell is a man of the people, rough, emotional, vulgar, ambitious, by reputation promiscuous, a personification of latent power and frustration.

There are similarities, also, in their intentions, methods, and achievements. Both were faced with an archaic system of loyalties in their people, O'Neill's being aristocratically contented with the outdated society of the Gaelic order and O'Connell's living as slaves in the social degradation that followed the final collapse of that old order. For O'Connell the answer was a utilitarian rejection of the Gaelic past, for O'Neill the invigorating transfusion of the Renaissance. O'Neill's people were without unity, without order, each chieftain living for himself and his own power, each either fighting the Tudors or aligning with them without any notion of the policy of the balance of power by which they exploited this basic weakness of Irish society. Before he could even trust them in a major conflict he had to give them the amalgamating power of some central idea by which he could overcome the deficiencies of the racial mind. The answer was a religious crusade. O'Connell's people, almost two hundred years later, were politically unformed also, without any absolute sense of themselves as a nation. By the idea of a democracy he roused them from their apathy and gave them the powerful conception of their own significance as a united force. Both men were also European in impact. O'Neill deliberately united his own struggle for independence with the widespread European movement of the Counter-Reformation, becoming thereby a focal point in a fight immeasurably more important in those terms than that of a local Irish chieftain struggling for local power. O'Connell in his defense of the principle of the freedom of the state in relation to the Church brought "democratic Ireland into the European world for the first time since the fall of the Stuarts."[13] In the various conspiracies that ensued among the Cardinals at Rome who were divided in their political loyalties he had brought Ireland into the region of foreign politics and increased his own stature as a popular leader.

Both men finally, and this is probably the greatest single aspect of their lives to be considered since it embraces all the others, were personifications of the basic drives of their people, united with them atavistically in a common sense of compression, frustrated talent, injustice, and hurt pride, motivated basically by the virtue of *pietas*. O'Neill had seen the Renaissance and had understood how far behind his own people were while "the rest of Europe had begun to move forward to the new ideas, new inventions, new codes, greater and finer elaborations in every branch of life—manners, education, architecture, social organization, politics, dress, food, philosophy, methods of war, letters."[14] He fought to inject some speculative energy into his people, to give them the liberating power of a general idea by which the native instinct could project itself fully, objectively aligned with European culture and tradition. In the same way O'Connell's struggle for Catholic emancipation was not merely a religious conflict. It embraced much wider and deeper issues. Religion was the symbol of contrasting concepts of life, values mutually contemptuous. Emancipation meant freedom to project the whole native genius in every way "as free nations affirm their genius, in educational institutions, political institutions, great buildings, social behavior, art and literature, and so forth."[15]

The defeat of O'Neill at Kinsale and the reversal for O'Connell at Clontarf produce opposing reactions in the author. In the case of O'Connell he would have preferred the colorful gesture; in the case of O'Neill, who did add the fire of the gambler to the caution of the "politician," he is disappointed that he should at this moment have allowed himself to be overborne by the emotional pleadings of his allies and did not remain firmly attached to his customary virtues of patience and discipline. In O'Connell the instincts of the gambler were already highly developed; his whole career had been filled with instances of bluff, daring, and aggressiveness. It was logical to expect him to be true to form at Clontarf and illogical to be disappointed when he was not. Similarly, the whole tenor of O'Neill's career had been patience, caution, reliance on time, and self-discipline, and therefore it was logical to expect him at Kinsale not to be guided so unwisely by emotional followers and to be disappointed when he was. Nevertheless, a logical solution will not suffice. In expressing his judgment upon O'Connell O'Faolain did not argue from the premise of a predetermined pattern of behavior. He merely called for the heroic instinct, the wasteful virtue, a quality that never depends on reasonable justification. It was, therefore, an instance of O'Faolain's romanticism overcoming his rational nature. His reaction to O'Neill's behavior *is* based on the evidence of an established norm and is strictly rational. Logically O'Neill should not have succumbed to the attraction of an outright military victory over a general as capable as himself. Romantically the idea is appealing. The difference in O'Faolain's reactions is a sign of development and change within himself, away from romanticism.

The fact that O'Faolain has been very successful as a historical biographer makes his relative lack of success as a novelist easier to explain. The two forms are so similar in the demands that they make upon a writer that there is good ground for believing that his inability to produce more than one really good novel is not altogether due to a personal weakness but rather to some external disadvantages inherent in the society in which he lives. Charles Neider has pointed out that to be able to create a literary portrait of any particular environment or period a writer has to make contact with his material and that to "make contact" in the poetic sense "signifies something very complicated, intimate—a penetration, carried to identification and self-substitution, so that something can be created which is called 'style' and which is always a unique and complete amalgamation of the artist with the subject."[16]

In the novels this involved and metaphysical process is not always complete, but in the two major biographies it has been more successful. *King of the Beggars* has been influenced by the work of the early Irish novelists, William Carleton, Charles Lever, and Maria Edgeworth, in its recreation of the conditions under which the peasants lived and of the manners and attitudes of the aristocracy. It has depended also on the general information available about the eighteenth- and early nineteenth-century philosophical, religious, political, and social beliefs, as well as on the numerous records of O'Connell's own life—letters, speeches, diaries, and so on. The intellectual problem of understanding the major ideas of the period and of estimating their effect on O'Connell was handled well. The work is spotted with some faulty interpretation and stress, but it would have taken an expert to untangle O'Connell's thinking and aims in some of the major issues of the day. In general O'Faolain has been able to present the man within a defining historical perspective. And certainly there was a sufficiency of incident in the life of this man to reveal his large and complex character.

The Great O'Neill presented the biographer with a more severe challenge because of the lack of evidence for the period and the man.[17] The final portrait, correspondingly more original than the portrait of O'Connell, demanded much more creative and imaginative energy from the writer. At the same time his intellectual conception of the subject's career has not been challenged on the grounds of historical inaccuracy or misinterpretation. The final achievement is a credible portrayal of the character of O'Neill within the logical reconstruction of the events in which he took part. And that reconstruction involved not merely the narration of incidents but a detailed and sensitive presentation of two civilizations and two types of warfare. In both biographies there is the evidence of O'Faolain's ability to fill in the background and to handle the general technical problems of structure and organization.

The two biographies are of interest not only because they show the skill of a novelist and the intellectual and imaginative power of the creative artist. In their contrasting conception of character and their stylistic attributes they illustrate the development that took place in O'Faolain between 1936 and 1942, between the writing of *Bird Alone* and *The Great O'Neill*. *Bird Alone* and *King of the Beggars* are optimistic works. The figure of O'Connell is the product of a writer who views his world with confidence and hope, and the luciferan posture of Corney Crone, the central figure in *Bird Alone,* is an assertion of individual pride in the face of all that may happen. Both works move with speed; both tend to be gigantic, even titanic, in their characterization; both reflect the author's aesthetic of personality. The novel is more restrained, but the biography revels in the hero's stature, in his appearance as the savior of his people, their creator and redeemer, their champion, their avatar. The culmination in a less than full martyrdom strikes the biographer as disappointing essentially because the poetic truth of the biography demands a fully heroic immolation of the self. The King of the Beggars is a figure compounded of heroes from the pagan and Christian traditions: he is his people's Moses[18] but also their Vulcan and their Hercules.[19] Like a figure in Greek tragedy his destruction is a necessary spiritual act for the survival of his people; the calamitous conclusion of this biography, the crack-up of the hero, the dissension among his followers, the ineffectual nobility of the Young Irelanders, and the terrible catastrophe of the Great Famine, is brought on illogically but with artistic truth because of the final failure of O'Connell, who will not lay down his life for his people, who will not let them share his martyrdom. O'Faolain tried to be strictly realistic but was guided by an inherent romanticism into this incredible and contradictory final judgment. In it literary truth triumphs over historical truth.

O'Neill by contrast is a much more sober, more disciplined, more restrained, and more integrated characterization. In this work the writer is in absolute control of his material and has come to terms with his romanticism. The tragic hero with the ironical perspective on his own involvement in a national movement is a personal portrait of an artist caught in a divided loyalty. It is an allegory of his resolute but clear-eyed acceptance of the advantages and disadvantages of such a position. O'Connell was by far the greater figure who "had all the joy of the creative artist in his life and work."[20] O'Neill is not as conscious of the "drive of history behind the individual."[21] One work is the reflection of a writer who still sees the possibility of a fully creative future; the other is the reflection of a writer who has come to realize that the integration of inherited affinities with intellectually acquired aims is not at all a simple process, not at all a private problem. O'Connell could move mountains; O'Neill has not the same faith. The difference between Corney Crone, the proud Faust, and Frankie Hannafey, the disenchanted reformer in *Come Back to Erin,* illustrate a similar change in point of view. In the second biography and in the third novel there is an increase in realism, objectivity, and technical control, but the biography succeeds in making the tension between the two sides of the divided loyalty an integrating factor for all the conflicts and divisions of the book—the two civilizations, religions, and types of warfare—but the novel fails to give dramatic force to the figure of the man caught between his atavistic attraction for his own people and his explicit desire for a more complex society. Frankie Hannafey is wrecked on the shores of sophisticated and shallow New York society, but Hugh O'Neill preserves his individuality and his irony amid the acclaim of Europe and the romantic distortions of his first biographer, Bishop Lombard.

The portrait of O'Neill is artistically more satisfying than the portrait of O'Connell because the propagandistic elements are not so obtrusive. O'Faolain is less concerned with hammering out social principles for a modern democracy than in creating a credible story of a particular human being. The result is the universal significance of a tragic type. There is an enlargement of human sympathy to be derived from the compassionate revelation of a man's inner struggle and inevitable involvement. The preparation for that commitment is finely achieved; lesser men are shown within the conflict of opposing civilizations and opposing modes of existence without any clear understanding of the magnitude and extent of the issues at state. O'Neill's story transcends theirs because his intelligence and experience prepare him and he goes into the catastrophe of that conflict in desperate awareness of all that is involved. The intensity and dignity of this creation, its imaginative integrity and moral truth, its allegory of the writer's own predicament, make it an outstanding achievement of O'Faolain's work.

Chapter 3

De Valera

The belief that public men serve as models for the whole nation inevitably placed the figure of Mr. De Valera in a central position in Sean O'Faolain's critical analysis of the new Ireland. Indeed the career of the writer had been closely bound up with this politician and statesman, and there is much evidence that the changing pattern of the relationship parallels and illuminates the evolution of the writer's response to the country as a whole. The theme of lost leadership that appears so frequently in his writings stems from his disappointment with the Republican movement and with its leader. Alternatively he has sought for figures in history—Wolfe Tone, Daniel O'Connell, Hugh O'Neill—as surrogate leaders. It would be difficult to overestimate the intensity of O'Faolain's youthful dedication to the cause of Irish nationalism and his loyalty to De Valera with whom, for him, it was associated. There is his own testimony that he "once held Mr. De Valera in an admiration 'this side idolatry,' "[1] and it was only after the Civil War that the divergence of the writer from the statesman began; it did not harden into a final condemnation until much later in 1945. That divergence was originated by his discovery of the absence of a clearly defined political or social policy behind the revolution.[2] It was intensified by his dissatisfaction with the manner in which De Valera tried to justify his acceptance of the Oath of Allegiance and by his growing discontent with the kind of society that was emerging in the new Ireland.

In 1931 O'Faolain redefined his political position as midway between the extreme Republican stand of those who wanted to continue the protest against the Treaty in arms and the constitutional policy of De Valera, who had moved into the Dail. He supported constitutional agitation in preference to further military activity because he wanted the country to have a period of peace in which to consolidate achievements and plan constructively for the future.[3] The fact that his support for De Valera was not complete must be kept in mind when reading his first biography (1933). It is very short work marred by propagandistic partisanship, and it is only by remembering the nature of O'Faolain's remarks in articles published about the same time that one can understand the true feelings behind the objective summary of the last chapter.[4] Published originally as a series of articles in the London newspaper, *The Sunday Chronicle,* it covers the main events of Mr. De Valera's career in a superficial and laudatory manner. O'Faolain commented later that it was written "as shamelessly pro-Dev and pro-Irish propaganda at a time when all of us who had stuck by De Valera from 1916 onwards at last saw our hero coming into power and all our dreams and ideals—as we foolishly and trustingly hoped—about to be realized."[5] The final chapter sums him up as an idealist and absolute nationalist, adhering not only to the Sinn Fein policy of complete self-reliance and separatism in politics but also adding to that the idea of separatism in language and culture; as prefiguring a Christian state within an individual culture based on the old Gaelic state; and as having a doctrinaire approach that led him to reduce too many problems to an abstract formula.

By 1934 O'Faolain had grown impatient with De Valera's absorption with absolute nationalism and his identification with a pure Gaelic past, because these caused him to formulate political ideas more in tune with the peasant background of the country than with the capitalistic, industrialized urban forefront. Such a philosophy left out of life "everything that was magnificent and irrelevant and proud and luxurious and lovely."[6] By 1935 he had decided that his countrymen were more absorbed in endless metaphysical debate about politics than with constructive social policies.[7] By 1936 he felt that within fifteen years of self-government the country had greatly changed.

In an important article in the *Yale Review* he maintained that the dominant figures in Irish life were the capitalist, the priest, and the politician—all of native stock. He pointed out that De Valera's limited economic program of protective tariffs for native products had created many petty capitalists and the Church, profiting by the loss of strength that civil war had caused, was more powerful than before the revolution, when an aristocracy alien in racial origin and religious identification had ruled. The native politician had naturally gained in prominence. The country was being given a nationalistic and religious bias that favored only the new middle class. Isolation from the outside world was advocated because of the possible danger to religion and culture. Insulation from the outside world was being advocated because of the possible danger to economic stability. Politician, priest, and capitalist were united under common aims that were advantageous spiritually, culturally, and economically. But the intermingling of sanctity with financial security and salvation with social stability caused O'Faolain to be somewhat suspicious.[8]

Much of his subsequent work was concerned with analyzing the elements of the new society that emerged from post-revolutionary Ireland. De Valera was inextricably bound up with this examination. *King of the Beggars,* published two years after the *Yale Review* article, mirrored the psychological characteristics of the Irish democracy and the practical and useful patterns of behavior that had been projected in Daniel O'Connell. In the following year, the second biography of Eamon De Valera attempted to illustrate the contemporary scene by the same method. Clarification of the type of mentality of the man who was to a certain extent the embodiment of the people's ambitions became important not only in seeking to understand the man himself but in understanding the character of the democracy he represented. The characteristics of the Irish mind were once again in evidence, the ability to dissociate one's self "from all responsibility for mental reservations, or, indeed, a power of dissociating one's self by means of mental reservations from the responsibility of what one is actually doing."[9]

The illustration of the existence of the Irish mind in De Valera was based on the examination of his behavior on five different occasions: his compromise solution as president of Sinn Fein in 1917 to the conflicting aims of the left and right wing elements in the Irish movement;[10] his Cuban proposal (1919) that England should adopt a British Monroe Doctrine in dealing with the Irish question, that is, stipulate that Ireland should never enter into compacts with other powers which might endanger her own independence nor allow any foreign power to get control in Ireland;[11] his theoretical arguments to uphold the "Second Dail" on the grounds that a minority of Republicans elected by a minority of the people, was the true government of Ireland and not the Free State government;[12] his method of accepting the Oath of Allegiance and his method of formulating ideas in the Constitution of 1937, which he drafted himself. Of these the last two are of particular significance in O'Faolain's critical assessment of the man and the people he represents.

Even in 1939 O'Faolain found De Valera guilty of confusing truth with falsehood in considering the matter of the Oath of Allegiance,[13] although he did not yet believe it to be indicative of "intellectual and moral obscurity."[14] This parliamentary oath had been embodied in the Treaty and had to be taken by members of the Free State Dail in the following form:

I, —————————, do solemnly swear true faith and allegiance to the Constitution of the Irish Free State as by law established and that I will be faithful to H. M. King George V, his heirs and successors by law, in virtue of the common citizenship of Ireland with Great Britain and her adherence to and membership of the group of nations forming the British Commonwealth of Nations.[15]

Because this offered less than a republic, De Valera and other
Republicans opposed the treaty in word and deed, refusing to
recognize the validity of the Free State Dail. Even when he had
broken with the Republicans and formed a new political party,
Fianna Fail, De Valera refused to enter the Dail as a minority
opposition leader because of the objection to the Oath of Allegiance. In speech after speech prior to the elections of 1927 he
denounced the Oath, insisting that he would never enter the Dail
while it existed. It had been suggested by those who had accepted
it that it differed from ordinary oaths and was not morally binding. To this he replied that it was sufficient for him that it began
with "I do solemnly swear" and was called an official oath. Why
go through mockery of that sort if it were not an oath?[16] The general election was held on June 9, 1927. On June 23 De Valera
and his followers entered the parliament building, but on being
brought to the room in which the signatures were customarily
signed and on being told that the signing was a formality, he
withdrew in protest and announced that they had been prevented
from entering the Dail as a political party "Because they would
neither take a false oath nor prove recreant to the aspiration of
the Irish people and renounce their principles."[17] Then the Dail
introduced and passed an Electoral Amendment Bill designed to
counter abstentionist policies. This decreed that every candidate
for election to the Dail should, on nomination, swear an affidavit
that if elected he would take the Oath prescribed by the Constitution. Thus De Valera had to make a choice between sacrificing
his principles or accepting political extinction. Already his followers had begun to desert him and to take the Oath. On August
11, 1927, he led his followers into the Dail and subscribed the
Oath. Five years later he tried to justify himself; it is this justification, so revealing of the character of the man, that has received
most critical comment.

Believing that "I swear" would mean an oath, I said, in my opinion,
it was an oath. My view was that it was an oath. But the Deputies
opposite had said quite differently. They said that it was not, that it
was a mere formality—they used the words long before I used them—
and had no binding significance whatever, that anyone could take it,

and that it meant nothing. I asked myself whether in a crisis like that I would be justified in staying outside if it were, in fact, true that this thing was a mere formality. I could only find out in one way. In order that the people's attention should not be attracted to it, instead of taking the oath—as they would have done, if they dared to stand over it as a thing the Irish people would stand for—publicly, as in other Parliaments, they hid it away in a back room, hid it away out of sight, so that the public could not know what it was. I said that at least we were entitled to find out. We published a declaration and here is the original document, signed by every member, in which we stated our attitude. The attitude was in fact this: the majority party of that time held that it was no oath at all; we are going to put it to the test. In order that our coming in here might not be misrepresented we made a public declaration as to what our intentions were. When we came to take this so-called oath I presented this document to the officer in charge and told him that that was our attitude—there were witnesses present for every word—that this was our attitude; that we were not prepared to take an oath. I have here the original document written in pencil, and in Irish, of the statement I made to the officer who was supposed to administer the oath. I said "I am not prepared to take an oath. I am not going to take an oath. I am prepared to put my name down in this book in order to get permission to go into the Dail, but it has no other significance." There was a Testament on the table and in order that there could be no misunderstanding I went and I took the Testament and put it over and said, "You must remember I am taking no oath."

A deputy having here interrupted to ask whether he did not sign the declaration, Mr. De Valera replied: "I signed it in the same way as I would sign an autograph in a newspaper. If you ask me whether I had an idea what was there, I say 'Yes.' It was neither read to me nor was I asked to read it."[18]

O'Faolain regarded the practical decision to enter the Dail as the inevitable move of the idealist who had been forced to compromise with the unidealistic world. He has never condemned De Valera for changing face completely. What he has found it impossible to condone is the pretense that there was no change of position. As early as 1934 he had defended Constance Markievicz's break with De Valera on the grounds of her inability to accept the "theology" with which he tried to justify his behavior —"she knew that no argument could now justify her in accepting the fruits of the Treaty that did not also stultify her and condemn her for her part in the civil strife. . . "[19]

It was easy enough to explain the decision of her simple, straightforward mind, but the second biography of De Valera did not arrive at any definite judgment either. The critical question of why he had not taken the Oath before the Civil War was not satisfactorily answered by saying that he did not think he would have to.[20] To the question of what he gained by entering the Dail as a minority leader in 1927 and not in 1922, O'Faolain rightly replied that he avoided the stigma of accepting the treaty and upheld the claim to absolute Republicanism. But to the further question of whether he did not forfeit that symbol in 1927, O'Faolain merely replied that he claimed that he did not but had acted under duress and had not really taken any oath. Realizing the inadequacy of this explanation, since it immediately led to the question of honesty, O'Faolain evaded a personal opinion by saying that the question of DeValera's integrity could only be answered by considering the enigma of the Irish mind.[21] By 1945 he was prepared to speak directly. In the first place he condoned the Republican protest in arms against a treaty that had been dictated by force and maintained that De Valera and his followers were entitled morally and politically to refuse majority rule. Whether that decision was politically advisable was a question he did not discuss. Once again he showed respect and sympathy for the idealist's dilemma but now strongly objected to his "prolonged practice by means of ingenious argufying that he never did what everybody knows he did, and that 'it is different now.' "[22] There should be an end, he said, "to this public smarm of righteousness about it all."[23]

It was this pretense that had continually made it impossible for O'Faolain to accept De Valera as a political leader of integrity and greatness. O'Connell, he felt, would have avoided the stigma of hypocrisy by stating openly that he disliked the Oath and the whole treaty position and would get rid of both of them by constitutional means.[24] His final statement in connection with the acceptance of the Oath was a logical result of his reservations about the integrity of the Irish mind:

One may forgive a man a hundred contradictions of behavior; what one does not forgive is when the evasions of his mind begin to disintegrate his soul. If a man, for example, takes an oath under duress, he may or may not justify his action. But if he keeps on deceiving himself and deceiving the public that he *never did it at all,* then all one can say about that sort of thing is what Bacon said about plain lies, that the man who tells them is brave before God but a coward before man. . . ."[25]

The Constitution of 1937 served O'Faolain as documentary evidence for De Valera's Irish mind. Calling it "unimaginative . . . commonplace . . . pedantic and circumscribed,"[26] he noted that it was characterized by distinctions rather than by assertions, by cautious negatives rather than by bold affirmations. Its author constantly interposed himself to interpret and qualify the various statements.[27]

The contrast between the character of Daniel O'Connell and that of Eamon De Valera as seen by this biographer is pronounced. For, although O'Faolain explicitly stated only the similarity of their Irish minds, he must also have been aware of the many implicit dissimilarities. An illuminating, if somewhat exaggerated, effect is produced when these are placed side by side. O'Connell is the extrovert leader inspiring a whole people, De Valera a pedantic teacher. Drawn to European ideas, O'Connell wanted to bring his people into similar contacts. De Valera, however, remained isolationist and provincial. O'Connell realistically swept aside the Gaelic language and all that it represented to accelerate the forward march of his people. De Valera idealistically and impractically identified with the Gaelic past. O'Connell fought the bishops on the veto question and expressed the people's will even when it was antagonistic to the Church. De Valera tended to implement clerical aims, no matter what the people thought. O'Connell wanted to embrace the whole of Irish life in an inclusive, nonsectarian, vigorous democracy, but De Valera favored an intolerant, inhibiting system. One was instinctively joined with his people, the other was inherently separated from them. One expressed their needs, the other frustrated them.

The implicit contrast with the character of O'Connell is striking. Almost as important in O'Faolain's mind is the contrast with that of Theobald Wolfe Tone, the chief figure of the United Irishmen, a Republican, a man of charming personality and with civilized ideas about life. He had a "merry, insuppressible, eager, all too human nature, so sceptical, so serious, so gay, so indiscreet, so utterly removed from all posing and false dignity."[29] He was to O'Faolain the only sensible definition of what Irishmen meant when they talked of being Republicans. From his *Autobiography* comes a vivid portrait, full of laughter and humanity. O'Faolain, who edited it in 1937, felt certain that Tone would not have liked the way of life De Valera had allowed to develop in post-revolutionary Ireland; would have resisted "the least sign of sectarianism, puritanism, middle-class vulgarity, canting pietism, narrow orthodoxies whether of Church or State,"[30] had he been first president of the Irish Republic.

There were two main aspects to De Valera's nature as seen by O'Faolain, his pedagogical manner and his provincialism—the one a remnant of his first profession, the other of his rural background. The presentation of De Valera as a teacher was of considerable importance since the tendency to explain was, on his own admission, rooted in his character. It weakened the value of his Constitution and accounted for the long-winded, expository nature of his speeches. O'Faolain believed that it hampered his political career since it caused him to treat his followers as immature.[31]

The other aspect this biographer stressed was De Valera's provincialism. Since he lived on a small farm in County Limerick during his formative years, he was influenced in many respects by the simple mode of life experienced in the hard, patriarchal, antique world of the 1880's.[32] De Valera himself referred often to the values he learned in that environment and their effect upon his thinking, believing incorrectly that because of those years of contact with the simple, rural way of life, he understood intuitively the needs of the people as a whole. Such a way of life could account for his simple frugal way of living and for the unimaginative concept of an Irish society based on the philosophy of a small farm. It could account also for the idealism and deep religious feeling that was apparent in his vision of a Christian, Gaelic Ireland, the "dreary Eden"[33] O'Faolain found so frustrating.

The 1939 biography tried to sum up De Valera's impact during the seven years in which he had been a political leader with a majority in the Dail. The one objective factor in which he could be most completely seen was the social revolution that had over-taken the country during his lifetime. O'Faolain's views on the middle class that consolidated itself during De Valera's time in office vary. On the one hand he may speak of its members as "a lot of well-meaning, good-hearted, good-humoured, not unidealis-tic, cute chancers with about as much cultivation as the heel of your boot";[34] or he will say "to be quite honest, because our new Irish, or shall I say our Raw Irish, are of decent stock, and we are still a fairly unspoiled peasant people, and we are, in the main . . . a pretty fine race, our middle class Ireland could be far worse than it is. . . ."[35] But on the other hand, in *The Irish* (1937) while outlining the process by which the peasants in the towns profited by the government's eagerness to develop native industries, he separated the particular aspects of the middle class as follows:

What is hard to endure is the combination, in this class, of vul-garity and insincerity. . . . They will indulge shamelessly in lobbying, political wire-pulling, do not stop at open corruption, kow-tow to clerical influence, make a constant parade of patriotism and piety, never utter, rarely support, and (with some honourable exceptions) do nothing to create an independent public opinion. Their influence on political and social life is pervasive. . . . I do not wish to paint a villainous picture. On the contrary these individuals are the most pleasant and sociable rascals in the world. They are kind and chari-table, and what is known as "good sports," so that no stranger or native who does not use his political uncommon sense would think them other than a splendid addition to the community, instead of, as they are, a splendid subtraction from the community—in the shape of fat profits at public expense. The most engaging and infuriating thing about these individuals is that they are tremendously patriotic. What they are doing for Ireland is their constant theme song; no mention being, of course, made of the percentage charged.[36]

The revolution of 1916–1923, had, in O'Faolain's estimation, a fundamentally social base. To fill the vacuum left by the depar-ture or depression of an alien middle class, came a *petit bour-geoisie,* as he had begun to suspect in 1936 and to fear in 1939, to exercise a predominating influence. He recognized that they could not have been expected to exert much cultural influence in the early stages; and that since their new wealth depended on the continuation of the status quo, they were unlikely to risk it by gratuitous displays of moral courage. The intellectual's fight for freedom of expression would receive hardly any comprehension from them. The ideal of public order and morality enshrined in the Constitution was more in keeping with their general outlook. They had, if anything, a vested interest in nationalism and isolation. As the years went by and their wealth and security increased, their alliance with the Church and the politicians became more firmly cemented. All three groups were nationalist-isolationist for, respectively, commercial, moral, and politico-patriotic reasons.[37] What he had sensed in 1936 had hardened into a social reality. If the relation between all this and the figure of Eamon De Valera is unclear, it will be clarified upon consideration of O'Faolain's most outspoken and most complete denunciation of the man whom he once held "this side idolatry."

The truth is that the people have fallen into the hands of flatterers and cunning men, who trifle with their intelligence and would chloroform their old hopes and dreams, so that it is only the writers and artists of Ireland, who can hope to call them back to the days when these dreams blazed into a searing honesty, as when Connolly told the wrecked workers of this city that he found them with no other weapons but those of the lickspittle and the toady and what his job and theirs was to make men of themselves. Surely, these are honourable footsteps to follow? Surely it is not to let the country down but to try to raise it up, to reveal the drab poverty level of life which has sent our youth stampeding to the wartime cities of Britain and now threatens another exodus of their wives and children. Surely it is the duty of our writers to keep hammering at such facts as that our children today are as hopeless putty in the hands of morons who have imposed on our generation a parody of an educational system beyond all ignorant, narrow and unrealistic, at which parents growl helplessly, at which the superiors of schools and convents can only wail and wring their hands, but in which the authors thereof obstinately and bearishly persist year after year against the protests of every class and creed? Surely it is not defeatist to protest to high Heaven against a censorship of bosthoons over letters and opinion in such a country?

It is the nature of writers to have a passionate love of life and a profound desire that it should be lived in the greatest possible fullness and richness by all men: and when we see here such wonderful raw material, a nature so naturally warm and generous as the Irish nature, so adventurous, so eager, so gay, being chilled and frustrated by constant appeals to peasant fears, to peasant pietism, to the peasant sense of self-preservation, and all ending in a half-baked sort of civilization which, taken all-over, is of a tawdriness a hundred miles away from our days of vision—when we see all that we have no option but to take all these things in one angry armful and fling them at the one man who must accept them as his creation, his reflex, his responsibility. In a nutshell, we say that this surely is not the Ireland that Wolfe Tone would have liked to live in, or even Dan O'Connell, for all his peasant coarseness and cunning, or the aristocratic Parnell, or any man like that old eagle John O'Leary, or that warm-hearted Jim Connolly, or any man who really loved men and life. And we accuse it.[38]

Such an indictment is comprehensive. The belief that public men serve as models for the whole nation was not altogether fair to a politician who had to work within the ambience of his own society and the limitations of his own character. De Valera has yet to find a biographer who will treat his political career within the perspectives of the various social, economic, political and religious ideas of his period. Until much preliminary scholarship has been done in these various fields and until the necessary documents and records are available to researchers it is virtually impossible to write anything like a representative study of the man or the period. In the meantime O'Faolain's second biography (1939), his two editorials (1945), and his extensive social commentary provide the most intelligible judgment. Even more important they help define the conditions within which Irish literature had been produced since the revolution.

Chapter 4

A Dreary Eden

Central to O'Faolain's analysis of the society that grew under De Valera was the contrast between the Ireland of 1900–1912 and the Ireland of his own time. Separate him from the basic idea that 1913–1923 was the dividing time between an extroverted, broad-minded, vital period and an introverted, narrow-minded, frustrating period and you undermine one of the essential factors in his mental image of the whole era. It was the new social milieu resulting from the consolidation of a native middle class that was the target for his critical attack in his historical biographies and in numerous other commentaries. He was stimulated partly by his awareness of what the country was like before the revolution, when life seemed emotionally more exciting and intellectually more stimulating. It was the kind of period in which literature could and did flourish. It was the Ireland of Yeats and Joyce, of George Moore, A.E., St. John Gogarty, James Stephens, and the Abbey Theater. In those days, he remarked in *Constance Markievicz,* "everything was in full swing—the theatre, the new literature, the new Gaelic movement, Sinn Fein, Labour. . . . Ever since then solemnity has killed the joy of life, and democracy wilts under the weight of its own conscience."[1] He spoke enthusiastically of that period in the first biography of De Valera, again in the second biography, and later in *An Irish Journey* and some editorials. There are, he said, "times in the history of every country when a liveliness in the air catches up the slightest dream and dilates it beyond measure . . ."[2] Political, social, and literary life were intense and challenging. Writers were faced with a stratified and fairly complex social scene.

In the second biography of De Valera, O'Faolain criticized his subject because he did not participate in Dublin life and missed the experiences of its many levels—the polite upper class, the club life, the sporting crowd, the large body of ordinary people in amateur theater, in the many pubs and cafes where one met the literary, theatrical, and political people.[3] Constance Markievicz was attracted to the vitality and color of that period in which the energy and assertiveness of the lower classes expressed itself in the Tramway Strike of 1913, in the founding of the Irish Citizen Army, and in the confidence of the socialist leader, James Connolly, whose presence accelerated the momentum of revolution. The Sinn Fein political movement attracted the writers, and for a time literature and politics were closely associated. But the excitement and promise did not survive the revolution and the social scene that later developed was much thinner. The sense of excitement and promise had subsided. The writer was left to work out his own destiny as best he could. His main problem was the diminished reality around him. Writers of the Irish literary revival had drawn freely from a rich store of legend and myth and history. The way had been prepared for them by the activity of poets, scholars, and translators in the nineteenth century. Even those who experienced the excitement of the Revolution and bitterness of the Civil War found passionate material ready at hand. It was the anticlimax of the postrevolutionary period that was cold to the touch. Now the writer had to think of what to write about; he had to find ways in which to handle a reality that was not immediately exciting, heroic, or supernatural. Looking back

in 1953 O'Faolain commented on the changed conditions that
faced the writer in his generation:

There is no longer any question about dishing up local colour. The
Noble Peasant is as dead as the Noble Savage. Poems about fairies
and leprechauns, about misted lakes, old symbols of national longing,
are over and done with. We have explored Irish life with an objectivity never hitherto applied to it, and in this Joyce rather than Yeats
is our inspiration. But to see clearly is not to write passionately.[4]

The writer was limited, first of all, in his choice of material.
He could make use either of the traditional, intellectually simple
life of the small farm or the new, undefined life of the town. Of
the two he would be instinctively drawn to the familiar, rural
background. Unfortunately that area had been overworked. The
Abbey Theater had presented the themes of the countryside, the
hunger for land, the greed, the mixed marriages, the religious
fervor, the small intrigues, and the family feuds. But the alternative was strange. Urban conventions were as yet embryonic, and
few clearly defined social patterns were visible. In addition,
O'Faolain's own conservative view of the novel made it difficult
for him to handle amorphous crowds. The novel, he believed,
finds its most congenial milieu in a closely organized, hierarchical society, and its usual role is to present the play of personality
on personality. It has to make use of the accepted or debated
values and conventions; it has to formulate the clashes between
the aberrants and the tradition. "How," he asked, "can one play
personality upon personality if the characters themselves are not
interesting personalities?"[5] Where writers at the beginning of
the century had found rich inspiration all around them, often
from the sense of contact with a folk-world of ancient traditions,
the writers of O'Faolain's time, faced with a changed environment
and a less congenial atmosphere, had to be analytical and rational.
They could hardly escape the sense of cultural shrinkage. Death
had taken the elder writers, and exile constantly depleted the
ranks of the younger ones. O'Faolain became increasingly aware
of the similarity between his environment and the world of
Hawthorne as seen by Henry James.

Just as James in his famous list had commented on Hawthorne's
provincial, simple surroundings by drawing an analogy with Eng-

lish life, so O'Faolain commented on Irish life by analogy with European and English life.

Here is a country with few monuments and these most drearily paid for, few traditions that have projected themselves, no palaces here, no triumphal arches, hardly a statue outside Dublin, no provincial Pinacoteca, or Piazza Dante or ancient amphitheatre, or towering cathedral, no Siena or Rouen, no gay cafe life, no mellow Dorset towns, few, if any, really pretty villages, no clever cooking, no wine. . . . And, yet, that good 'feel' is there.[6]

In *The Liberal Imagination,* Lionel Trilling comments on James' enumeration of the things lacking to give the American novel the thick social texture of the English novel apply equally well to O'Faolain's list: "that is, no sufficiency of means for the display of a variety of manners, no opportunity for the novelist to do his job of searching out reality, not enough complication of appearance to make the job interesting."[7] O'Faolain has been particularly conscious of the achievement of Balzac and would agree with Trilling's comment on the evidence in Balzac's novels of "life in a crowded country where the competitive pressures are great, forcing great passions to express themselves fiercely yet within the limitations set by a strong and competitive tradition of manners."[8] James was sympathetically aware of the thinly composed, democratic, and simple world of Hawthorne and knew it takes a great deal of history to produce a little literature and a complex machinery to set a writer in motion. Irish writers, O'Faolain pointed out, could very well understand the implications of the Jamesian concern about "social dreariness," "Juvenility," and "the life that has begun to constitute itself from the foundation; begun to *be* simply."[9] James had remarked, too, on the difficulty of a provincial writer having to face such a society with the necessary enjoyment of the artist in his material, of his having to work empirically without the value of companions with identical purposes, without the stimulus of suggestion and emulation. It was partly to avoid this lack of companionship that Irish writers emigrated or spent long periods out of the country. But there were other aspects of Irish life that made exile attractive and increased the discomforts of those who remained.

Edward Garnett's introduction to *Midsummer Night Madness*

drew attention to some of them. Alternating between praise of
O'Faolain as a young writer of ability and promise and pity for
him as a native of a country in which there was little awareness
of literary standards, Garnett formulated a general picture of the
circumstances within which O'Faolain would have to work. Ireland, he observed, stood at the bottom of the cultural world with
an abnormally conservative literature and a national mind paro-
chially indifferent to critical standards and to its own literature.
Irishmen, he went on, were apathetic in supporting art and sus-
taining critical values; they had a puritanical attitude toward
sex; they supported an isolationist policy of shutting out all non-
Gaelic expression; and they tolerated a lack of freedom in the
discussion of social, literary, and religious values. The prompt
banning of *Midsummer Night Madness* must have struck him as
a grim but not surprising confirmation of his judgment upon his
fellow-countrymen.

Actually there was no shortage of evidence at this time or at
any later time. Public bodies in County Mayo had refused to
allow a Protestant girl to be County Librarian and had forced
their will on the government. In Galway the works of George
Bernard Shaw were banned on moral grounds. In Limerick they
seized the English newspaper, the *Sunday Times,* because it contained an article on birth control. And because the English *Daily
Mail* published a sympathetic review of a materialistic life of
Christ, it was forbidden entry to Ireland. O'Faolain's explanations
for these actions excused them on the grounds that they were
those of a people unaccustomed to exercising their democratic
rights; they were, he explained, the outcome of an "uninstructed
Puritan Catholicism . . . the blind gropings towards the creation
of a national mind."[10] Nevertheless, minimize them though he
might, they were symptomatic of a kind of narrow, restricted
mentality that had little sympathy for the writer.

De Valera's abstract ideal of a Gaelic, Christian state favored
isolationism in culture. Two books by Daniel Corkery gave formal expression to a doctrinaire criticism that was characteristic of
a widespread attitude. *The Hidden Ireland, A Study of Gaelic
Munster in the 18th Century* (1925) popularized peasant culture

in a romantic way. It was attacked by O'Faolain in several articles and in *King of the Beggars,* mainly because it overrated the literature of the seventeenth and eighteenth centuries and set poor standards for those interested in learning the Gaelic language.[11] *Synge and Anglo-Irish Literature* (1931) formulated the official attitude more completely. It expressed a preference for exclusively Gaelic literature and condemned Anglo-Irish literature as a partial and inadequate interpretation of Irish life. Corkery belittled the writing of the Irish literary revival as colonial. He argued that since it was written by Irishmen who did not live in Ireland and did not write primarily for their own people and were evaluated mainly by non-Irish critics, it could not be regarded as an Irish literature. A "normal" literature, Corkery maintained, lives and dies by the judgment of its own people first of all; an "abnormal" literature lives and dies by the criticism of people who are not Irish and therefore it is not "national."[12] Government subsidies encouraged writers in Gaelic but not those writing in English, and the creation of an official literary censorship (1929) marked the blending of moral and patriotic elements in a combined attack on the writers. O'Faolain rightly explained that the official censorship favored the Gaelic revivalist, who feared the influence of European and especially English literature for nationalist reasons, because it might hinder the encouragement of native Gaelic literature. He explained that it also favored the Catholic Actionist, who feared the same influences for moral reasons.[13] Official literary censorship also had the unfortunate effect of sanctioning the existing censorship by local groups and signalled the increasing influence of what they represented.

Censorship was certainly one of the irritating factors in Irish life, but it did not hinder any Irish writer of ability from doing whatever his artistic conscience decreed. In fact it became a kind of humorous accolade: the better the book the more likelihood there was of its being banned. Irish writers of distinction, such as Austin Clarke, Liam O'Flaherty, Frank O'Connor, and Sean O'Faolain, continued to produce work of sufficiently high caliber to merit the disapproval of the censors. Nevertheless, the situation was not altogether humorous. The immediate effect was to cut the serious writer off from his primary audience. It was also distressing to be branded officially as a menace to public morality, to have one's books excluded from public libraries, from Irish bookshops, and forbidden entrance to the country as a whole. In reality the Censorship of Publication Act ought to have protected the serious writer. As the law stands a book can only be banned if it is in general tendency indecent or obscene or if it advocates unnatural methods of birth control. The censors are supposed to take into consideration the overall literary or artistic merit of the book.

In practice, the serious writer suffered unfairly and found himself all too readily listed with the pornographers. The censorship board was guilty of many blunders, such as its banning of Halliday Sutherland's *The Laws of Life* in 1943. They had not realized that the book had received the imprimatur of the Westminster Diocesan Council six years earlier. But it was the debates on this issue in the Irish Parliament that vindicated the writer's constant complaint that the censorship law worked unfairly. The Minister for Justice flatly declared that he was the law, "that whether or not a book was legally banned he would over-ride or ignore the Act of Parliament and ban it on other (unspecified) grounds."[14] Books were being improperly proscribed under cover of the law. Censorship, official, local, and private, was merely one of the manifestations of a general antagonism to the writer, and it was the cumulative effect of the latter that was dangerous to his creativity.

The writer's awareness of many elements in the community hostile to the freedoms of the artist had the potential danger of making him embittered and distorted in outlook. Such forces threaten creativity. O'Faolain feared as early as 1934 that his own unsympathetic response to certain facets of Irish life might impair his sympathy with humanity itself.[15] In 1953 he asserted that it was the attempt to maintain a fair balance in himself toward his material that made the real difficulty for the Irish writer.[16] Dissatisfaction is a dangerous condition of the writer. It is a measure of O'Foalain's courage and sense of public duty that he devoted so much energy to polemical, controversialist work. He believed the nation and the artist needed each other and once stated a "purely hypothetical example" of the extreme condition that might conceivably arise in Ireland or elsewhere:

. . . suppose a writer to be living in a country in which the politicians are corrupt, in which religion is used for temporal reasons, in which the machinery of the law is employed to give an almost despotic power to the State, in which the poor are kept quiet with bribes, in which everything is cloaked with a great panoply of patriotism, but in which the individual soul is inert and timid and silenced? No matter how fair the face of that imaginary country, no matter how materially prosperous it may be, your artist will have to fall silent, or, as often happens, he will take ancient historical subjects remote from his immediate surroundings, or he will go off into fantasies or end in flippancy and bitterness, and all the natural poetry of a "full human life" will vanish from his heart.[17]

His urge to interpret the social scene was not limited to his need as a writer to understand it. He believed that by defining its elements he could release the country from narrow, outdated loyalties in much the same way as Hugh O'Neill and Daniel O'Connell did. Intellectual leadership had not come from the state or the Church and the responsibility therefore fell on the writer. He had the important job of fighting for the rights of the individual. O'Faolain's social commentaries ranged over thirty years, and in 1947 he could claim with justice that he had helped to clarify intelligible and recognizable elements within the community: liberals, chauvinists, bureaucrats, pietists, professional peasants, native middle classes, the frank and brutal racketeers, "friends," and "enemies."[18] Much of that clarification resulted from his outspoken and intelligent editorials in *The Bell* magazine, which he founded and edited from 1940–1946.

Social and political problems, however, were not his primary concern. Insofar as the magazine had any definite policy at the beginning, it was intended to receive the impression of the life of the country, assuming, as it hopefully did, that life would stamp an impression. The first issue appealed for articles on the "intimately known corners of life," that is, on the familiar things that appeal to the individual. O'Faolain intended to accept the situation but to see it clearly, to get the facts and thereby understand the picture.[19] The theme of acceptance ran through the editorials and was a reply to the idealists and absolutists who dreamed of an Irish greatness and clung to the romantic and glorified vision of prerevolutionary years. The editor's realistic opinion was that Ireland could never hope to be one of the great nations of the world, and so the magazine eschewed noble theories of civilization and advocated

. . . the simple things of life which are those theories made flesh, the seat by the fire, the ritual of the table, the enjoyed book in the clevvy, the satisfaction of eye and mind, the quiet hour in the church whose grace itself is a prayer, dress, habits, the arts in their simplest and noblest expression.[20]

A literature dealing with these themes was what he hoped to encourage, but only Frank O'Connor, Liam O'Flaherty, and he were capable of producing short stories of such an intimate kind. At the same time he appealed for elegance, articles on fine food, fine dress, fine furniture, fine drink, all things that delight and satisfy the senses.[21] In all, he was seeking for a desirable image of life which would be natural to the country. He wanted the magazine to be in tune with popular life, to get from it assurance of normality, balance, and truth.[22] He was trying hard to avoid the doctrinaire approach of Corkery and the professional Gaels, who tried to impose preconceived standards and aims upon the people. He wanted to get back to the roots of the new Ireland, beyond the social revolution, to rediscover the instinctive virtues of the people. For a long time he refused to state where *The Bell* stood on intellectual, political, or social issues.[23] His attitude was that the country was at the beginning of its creative history and at the end of its revolutionary history, and consequently Irish standards and tastes were confused and undeveloped.[24] He quoted Boswell with approval:

The true state of every nation is the state of common life. . . . The great mass of nations is neither rich nor gay: they whose aggregate constitutes the people are found in the streets, the villages, in the shops and farms, and from them, collectively considered must the measure of a general prosperity be taken. As *they* approach to delicacy a nation is refined, as *their* conveniences are multiplied a nation, at least a commercial nation must be denominated wealthy.[25]

As "A Magazine of Creative Fiction" *The Bell* was not a success. The hope of being able to record life in a faithful, realistic manner gave way finally to despair. By comparison with Yeats's *Samhain* "full of poetic vision of ideal life and noble theories, interesting aesthetic ideas,"[26] or with A.E.'s *Irish Statesman*, O'Faolain felt that a literary magazine could not be produced in the Ireland of his own day. It was just one more sad proof that the country had changed. He could only surmise more and more that a "weight of inertia, some large psychological frustration"[27] prevailed all over the country and the energy of the people could not be released until it would disappear. In April 1946 he resigned as editor with that unhappy thought. The sense of the intellectual shrinkage in the country remained with him, an awareness of a contraction in the society around him.

The basic cause of this decline was the inability of the new middle class to produce sufficient intellectual energy to reproduce itself in literature. The peasants could not be expected to provide leadership and generative ideas, and although they continued to drift into the towns, they found little clear-cut guidance there. Nevertheless there was material for the writer in Dublin at least. There one encountered

. . . the emerging society of a native government, a corps diplomatique, a Church of unbounded influence and occasional panoply, a growing middle-class full of energy, a raw, new industrialism, a decaying gentry, and an *ancien regime* that hums with echoes; and there are the problems that go with these things—men fumbling for power, men fumbling for place; men fumbling for standards, moral, social, cultural; men fumbling on all sides to find out what it is all about, and what it is all leading to. . . .[28]

None of this had appeared in *The Bell*. Nor had it appeared to any appreciable degree in O'Faolain's fiction. The whole difficulty for the writer was that this period really was one of pause before change. There was the sense of new beginnings being made. The writer was caught in the general contradiction and confusion, the general uncertainty about standards and taste. He was forced to be empiric, hoping at best to make writers coming after "by our very failure, to see and to say how much better it could be done."[29] O'Faolain himself could be quite clear and appreciative of the many attractive qualities of the country. On the level of *l'homme moyen sensuel* the lazy tempo, friendly air, good-heartedness, and warm charity were very attractive. Unlike the artist or the intellectual he would not be restricted by the one class of petty bourgeois, uncultivated businessmen, by the puritanical Church, or by the old-time, thoughtless politicians. A generation of isolationism and obscuranticism that had, as O'Faolain kept pointing out, changed a lively nationalism into a cantankerous provincialism[30] would fail to dampen his enjoyment of the amicable, argumentative, hot-headed, roguish, kindly Irishman.[31] Significantly the literature failed to reflect the humor. O'Faolain concluded that hypermoralists and hypernationalists had deflected the artist from seeing life steadily and seeing it whole.[32]

O'Faolain's achievement as editor of *The Bell* ought not to be measured solely by the nonappearance of the creative revolution in literature and life that he had hoped to encourage. That failure tended to confirm his gloomy opinion about Irish life and thus make his own creative efforts more difficult. But his judgment on *The Bell* was too severe. His analogy of postrevolutionary Ireland with the days in which the literary revival flourished side by side with a confident national spirit is unjustifiably hard on himself and his period. Apart altogether from the general mood of the country after 1923 and from the depressing vulgarity and hypocrisy of the middle class, it was hardly to be expected that the level of achievement of a Yeats, a Synge, a Lady Gregory, and a Joyce could be maintained indefinitely. Even large countries with a rich literary and cultural heritage never achieve sixty years of unflagging literary output of a high quality. It was too much to expect a small and shrinking nation in the first flush of independence and the uncertainty of nationhood to produce a James Stephens, a George Moore, or an A.E. in every generation. The flowering of Anglo-Irish literature in the 1890–1920 era was a phenomenon unlikely to be repeated in the 1920–1950 period or for some time. At the same time, O'Faolain's sense of a dilution in national life was justified.

His enthusiasm for the idea of a new revival was influenced to some extent by the achievements of A.E., who as editor of *The Irish Statesman* (1923–30) had given encouragement to almost every major Irish writer of the time. In his pages also had appeared the early work of a large number of young men: Seamus O'Sullivan, Padraic Colum, James Stephens, Frank O'Connor, and O'Faolain himself. O'Faolain's constant search for a desirable image of life resulted from his realization that there had been a general weakening in the quality of Irish life and a consequent impoverishment of each man's mind and life. His vision of a nation was consistent with A.E.'s:

A nation is cultivated only so far as the average man, not the exceptional person, is cultivated and has knowledge of the thought, imagination, and intellectual history of his nation. When there is a general culture its effects are seen in the houses, the pictures, the homes and gardens, the arts of life. Almost insensibly beauty enters the household and what is meant by civilization is apparent.[33]

O'Faolain hoped for some sign of an emergence of a distinctive, national culture. In this he was carrying on the work of A.E., who had combined mystical meditation and theosophical pursuits with a practical and mundane ideal of rural cooperatives. The older man's influence was apparent in much of O'Faolain's thinking— his dislike of the naturalist tradition in literature, his mystique of an ancestral heritage, his concept of a nation, his preference for intuition over rationalism, and above all his highly developed social conscience.

O'Faolain saw himself living at a period of transition and potential change; he saw himself as a pivotal figure in the manner of O'Connell and O'Neill. One phase of national evolution had ended, and he wanted to see the new phase begin, wanted to help create the conditions in which the national imagination could be defined in satisfying terms. Artistic achievement, expressing the realistic attributes of the national self, together with historical reassessment, could provide an emergent pattern and a foreseeable future. *The Bell,* he felt, could participate in this new departure, could help in the search for a national identity. His persistent quest for a desirable way of life in which the individual could express himself with dignity was part of the general pattern of his work.

The intensity of our minds is the measure of the growth of our lives. And it cannot but be that by searching life for the material of literature, and by searching our literature for the pattern of our lives . . . we shall extract the instinct of our race for certain affectible things that it is natural for us all to like and to prize.[34]

He believed firmly that the individual must revolt against the tyranny of tradition in defense of his own individuality, that tradition must be questioned and analyzed to be kept productive.[35] "Those who examine nothing and question nothing," he declared, "end by knowing nothing and creating nothing."[36] Unfortunately, there was an influential and vociferous element in the country, and particularly in the urban centers, that was determined to hinder the dialectic of past and present. A complex phalanx of hyper-nationalists, hypermoralists, and Celtophiles had for more than twenty years favored the preservation of the status quo. A form of thinking characterized by O'Faolain as "Delphic Nationalism" preferred a comfortable identification with a cultural unity of ancient Celtic times to a realistic acceptance of the facts of nineteenth-century political and economic change. The bulk of O'Faolain's historical treatises sought to undermine this approach by pointing to a national tradition that would include all aspects and levels of Irish life, Catholic and Protestant and Nonconformist, townsman and peasant, cottage and big house, and all strands of thought, including English, French and American.[37]

What is most evident in his writing is a deeply rooted love for his own country and his own people The ineradicable *pietas* that drove Daniel O'Connell to live a life of self-sacrifice and dedication, that forced Hugh O'Neill to risk death and failure, also motivated this writer to public expression of his reservations about the quality of life in his own country, a thankless undertaking for which he has received all too little recognition. But his identification with a figure like Daniel O'Connell was fatal to his peace of mind as an artist. A writer cannot be creative in the magnificent manner of a popular demagogue. His triumphs are not determinable by the evidence of parliamentary victories or the size of mass demonstrations of affection. To be overactive in the sociopolitical sphere is a danger to the creative artist, one that men like Joyce and Frank O'Connor were careful to avoid. But O'Faolain's temperament and character left him little choice. His reforming zeal was responsible for his search through history for remedies for contemporary failings; it produced his unflattering comparisons of European civilization with Irish civilization; it caused him to be irritated by the slowness and deficiencies of his own people; and in all of this he was being somewhat contradictory since few people knew as well as he the exonerating conditions in which Irish life existed and the natural limitations it encountered. Yet such inconsistencies were a natural part of his work and character, and one would not wish him to have been less agonized by the conflicts since out of their tensions emerged his sharpest definition of Irish society and his most forceful studies. Unfortunately such a highly sensitive social conscience made his task as a creative writer proportionately more difficult. It is understandable that he should have constantly expressed his awareness of the need for maintaining an equilibrium between the self and the environment as essential in the writer's life.

PART II

Imagination and Faith: The Short Stories

Chapter 5

Introduction

Since his novels and historical biographies come within the same ten-year period (1932–1942), it is really only through the short stories that O'Faolain's development as a writer can be fully traced and evaluated.[1] In the section that follows that task is attempted by means of a thematic and technical analysis of stories representative of significant alteration in vision and method. Thus "Reluctant Rebels" (6) dicusses two stories from *Midsummer Night Madness* (1932), his first collection, to show his efforts to deal with the experiences of the revolution in a detached and objective manner. "A Broken World" (7) concentrates on the prologue story of *A Purse of Coppers* (1937), his second book of stories, to show the emergence of a distinctive, pessimistic point of view and noticeable technical ability. The issue in this collection is that of individual freedom, not from the romance of revolution, but from the frustrations of a stagnant postrevolutionary society. The technical gains in this collection underline O'Faolain's increased understanding and appreciation of the short story as an art form. "Admiring the Scenery" (8) summarizes his theories about the short story and illustrates his own practice.

The depressing outlook of these stories is mainly the result of his involvement in the revolutionary movement. The detachment that he finally achieves was hard earned. He has summed up his progression from anger and frustration to objectivity and sympathy in *Vive Moi!*

... being privileged to see man at his best I had been given an exceptional vision of the potential wholeness and integrity of human nature in a moment of intense awareness forced on us all, collectively, by a crisis in our country's history; ... I had thereby been blinded to the virtues of ordinary, average, common life as it is outside of such rare hours; and ... when the hour passed I felt at first bewildered, then dismayed, and finally filled with a wholly unreasonable anger at my fellow men.[2]

"The Silence of the Valley" (9) shows the effect of that release from bitterness in the tone and interests of the stories that appear in *Teresa* (1947), *The Man Who Invented Sin* (1948), and *The Finest Stories of Sean O'Faolain* (1957). Now he concentrates on the variable nature of man, and this attentiveness to the delightful complexity of human nature lightens the tone of his stories. Their narrators, unlike the compulsive and haunted figures in *A Purse of Coppers,* stand apart, in detached and understanding sympathy, from what they describe. "A Design for Confusion" (10) discusses his comic and satiric treatment of Irish character and "Lovers of the Lake" (11) shows how his amused interest in the confusions that beset the contemporary Irish leads him to a profound treatment of the psychological and moral condition of two adulterous lovers. The final chapter, "Some Bright Destination" (12), reveals even greater refinement of feeling and technique as he meditates on the universal themes of growth and change as experienced by every man, themes illustrated from his most recent collections: *I Remember! I Remember!* (1961) and *The Heat of the Sun* (1966).

The stories give rich and satisfying evidence of his growth and development. In his best work he has been motivated by a complex and infinitely compassionate view of the human situation:

I would . . . try to write, however tangentially, about those moments of awareness when we know three truths at one and the same moment: that life requires of each of us that we should grow up and out whole and entire, that human life of its nature intricately foils exactly this, and that the possibility of wholeness is nevertheless as constant and enormous a reality as the manifold actuality of frustration, compromise, getting caught in some labyrinth, getting cut short by death.[3]

Chapter 6

Reluctant Rebels

Midsummer Night Madness (1932), O'Faolain's first collection of stories, takes place during the Anglo-Irish War and the Civil War. It provides the kind of tense and varied action one might expect from an account of those disturbed times: guerilla fighting, executions, reprisals, seductions, bombmaking, and the accompanying violence of word and action. To that extent the stories are the work of a young man who has revelled in the excitement, felt the thrill of his commitment, and tries to recapture experience. They are records of how it felt to be young and alive to experience. They have, however, another and more profound interest. What primarily distinguishes them is not their sense of joyful participation, the bliss of being alive at that hour, but their unexpected insistence on withdrawal and detachment. The central figure is a romantic young rebel who had responded warmly to the cause of independence but has come to question the wisdom of that response. Under the stress of the external action he is driven to analyze his own motives and to search for a meaning and a purpose behind the whole movement. This search emerges even in the earliest story and reaches a conclusion in the final one.

These two stories, "Fugue" and "The Patriot," serve as terminal points in the young rebel's progress from identification with romantic nationalism to the rejection of abstract political causes. The fact that the first story deals with the Anglo-Irish War and the last with the Civil War strengthens the change in attitude: one comes from a period of national unity and optimism, the other from a period of disillusion and bitterness. The theme of gradual alienation, however, transcends these chronological differences. The final rejection of politics is not more positive only because it deals with the collapse of the Republican protest against the treaty, although that accounts to a great extent for O'Faolain's own change of attitude. The whole collection moves toward that final decision; the young rebel's discovery of a personal attitude, an individual stance, is its unifying and recurrent theme.

"Fugue" is a tribute to a time, an attitude, and a tradition. Dreamy and idealistic, a conscious phantasist and a poet patriot, the central figure is the epitome of all the young rebels in this collection. His is the timeless story of the rebel on the run, hunted by the enemy, sheltered by the people, exposed to the chances of war and the changes of weather. What gives this particular version its distinctive quality is the poetic, evocative manner in which the story develops. Around a dominant image of a dark-haired girl whom he encounters, the rebel-narrator weaves nostalgic thoughts of domestic peace. All the other chance contacts of the day, threshers, carters, and families, express the regular cycle of normal life from which he is excluded. His days and nights are filled with the irregular, nerve-racking movements of the hunted man. The contrast of his life with theirs, his loneliness with their security, his cold and misery with their warmth and fulfillment, forms an interwoven, delicate rhythm. He is a poetic, introspective observer, responsive to the changing aspects of the countryside, aware of the transience and impermanence of life, and liable to find correspondences in literature and legend for his own feelings.

In the foreword to the *Finest Stories,* O'Faolain pointed out that the stories in *Midsummer Night Madness* are full of "metaphors and abstractions, personalizations and sensations which belong to the author rather than to the characters." He had, he explained, been dazed by the revolution, a period "too filled with dreams and ideals and a sense of dedication to be an experience in the meaning of things perceived, understood and remembered." On the whole his comments are valid, but they are not quite fair to "The Patriot," which is a maturer and more objective treatment of the reluctant rebel, marking the climax in the movement through these stories toward the rejection of abstract causes in favor of human relationships. Like "Fugue" it uses a pattern of imagery drawn from the countryside, domestic fulfillment, and the moods of the young rebel. But it combines the fragile romanticism of the earlier story with carefully constructed incidents that give life and definition to his inner conflicts. It treats his growing feeling for the dark-haired girl with detachment and strengthens it by the introduction of Edward Bradley, an extreme nationalist. His magnetic appeal to Bernie, the rebel, is opposed to Norah's. The story is an account of how, eventually, love triumphs over patriotism as Bernie moves away from Edward and what he so passionately represents.

That development is projected in three carefully related sections, each of which counterpoints Bernie's response to Norah with his response to Edward. The story moves from an introductory paragraph dealing with the present, through two sections dealing with past experiences, and then back to the present. The circular movement is structurally effective: the short final section about the honeymoon of the lovers, the triumph of love over abstractions, is meaningful in relation to the past. The two preceding sections are dramatically related to it, being necessary supports for its resolution of the conflict they present. Because the small seaside town of Youghal was where the lovers "had spent the gayest days of their lives," they return there for their honeymoon, "as if to crown all their happinesses." That final happiness can, in other words, be best realized only where the past exerts its fullest pressure. Memory is thus deliberately evoked: by the lovers because it intensifies and even justifies their enjoyment of love; by the writer because it integrates the two time levels of the narrative, effecting a solution that is artistically satisfying and aesthetically justified.

The counterpoint development of Bernie's attraction to Norah and to Bradley is complicated by the evidence that Edward is also attracted to her. The result is a more human portrait of the fanatical idealist: Bradley's nationalism does not consider what individuals must suffer to achieve his aims. He evokes sympathy here because his frustrated interest in Norah indicates how much he has sacrificed through his ideals. What Bernie ultimately wins, as the very last scene so poignantly and so justly reveals, Edward is deprived of forever, and the price shows in his intensity, his premature greyness, and his narrow political passions.

Bernie's increasing detachment from Bradley, so clearly projected in incident, is also illustrated through contrasting imagery. Foremost in the imaginal design is Bernie's vision of Norah, his dark-haired girl, seen and lost in their first encounter but found again when he returns to Youghal as a rebel. It is the summer flowering of their love in the woods across the bay that creates the richest associations. In that idyllic pastoral scene they find a sympathetic and responsive setting for their love. But the first section ends with the blotting out of its light and peace by the smoke from the burning barracks.

Section two provides a contrast: Bernie's youthful nationalistic bravado changes to the soul-searching loneliness of the hunted rebel in the mountains. The new setting is appropriate to his new mood and under the pressure of its desolating wintry aspects, his attitudes toward the fighting and finally toward Bradley himself change. At first he is lost in the dream of the rebel life, thoughtless of home or friends, living "aimlessly" and "uselessly." He has no consciousness of time but lives by instinct, "until as a human being he almost ceased to be, enveloped by the countryside as if he were a twig, a stone, or ear of corn." He is saved by the intrusion of memory, as in a series of opposing images, he juxtaposes his present conditions with the days in Youghal with Norah. Now it is February; he hates the cold, naked mountains; he is hunted incessantly. A letter from Norah reminds him of their sylvan love. His decision to seek reassurance is motivated by the thrust of the contrast between his present circumstances and those evoked by her letter. But even Bradley's passionate plea to the soldiers cannot dim her memory. The change being effected in Bernie now and later contrasts with the static, undeviating passion of Bradley, who orates fiercely in each section, the fire of his nationalism undimmed by time, physical change, or human relationships. When Bernie and Norah return to Youghal, it is February but here the imaginal design offers hope: the setting is again congenial and full of personal associations. In place of the black pall of smoke that shut off section one, spring is a felt pressure here.

Section three, the honeymoon, reinvokes all the attendant images of their previous happiness. It is Easter, the catkins are visible, lambs have been born, the furze is yellow, and they see everything with new delight. Spring's transforming and creative force supports the renewal of their love, their deliberate recreation of its earlier growth and intensity. There delight is conveyed in innumerable ways: in the happy, offseason peace and silence of the town, in the miles of deserted sand, the movements of birds, the long silences, the soft descent of night and its promise of love's fulfillment. Bradley's political passion scarcely enters their consciousness, "As by one thought they moved quietly out through the cheering crowd into the darkness." In the final scene the description of Bradley driving past the window of their bedroom out to the country and the dark night, shaken by his own particular passion, contrasts with the consummation of the young lovers; Bradley drives into the "dark night" but Bernie turns to Norah "where she gleamed even in the dark."

Midsummer Night Madness, besides indicating the quality of O'Faolain's writing in its early stages, reveals his romantic temperament. The weighted style, the poetic language, and the subjective, introspective quality of the young rebel reflect the writer's sensibilities. The transition from "Fugue" to "The Patriot" showing the growing detachment from violence, also shows a growing artistic detachment. It is part of the writer's search for objectivity, a search that is continued through the next volume.

Chapter 7

A Broken World

Implicit in the rebel's demand for personal freedom is the writer's search for self-definition and the discovery of an individual literary personality. The hopeful thrust of the early stories, their lyric optimism, carries the young hero beyond his immediate difficulties, and there is no suggestion that life thereafter may bring problems beyond his capabilities. But for the writer who is at all serious about his work, there can be no final solution, no absolute possession of his dark-haired girl. She changes shape with the years and has to be endlessly pursued. To have won a certain amount of detachment and adjustment in the matter of romantic nationalism was to have acquired a certain amount of technical skill and artistic maturity. But by the very nature of the writer's trade and the demands it makes on the whole man, personal growth would have to be accompanied by increased literary control.

To state, therefore, that *A Purse of Coppers* (1937), the second collection of stories, shows greater objectivity is to imply a corresponding maturity in the manner and methods of the stories. And certainly the range of the new stories goes well beyond the conflicts of "Fugue" or "The Patriot." A whole new landscape is explored. Instead of the problem of the individual demanding the right to do what his heart wants, a rather simple problem treated without much complication or subtlety, the question of individual freedom is now placed in much wider focus. Against the restrictive background of Irish society as it emerged from the revolution a whole series of stories pursues the question of how human nature reacts under frustration.

What happens to the reluctant rebel when the smoke of battle has cleared away? How does the sensitive, intelligent, creatively alive individual survive when he is surrounded by forces that restrict his growth and hinder his potential as a human being? If his demands for personal freedoms have been so intense in the past, how is he affected emotionally and morally under the new conditions? This is not to suggest that the characters in the new stories are all former rebels (few are), but there is a continuity of theme, a distinctive stance, and a single artist-observer. The fact that he has fought for national independence, has been committed in the past to the country's interests, makes its subsequent condition of particular, even distressing, importance. Detachment and adjustment are not so easily won; the bridges of one's youthful ideals are not so easily burnt. By the time he was writing these stories the best O'Faolain could do was "grin a bit at my solemn self and at my solemn countrymen." There was, in fact, little enough to be humorous about in the new subject, particularly if one were as seriously involved with it as O'Faolain was.

For one thing, the new questions he asked led to unhappy and rather terrible answers. What might happen to that hypothetical figure with the intense intellectual and imaginative needs? The frustrated man, out of tune with his age, might be alienated from his people, his colleagues, his work, his country, or his religion, since they inevitably reflect elements in the society that he dislikes. He might be driven in upon himself, forced to feed upon his memories of a more congenial time or upon comforting self-delusions and phantasies. If really pressed, he might be driven into insanity.

These are not the only possible answers, but they are some of those considered seriously in *Purse of Coppers*. They exert considerable pressure on O'Faolain as an observer of society, critically alert to its influences on himself or on any creative being. "Fugue's" lyrical form absorbed the action of the story into the consciousness of the hero-narrator. "The Patriot," on the other hand, adopted the voice of a person, but the process of detachment was not complete: Bradley's inner vision of the world was not realized, whereas Bernie's was consistently present. In both stories the presence of a subjective, closely involved writer could be felt. Now, with the external reality of his subject, comes the challenge of finding adequate structural and organizational patterns. The complexity of that challenge can be seen at once in the opening story, which serves as a prologue to the whole collection.

The setting for "A Broken World" is the carriage of a train journeying toward Dublin through a snowy landscape. Inside are three people, the narrator, a priest, and a peasant. The theme is the loneliness of Irish life after the revolution. Loneliness is a key term for this story and for the whole collection; it is an inclusive concept for the various forms of alienation and suffering that can be experienced in a repressive environment. In this first story the general historical causes of the disruption in Irish life are carefully stated, for this is the introduction to all that follows. The story is important since it formulates the general social and historical background. But in addition to its richness of content the story has a more literary interest. The drama of the growing responsiveness of three strangers to each other intensifies the theme. There are, in fact, two stories: the first person narrator tells of his encounter with the priest and the peasant and its effects on his outlook; within that "frame-story" lies the personal narrative of the priest, who relates his experiences of Irish life as a young man in his first parish and their effects on his outlook. The interplay of attitudes and responses brought out through these contrasting but closely related narratives gives vitality to the drama of growing responsiveness.

Each story moves toward its particular truth, both the intended truth of the narrator and the truth of his unintentional self-revelation. Each focuses on the central question of loneliness, which is ironically heightened by the unity of response created among these strangers through story-telling. An artistically created cohesion of priest, peasant, and writer, marking the climax of the priest's story, is bluntly destroyed. But the first narrator is moved by the priest's story of loneliness set in the context of all Irish life to demand and hope for a solution. At that point, the climax and the conclusion of his own story, the story expands to include the reader as well, who if he seeks to explain the effect of these two interlocking stories on himself becomes another link in an apparently endless sequence.

The initial propulsion for this chain reaction is given in the first words of the story—"That's a lonely place!" The silence of the carriage has been broken suddenly by the priest, who responds to the association of a passing scene, a mountainy farm and a small chapel. In the unexpected force of that exclamation lies the clue to the man's character. He is a compulsive talker, haunted by the memory of a particular experience from which he has never recovered. Unburdening himself to this indifferent, even resentful, audience, he reveals the inner frustration that his appearance implies.

The priest's story is personal, and he uses it as an *exemplum* for the philosophical thesis that where there is no moral unity there is no life.

Life is a moral unity with a common thought. The *compositum* of one's being, emerging from the Divine Essence, which is harmony itself, cannot, unless it abdicate its own intelligence and lives in chaos, that is to say, in sin, be in disunity with itself. Since society, however, is an entity composed of many members, life becomes a moral unity with a common thought.

His first parish was in a lonely, hilly region, among a poor, hardworking people subject to emigration and a falling birth rate. Its restrictions made him lonely. In his visit to the neighboring parish in the valley, he finds better land, good natural growth, and bigger farmhouses. Further down still are the deserted estates of the gentry, who have been driven out by the revolution. Thousands of acres of good land lie unused. The priest returns to his poor parish "Much improved in spirits. You see, I had extended the pattern of life of my own parish. I saw how, how—I mean, how the whole thing had worked, hung together, made up a real unity. It was like putting two halves of a broken plate together. . . ."

The drama of the interplay of the characters begins with the initial exclamation of the priest and his pointing through the window at the mountainy farm. The narrator, following that signal, noting the uncommunicative quality of the other's speech ("He might have been talking to himself"), sees "a lone chapel and a farmhouse." His complacent reply—"It is lonely. But," I said easily, "sure every parish is a world in itself"—sets the other off on his pedagogical tale. His greater experience of life and his earned right to instruct the narrator is shown in his admission that he too used to believe as the narrator does. Now he has discovered that "where there is no moral unity there is no life." At this state, the narrator is unimpressed by the other's assertion of his thesis; he simple notes his manner ("He was cock-assuredly positive") and wonders idly if he is a professor from some seminary. The details of the priest's appearance, seen through the objective eyes of the narrator, emphasizes the hellish, pedagogic character. But from this early impression there is a subtle and gradual change; the initial unflattering image of the priest (a skeleton of a man) is denied by the revelation of character through his narrative; and the initial boredom of the narrator changes to spellbound attention and sympathy.

The priest's narrative is dense with detail. His contrast of the poor, hilly parish with the rich, valley parish is full of informed and informative facts. These reflect his intellectual ability, but they also indicate his warm and responsive nature as a young man and prepare for an understanding of his personal tragedy. Through the manner of his narrative we find explanations for his unpleasant appearance. In particular, when he moves from the coldly factual account of the historical and social aspects of the poor parish, his inner fire appears. Once he was a poetic, sensitive man ("I didn't say *they* were lonely"); when he describes his visit to the neighboring parish the language glows with remembered feeling:

"Do you know, the contrast was amazing! When I climbed down to the valley and the good land! And it was the trees that made me realize it. Beeches instead of pines. Great, old beeches with roots like claws on the double ditches. The farmhouses, too. They were large and prosperous with everything you might expect to find in a sturdy English farm—barns, ducks in the pond, thick-packed granaries, airy lofts, a pigeon croft, a seat under the arbor, fruit gardens."

His imagination revives also when he describes his visit to the deserted estate: "It was a lovely spring evening. The sky was like milk. The rooks were cawing about the roofless chimneys just like the flakes of soot come to life again."

The spell of his story works slowly, paralleling our own absorption in it and our own realization that beneath the forbidding exterior lies a tragic, explanatory tale. At first the narrator forces himself to attend. Then he notices the reaction of the third member of the group, hitherto unmentioned, who "contemplated the priest's face with an air of childlike wonderment." A wink from the peasant makes him realize the priest is known as a local "character," meaning in Ireland an odd person whose actions amuse. Now the narrator listens more willingly, enjoying the reactions of the peasant but not yet involved himself in this dramatic interplay. He is still the indifferent, captured listener, but he is now indulgent and slightly entertained. The peasant has already not only become interested but also begun to react to the story of national decline. He follows only those parts that deal specifically with problems familiar to himself but is bewildered, for example, when the priest traces an imaginary history of one of the gentry. The narrator, on the other hand, apparently a man of some education and intelligence, follows the priest easily.

But when the priest speaks feelingly of incessant subdivision of land and constant intermarriage among the poor people, which contrast so strongly with the social customs of the gentry, all three are united in that common identification with familiar history; all share a sense of national injustice. ("The farmer leaned forward, listening now with great interest. Our three heads nodded with the jolt of the train.") When he talks of population decline and the deserted cottages, the farmer asserts that his own locality reveals the same evils.

The priest's narrative divides into separate but related sections. In the first he describes his parish and gives historical causes for its condition. It concludes with his restatement of his thesis: his parish was too incomplete, his parishioners were too dependent on others. But here the narrator, showing his intelligent response, demands a fuller exposition. "But did that make their lives lonely? You said they were lonely?" To which the priest says "I didn't say *they* were lonely." In the second part he describes his visit to the neighboring parish and his vision of a once unified world. In that other parish with its burnt-out ruin of a Big House, he looks across the valley at his own people. He gains a new perspective:

". . . They could have sat there and drunk their tea and seen my people—the poor Ryders, and Greenes, and O'Tooles—making little brown lines in the far-off fields in the plowing time."
"They could? O, begobs, Father, so they could!"—and a mighty spit.
"Or at night, on summer evenings, they could have sipped their brandy and coffee and seen the little yellow lights of our cabin windows, and said, 'How pretty it is!' "
"Begobs, yes! That's true!"
If anyone entered the carriage then he would have taken us for three friends, we were huddled together so eagerly.

It is the climax of this subtle interplay of human feelings. For a short, radiant period the three respond to what is deepest in all of them, the peasant to the particular oppressions of his class, the priest to his remembered moment of truth, and the narrator to that vision of a full life the priest gives him. For one short paragraph the contrast of vision and reality is maintained. The setting is still the same and the passing scene returns its imagery of coldness, decay, and desolation. ("The white, cold fields, were singing by us. The cabins so still they might be rocks clung to the earth. The priest was looking at them and we were all looking at them, and at the flooded and frozen pools of water divided by the hedgerows.") They are united in a common thought. "By his talk he had evoked a most powerful sense of comradeship in that carriage, whether he meant to or not: we felt one."
It is the most perfect union of the story. For immediately the priest disturbs it and the narrator "angrily" demands that he

explain his idea of moral unity and common thought. Obviously his image of a former wholeness, of a hierarchical society, is a thing of the past. The farmer losing the thread of the talk, gazes at them "with dull, stupid eyes." The priest is strangely non-commital; the narrator presses him—won't the people who remain make their own unity? The priest shakes his head. The farmer listens stupidly. All the priest does is send a warning look to the narrator, faintly indicating the peasant. "Then he actually began to laugh, a cold, cackling laugh, an extraordinary, inhuman kind of laugh that ended in a noise like a little groan." Very soon the train stops and the priest has left.

After the surge toward greater intensity that has characterized the development of the story, the narrator suffers a feeling of anti-climax. Roused from indifference by the powerful appeal of the priest's story and intensely interested by the end in its idea of life as a moral unity, he realises that the poetic truth of the story demands a more exciting conclusion. The whole characterization of the priest as built from within his own story is an incitement to action. That final vision of a world complete in itself, inde-pendent of humiliating authority, calls for a fulfillment. Yet the man responsible for calling it into being has abandoned it. In that abandonment lies a further clue to his thwarted nature, which was stressed in his final cackling laugh.

Under the questioning of the narrator, the farmer admits to knowing the priest: the priest is silenced because he encouraged the people to take possession of the deserted estates. He had tried to realize his vision of wholeness. His failure and the terrible penalty he incurred explain his external marks of suffering, explain them and soften them. The short, separate sequence between the farmer and the narrator has a larger purpose than merely providing relevant information about the priest. Under aggressive interrogation by the narrator, the farmer reluctantly and indifferently answers. The movement toward increasing com-munion that marked the first section of the story is abruptly re-versed here. What emerges most clearly is the lethargic, vegetative quality of the Irish countryman. No mode of inquiry can rouse him. The narrator passes rapidly from calm, to annoyance, to eagerness as he mistakenly thinks the farmer will be interested in the question of land ownership, to anger, and finally to disgust. The farmer hears his questions "without interest," "still without interest," "it was a matter of no importance," "puffing at his ease he was looking idly at the passing fields," "his lethargic mood," "relapsed into indifference," "and went to sleep under his hat."

The frustration of the narrator is evident in the tone of these descriptive phrases. He looks at the farmer and sees him as a natural projection of rural life, molded by its work and its seasons, primitive in his dependence on the land. His easy mystical relationship with the rural landscape is stressed in the final paragraph. At a station no different from all the others he suddenly rouses himself from sleep and "as if some animal magnetism in the place stirred him, he rose and stumbled out. . . . He was exactly like an old black mongrel loping home."

The bafflement felt by the narrator is an important element. For in the peasant's unimpressionable, unintelligent character lies the frustration of much of Irish life, which has depended heavily and not too successfully on rural productivity for economic growth and security. High-minded and generous natures, such as the priest's and the narrator's, men with reforming instincts, are inevitably frustrated by men such as this animal-vegetative-mineral peasant.

There is one final contrast. The farmer passes through the station: "He did not speak. He did not raise his head to see if it was his station. He saluted no one." While serving to illustrate the peasant's instinctive sense of belonging, this also acts as a counterpoint to the priest's exit:

A manservant, touching his cap, took the bags. The stationmaster touched his cap to him. The porter receiving the tickets touched his cap to him. The jarvey, who was waiting for him, bowed as he received the bags from the manservant. Black, tall, thin, and straight as a lamp post, he left the lit, snow-bright station with every downlooking lounger there bowing and hat touching as he passed.

It is a pathetic, final image of this tormented, frustrated man. He had complained of his parishioners because they were too subservient ("Too respectful, tipping their hats to everyone."), and even in his silenced state, when secretly regarded as a figure of amusement, he is paid the excessive formal reverence. He is thus isolated from the people he has tried to help, because of whom he is suffering. It is a final irony that lingers after he has gone.

What of the narrator, now alone in the carriage? He, in turn, becomes a haunted man, expelled from his complacent view of life. Led to the sight of a promised land by the priest, he can only hope for a redemption. For a while he tried to rationalize his feelings and attribute them to transient causes but in the end he has to accede to the truth of the priest's story, "that under that white shroud, covering the whole of Ireland, life was lying broken and hardly breathing." As he leaves the train in Dublin he sees the people in a similar state, half-dying, barely holding on to life. His view is hopeful. Unlike the priest, corroded by the knowledge of failure and the memory of a youthful dream, he sees Ireland ready for a "dawn," the final word of the story. Now transformed by his encounter with the priest, he longs for a force that will release the country to moral unity.

What image, I wondered, as I passed through them, could warm them as the Wicklow priest had warmed us for a few minutes in that carriage chugging around the edge of the city to the sea? What image of life that would fire and fuse us all, what music bursting like the spring, what triumph, what engendering love, so that those breasting mountains that now looked cold should appear brilliant and gay, the white land that seemed to sleep should appear to smile, and these people who huddled over the embers of their lives should become like peasants who held the hand of Faust with their singing one Easter morning?

The story ends on a wave of romantic hope. But it has not been characterized by such a response. The contrasting styles of the two narratives bring out the dual nature of O'Faolain himself. The priest is noted for his keen, analytical mind, a sharp eye for social and political life, a studious bent; he represents the realistic side of O'Faolain. The narrator, moved so turbulently by the evidence, represents the romantic side. Each side is strongly present, each as innate as the other.

The tone of damnation persists in many of the stories in this collection; the satanic overtones of the priest's character appear in other figures. The idea of lost innocence, so much a part of the young rebel's dissatisfaction in *Midsummer Night Madness,* emanates within *Purse of Coppers* in the character of the haunted hero, the compulsive talker, the man ravished by the knowledge of a time, place, or condition in which he has been or could be happy. Loneliness, as the priest in "A Broken World" insists, is a condition of sin, in which those incapable of achieving a full projection of themselves as a compositum become disordered fragmented caricatures of men, live in the chaos of sin and produce disorder in those about them. In a society, such as that of postrevolutionary Ireland, that impedes a man's development, loneliness, the sin of disunity, blooms in corruption.

Many stories focus on the problem of the self and a restrictive society. In "A Born Genius" Pat Lenihan, failing to escape from the poverty and provinciality of his life in Cork, is drawn into masochistic wanderings. He seeks out places in the city associated with English settlers, identifying with them as exiles "doomed to the torture of empty days and companionless nights." John Aloysius Gonzaga O'Sullivan, the compulsive talker in "The Old Master," longs for the prerevolutionary days of a more cultured and hierarchical society. Instead of Lenihan's inner-directed bitterness, O'Sullivan compensates for the pressing horror of his insufficient world by promulgating escapist phantasies. Hanafan in "Admiring the Scenery," physically signifying his internal suffering, cries out from his inferno of self-perception that every man lives out his own imagination of himself and that every imagination must have a background. Of course the point is not just any background but one suited to the individual's needs, against which he can possess himself in pride and dignity as a full man.

The sense of sinful disorder is constant. The Canon in "Sinners" is more of a random assembly of rules and suppositions than a whole man with a sensible response to life. Minor scruples and prejudices interpose themselves between his role as God's minister and his identity as a human being. When he leaves the confessional having fully revealed his lack of self-integration, he passes through the church with "his hand under the tail of his surplice, dancing it up and down." That revealing image of the satanic tail appears again in the later story "The Man Who Invented Sin." Again a priest has exercised excessive authority and produced a sense of sin where there had only been innocence. And again, as he moves, "his elongated shadow moved behind him like a tail." In "Discord" the black arm of Father Peter comes between the heads of the lovers whom he leads through the widening circles of an inferno of death, disease, and old age from which they retreat hastily to the refuge of each other's arms and wilfully transform him into a "fat Punch like the Devil in the play."

Disorder is endemic. "Sullivan's Trousers," a satire on De Valera's policy during the Economic War with England, is a fusion of sanity and insanity, absurdity and common sense that represent the chaotic nature of the country's ideologies at that period. "Mother Matilda's Book" is another extravanganza, in which an aged nun reduces the history of her order to a highly personalized saga. The series of reversals and counter-reversals that characterize the action support a general picture of disorder.

Chapter 8

Admiring the Scenery: Theory and Practice

The theme of self and society is clearly related to O'Faolain's interest in the writer's struggle to achieve and maintain an equilibrium between his personality and his environment. His approach to the whole question of the artist and his world is an acknowledged reflection of Flaubert's statement that the secret of masterpieces lies in the concordance between the subject and the temperament of the author. A good short story, he believes, is produced by "punch" and "poetry," a combination of reality (plausibility) and the personal voltage of the writer that lights up the material in a distinctive, ultimately indefinable way.[1] His definition of personality is like that expressed by the priest in "A Broken World":

All we can do is to state a personal feeling that the distinctive mark of personality is harmony in the internal art of the individual, the whole *compositum* as a Thomist would say, moving in a unity of being, with an undivided force of energy, towards its own ends.[2]

The constant task of the writer, therefore, is to establish a rapprochement between himself and the circumstances that condition his life so that his literary personality may flourish intact.

The evidence that a particular sensibility has discovered a subject uniquely suited to itself is an important element in evaluating a story. O'Faolain's view of the relationship between subject and temperament is that the writer imagines the subject into his own likeness. He can, therefore, very often be identified in relation to particular situations and types of character. Their presence defines the nature of the literary personality to which they have appealed and through which they have emerged as distinctive creations. A writer's work can be said to have imaginative integrity when it contains a pattern of recurrent situations and characters. It can be judged in the light of the nature and the quality of the particular view of life they express. Through them one may discern a writer's faith. "A faith," O'Faolain explains, "for literary purposes, means any feeling for life or any way of seeing life which is coherent, persistent, inclusive, and forceful enough to give organic form to the totality of a writer's work."[3]

Purse of Coppers treats the question of self and society in various ways and with a distinctive bias; failure and frustration are endemic. The response is predominantly negative: Lenihan in "A Born Genius" broods in defeat, totally unable to come to terms with the conditions that hamper his freedom; O'Sullivan in "The Old Master" chooses the escape route of phantasy and self-deception that lead to a *folie de grandeur*; Hanafan in "Admiring the Scenery," the most rational and sensitive of the three, with the most balanced response to life, suffers from the knowledge that his environment cannot satisfy his imaginative needs. External marks of frustration prevail but the artist himself is not defeated. Out of the negative factors that appeal to him, and despite the general feeling of hopelessness, he continues to create ordered and disciplined work.

The successful manipulation of the self for an artistic purpose is primarily an internal struggle; it is discernible in the technical struggle through which the writer gains mastery over the methods of his forms. *Purse of Coppers* besides being an allegory of the internal struggle, is also a revelation of the development in technical skill; it shows the writer adjusting to his materials, seeing how they can reflect his environment and his own distinctive relation to it. The development is away from the romanticism of *Midsummer Night Madness,* from the overdescriptive to the concise, from an emphasis on the impact of the subject to a smoother, detached style. The ornamental and scientific use of detail is found in earlier stories in *Purse of Coppers*—"My Son Austin," "A Born Genius," and even "A Broken World"—but O'Faolain gets away from the naturalistic style. He prefers the kind of meaningful compression that allows the reader's imagination to dilate with suggestion. Thus instead of giving a full description of a character, he gives a few details that suggest the whole man. Weaker and earlier stories constantly exceed the limitations of the short story form; they try to include the perspective, scope, and relative casualness of the novel. From 1936 on, however, he faces up successfully to the limitations and the challenges of the shorter form. Stories such as "Sinners," "Discord," and "Admiring the Scenery" are masterly in technique.

"Sinners" is controlled throughout by a disciplined dialogue that quietly and carefully represents the varying shades of feeling and thought emerging through the Canon's interrogation of the frightened servant girl in the confessional. Her employer has told him the girl has stolen a pair of boots, and he remembers he refused the girl absolution the previous Saturday because she did not seem sorry enough for being away from confession for five years. This foreknowledge complicates his approach, since he is bound under the *sigilium* not to make use of such information.

"My poor child," he said, ever so gently, dutifully pretending to know nothing about her, "tell me how long it is since your last confession."
"It's a long time, Father," she whispered.
"How long?" To encourage her he added, "Over a year?"
"Yes, Father."
"How much? Tell me, my poor child, tell me. Two years?"
"More, Father."
"Three years?"
"More, Father."
"Well, well, you must tell me, you know."

In spite of himself his voice was a little pettish. The title "Father" instead of "Canon" was annoying him, too. She noted the change of voice, for she said, hurriedly:

" 'Tis that, Father."

" 'Tis what?" asked the Canon a shade too loudly.

Descriptive material in this passage is minimal yet the dramatic interplay, kept in a minor key, shifts gradually and perceptibly. The Canon's losing battle for self-control and his well-meant intention undermined by his scrupulous conscience are balanced humorously against the increasing fear of the main. As his defenses weaken, hers strengthen. Later, leading her through the ten commandments, in growing irritation at his own stupidity for using this approach, he finally reaches an area of relative certainty:

"Stealing?" prompted the Canon, and he waited for her to say that she stolen Mrs. Higgins' boots.

"I never in my life, Father, stole as much as the head off a pin. Except when I was small I once stole an apple in the nuns' orchard. And they caught me and gave me a flaking. And they took the last bite out of my mouth."

"You never stole articles of dress?" threatened the Canon, and he suddenly realized that there were only three very unlikely commandments left. "Clothes? Hats? Gloves? Shoes?"

"Never, Father."

There was a long pause.

"Boots?" he whispered.

The opening paragraph of this story also shows the economical and oblique manner in which O'Faolain now uses words:

The Canon, barely glancing at his two penitents, entered the confessional. From inside he looked wearily across at the rows of penitents on each side of Father Deeley's box, all still as statues where they sat against the wall, or leaned forward to let the light of the single electric bulb, high up in the windy roof, fall on their prayer books. Deeley would give each about ten minutes, and that meant he would not absolve the last until near midnight. "More trouble with the sacristan," sighed the Canon, and closed the curtains and lifted his hand towards the slide of the grille.

This comes to terms at once with the situation. The main character is introduced and unobtrusively much of his character appears. There is the contrast between his curate's popularity

("rows of penitents") and his own lack of appeal ("two penitents").
There is the fact that he notices it and that it has an effect on
him ("barely glancing . . . looked wearily across"). There is
the suggestion of lack of electrical fittings and the implication
that the Canon is economizing on small things. His petulance
appears in his reflection on the length of time Father Deeley gives
to each penitent and implies his own mechanical nature, which
favors efficient frugality rather than time-consuming human contact and sympathy. Characteristically, he sees people as statues, a
point of view that reflects his own inability to attain life. Weariness, petulance, defeat, a concentration on trivial rules and regulations, all these prepare us for his failure in the confessional, for
his authoritarianism, his irritation, his vanity, his misunderstanding, his cruelty, his disgust with human nature that will not fit
in with his suppositions.

"Discord" resembles "Admiring the Scenery" in that it is a
meeting of three characters who do not form a background for
each other. Two young people on their honeymoon in Dublin
visit a priest. His laughter and enjoyment are incongruous against
the background of slums, broken lives, madness, and death that
surrounds his life. Basically, he wants a quiet parish in the country. However, custom has diminished the ugliness of his familiar
inferno but for the lovers the descent into the underground crypt
leads them uncomfortably close to the knowledge of death and
age for which they are altogether unprepared. The story is developed through juxtaposition of these contrasting attitudes.

. . . Suddenly they saw a wild-bearded, hollow-faced man standing away
back in the nave, praying devoutly. His beard was soft but tangled;
his hair was to his shoulders; he held his two arms aloft as he prayed;
his eyes shone. Curiously they watched him, a little frightened.
   "Who is he?" asked the girl of the priest.
   "He's daft," whispered the priest. "An ex-soldier. He sometimes
preaches to the empty church. Come this way."
   "He'd terrify me," said the girl.
   Peter laughed again as he led them down another flight of stairs
through an old trap door.
. . . Somehow, since they had met the priest, several years had been
added to both of them. They had come upon one of those moments of

life when, like the winter butterflies in the high corners, they felt the hurt of cold. Breezily the priest returned, coated, buttoned, slapping his hands.

"Admiring the Scenery" is perhaps the most successful of these stories from O'Faolain's point of view, since it combines a gentle, poetic atmosphere with a realistic or plausible situation. It represents the emergence of a balanced approach made up of a realistic use of detail and a romantic sensibility. The revelation of character is carried out by an unconscious unmasking of the narrator, Hanafan, by himself. The familiar device of the story within a story is presented with a skillful juxtaposition of present and past, or outer story and inner story, so that the setting, the responses it produces, the characterization, and the themes fuse and correspond. The setting of the outer story, the beautiful evening, is similar to the setting of the inner story, the beautiful night. Hanafan, responding to the present scene, sets out to relate the loneliness of the stationmaster on the former occasion and how this was momentarily transcended; at the same time, Hanafan reveals his own loneliness and the dissimilarity of the present occasion; the inability of these three people to form a background for each other heightens the sadness. On both occasions Hahafan quotes poetry: on the present, the first two stanzas of Gray's "Elegy in a Country Churchyard;" on the former, a section from Sir Thomas Browne's "The quincunx of heaven runs low and 'tis time to close the five ports of knowledge. . . ." The contrast here also relates to the different emotions aroused by the two scenes. The elegiac tone of Gray's poem, its weariness and regret, contrasts subtly with the wonder and imaginative delight of the Browne passage and sets off the two occasions exactly.

This contrast is also made in the description of the settings; the present scene, "before sunset in early spring, a soft evening of evaporating moisture and tentative bird song;" the former, "one hard, moonlight night in December. . . . The snow was white on the hills. It was blazing. . . . A deep, rich night, and no harm in the winds, but they puffing and blowing." Both descriptions set the mood for the occasion: the softer gentler tone for the present, its tentative quality; the harder, more joyous quality of the former, its successful integration of personality and mood. The act of admiring the scenery is not an intellectual one, not a projection of the idea of the beauty into one's consciousness. It is, as Hanafan shows by his narrative and his own behavior, an emotional, sensory response. The mood of the story is muted and soft, a reflection of the evening. The communication of a distinct personality subsumes the whole work so that the relationship between the punch and the poetry is evenly and effectively maintained.

The emphasis in *Purse of Coppers* moves away from the social context and centers on human nature instead. "Admiring the Scenery" and "Discord" illustrate this change. This shift in perspective becomes more evident in later stories and indicates an increasing ability of the author to separate his reactions to uncongenial circumstances from his literary activity. A greater detachment is the reward of such self-discipline, and it is surprising to find an author who is capable of much polemical writing and much hard social commentary becoming so gentle. His sensitivity to the context of human behavior, his warm sympathy for his own people and his understanding of the conditions of their lives predominate.

His understanding of the technical aspects of the short story developed rapidly after 1936. It may have been that his growing realization of the difficulty of handling his material in the novel form led him to regard the shorter length with more interest and a more critical awareness of its techniques. His first writings on the short story appeared in *The Bell* (1944) and were later expanded and incorporated into *The Short Story* (1948). In this work he formulates some of the theories that are evident in his writings. He understands, for example, the function of conventions and the various ways in which writers try to make fiction seem plausible: the device of the preamble in which the writer tells how he came into possession of the facts; the device of the first person narrative, overused by O'Faolain in the early stories in *Purse of Coppers*. Maupassant, as O'Faolain points out, had shown how these various introductory remarks and other references to time, place, or occasion could be avoided simply by coming to terms with the situation. Later stories in *Purse of Coppers* consistently avoid the elaborate introductory approach. *The Short Story* also comments on the kind of technique favored by Chekhov, which had been influential in improving the quality of these later stories. This is the method of informing by suggestion or implication, the most important of the shorthand conventions used by modern short story writers. It makes for compression and for the pleasure of discovery and imaginative dilation. The excitement of this genre lies in its compression. The writer searches for language that will suggest; he avoids excessive detail and prefers implication to explanation.

In "Discord," for example, the young lovers have come to visit Father Peter. "Always awkward with the newly wedded, he had led them straight to the window immediately they entered the room," and there "his black arm pointing between their heads, led their eyes over the aerial plain." The discord between the young people and the priest is introduced here with slight touches: the black arm dividing them, the phrase "led their eyes" suggesting compulsion and restraint, and the repetition of the word "led" reinforcing the idea of mutual uncertainty and embarrassment. These imply the character of the priest. All his subsequent cheeriness does not overcome this initial insecurity, and the sense of a forced situation—forced cheeriness, forced kindness—becomes increasingly evident until the image of discord is inclusive of a whole way of life and the character of the man. His compulsive pattern of speech and behavior signifies an attempt to survive, to retain individuality, amid the misery and decay, the sin and frustration, the loneliness and compression of his life. His natural good nature has been corroded by his environment, but the lovers neither understand nor want to understand the tragic nature of their friend; they dismiss him as a comic caricature and, like the lovers in "The Patriot," seek for happiness and forgetfulness in love.

O'Faolain's stories after 1936 are full of gentle, humorous scenes in which character is revealed against a careful counterpoint of idea and imagery. His very personal fusion of realistic observation with romantic sensibility is expressed in this method. In "Teresa" the two nuns are returning from an unsuccessful pilgrimage to Lisieux. Teresa, the young postulant, has discovered that she is unfitted for the hardship of her order but now in the presence of her comfortable, chocolate-chewing companion and looking across at the worldly delights of Dinard she announces a new decision. The intense feelings of the older nun are reflected by the sounds and movements of the waves, by her controlled whisper, by her tightly shut eyes, and by her final exclamation:

"I have decided to join the Carmelites," said the novice.
They halted. They looked across the sea wall into the blue of Dinard. A few lights were already springing up over there—the first dots in the long golden necklet that already they had come to know so well. A lone sea gull squaked over the glassy water. The sunset behind the blue pinnacles of the resort was russet.
"And what's wrong with our own order, Sister dear?" asked Patrick of the vacancy before her.
"I feel, dear Sister Patrick," judged the novice staring ahead of her, "that it is too worldly."
"How is it too worldly?" asked Patrick in a whisper.
"Well, dear Sister Patrick," pronounced the novice, "I see, for example, that you all eat too much." The little wavelets fell almost inaudibly, drunken with the fullness of the tide, exhausted and soothed by their own completion.
"I shall tell Mother Mary Mell that you think so," whispered the old nun.
"There is no need, dear Sister, it will be my duty to tell her myself. I will pray for you all when I am in the Carmelites. I love you all. You are all kind and generous. But, dear Sister, I feel that very few nuns really have the right vocation to be nuns." Patrick closed her eyes tightly. The novice continued: "I will surrender to the divine love. The death I desire is the death of Love. The death of the Cross."
They heard only the baby tongues of the waves. The evening star blazed in the russet sky. The old nun saw it, and she said, in part a statement, in part a prayer, in part a retort:
"Sweet Star of the Sea!"

The ironies here are almost too subtle to explain: the worldly shallow Teresa; the good-natured, disciplined old nun; the parable of the gay life across the water; the religious connotations of the evening star; the too polite manner of address; the natural calm of the ocean and the beauty of nature contrasted with the enforced restraint of the old nun and her charity in the face of attack; the clichés of the young nun's adolescent religious intentions associated with the baby tongues of the waves and the final triumph of the old nun over her silent inner conflict, her struggle for self-control associated with the blaze, the purity, and the radiance of the symbolic star. Over all O'Faolain moves with a gentle, warm, and compassionate understanding, controlling the emotional nuances, expressing the growth of shades of feeling and decision, sure of his judgment which he reveals implicitly. In such sequences his technical mastery is superb; situation and construction merge into a single movement.

The Short Story also discusses the conventions by which writers suggest that the endings are not disjunctions but continuities; they seek to provide an illusion of permanence. There are a number of ways in which this can be done; O'Faolain makes use of at least three. There is the poetic ending that floats the narrative into a "poetic" continuity of place whose image remains after the conclusion:

The dawn moved along the rim of the mountains and as I went down the hill I felt the new day come up around me and life begin once more its ancient, ceaseless gyre.

The last sentence of "Sinners" leaves a similar impression of place: "He turned towards the dark presbytery deep among the darkest lanes." Such a conclusion corresponds also to those endings which merge the episode into a general moral picture. In "The Old Master" John Aloysius has been treated as a figure of amusement to his contemporaries, but the final sentence places his activities and their response to them in a moral perspective. For, as O'Faolain writes, it was only after his death that people began to think of him as a human being. "I wonder," he adds, "is there any wrong or right in that? Or is it, as John would have said, that one kind of life is just the same as another in the end?"

Most modern writers, he observes, do not use such easy or obvious devices. Chekhov was able to invoke the "poetic" mood of place and to imply a general moral or idea, but he also developed the method of using transitions from one tense to another to suggest life going on as before, from the past to the present with the suggestion of continuity in the future. Even as early as "A Broken World" O'Faolain had absorbed this practice:

The train could be heard easily, in the rarefied air, chugging across the bridges that span the city, bearing with it an empty coach. In the morning, Ireland, under its snow, would be silent as a perpetual dawn.

But he is not tied by such conventions. Modern writers do not always take care to provide a sense of continuity. As the short story form has become more widely read the conventions have needed less and less concealment. For not only does the reader share knowledge of these devices with the writer but also by tacit agreement he suppresses it, or some of it, and the writer relies on the sophistication and intelligence of the reader, his sensitivity to suggestion and implication, his ability to distinguish nuances of observation and revelation. "Every writer appeals therefore to a complex mass of emotions, of sensory experiences, of accepted, or acceptable ideas whose existence he presumes." As a result, writers often make no effort to save the story from a sense of disjunction; many of O'Faolain's good stories are like this, "The Fur Coat," for example. But the ability of modern writers to be so free may be a result of the older conventions remaining implicit: "That 'so it goes on' (though there is now no need to say so); or that it is a moral tale, or a comment (though now there is no need to be explicit about it); or that it is 'typical', i.e. that it is a tale of, perhaps Java or Italy, but that it is a microcosm of everywhere."[4]

Characterization, O'Faolain also observes, can be no more than assumed in a short story; there is no time for development, no time for unnecessary details or elaborate description. In place of detailed characterization there may be a situation that expresses character or temperament; or conversation that reveals it; or gesture that expresses it. Thus "The Fur Coat" expresses the natural human desire of a woman for some luxury in a life that has been full of privation and her consequent inability to accept the luxury without guilty feelings. "The Trout" uses the discovery of the fish in the dark and terrifying wood to express the young girl's transcendence of childish fears and her first radiant discovery of courage. "Sinners" and "Teresa" are examples of the controlled use of dialogue to reveal character. In "The End of a Good Man" Larry Dunne shoots his favorite but intractable pigeon and in that gesture expresses his anguish and hurt pride. In "Childybawn" Benjy goes back to Angela and becomes engaged but then keeps her waiting five more years until his mother dies, thereby expressing his lasting failure of human sympathy and his deeply rooted selfishness.

The Short Story gives some indication of the technical aspects of O'Faolain's work. In practice he was able to exceed or surpass many of these principles. His best early stories tend to follow a concise, restrained, and economical manner as in "Admiring the Scenery" or "Discord." But many of his later ones, "One True Friend," "The Silence of the Valley," "Childybawn," or "Lovers of the Lake," extend far beyond the limitations of form and method outlined in this book. The varied nature of his stories as a whole, their tendency to go beyond his own principles of conciseness and lack of full characterization, their ability to dilate into philosophical, moral, and social considerations, and their lack of similarity in length may indicate that he has never found any particular scale within which to express himself completely. But they also attest to his artistry; he knows when to follow the principles he has learned and when to modify them to suit the requirements of a particular story.

Chapter 9

The Silence of the Valley

The dominant pattern in *Purse of Coppers* exposes the individual's condition in a straightforward, unambiguous manner. It establishes an alienation so complete that it becomes an impasse beyond which there seems to be no accessible line of development. However much the artist in "A Broken World" might desire the images, sounds, and rhythms of a resurrection, the cries of the doomed and the lonely sounded on all sides in the stories that followed. Since the landscape was shadowed by the presence of disunity in men and in society, the artist's hope of a better time remained as an epilogue to that pilgrimage through the land of the lost.

For the writer the impasse had to be surmounted. The simple method of describing individuals doomed within the restrictions of an insufficient environment could hardly be repeated indefinitely. As artist he would feel more and more the disadvantages of so much social commitment. His intense sense of disruption coming from his awareness of the contrast between his own increasingly cosmopolitan outlook and the extreme nationalism that characterized his country gave his work its atmosphere of negation. Then, too, his dedication to the country made him sensitive to its progress, impatient with its mistakes, and eager for quick reforms. His constant problem of maintaining an inner harmony was aggravated by his reforming instincts. Yet somehow an answer had to be found to Hanafan's demand for an adequate world.

The appearance of "Lady Lucifer" (1941) shows O'Faolain working out a rationale. In the course of this story the whole problem raised in *Purse of Coppers* is discussed. The alternative solutions are traditional: exile to a more adventurous and competitive existence where one can realize one's self to the fullest extent, or retirement within the hermitage of an accepted insufficiency. The chief character is a specialist in mental diseases, a rational, scientific Irishman, who has travelled much outside the country. Like many characters in *Purse of Coppers* he is a man of divided loyalties—emotionally and atavistically drawn to the country of his birth, imaginatively and intellectually attracted to the wider world outside. His defense of that attraction contrasts with his enjoyment of the quiet, rural setting in which the story takes place. Men of ambition, he argues, need a full life; man's pride in himself demands it. The Irish, he says, have too much humility and therein lies the cause of their failure. His argument contains familiar references to loss, damnation, and inner disunity:

Pride and humility aren't opposites. They're two sides of the same thing. . . . If a man is born proud he must feed his pride. It was something given to him. Once he starts the humility tack he's lost. Lost and damned. Drowned in the opposite of his own pride. Show me your humble man and I'll show you the pride coiled up in his humility devouring it like a worm. Show me your proud man and I'll show you the humility flowering beneath his pride like a crocus under the snow. . . .[1]

The significant point about the doctor's defense is that it enables him to face up to his divided state successfully. He is the first to move beyond the condition of loss. He does so by an acceptance of human nature as inherently composed of opposing forces.

Like the priest in "A Broken World" he is concerned with the *compositum* of one's being, the full life. For both, anything that denies the achievement of a full personality is harmful, mentally and spiritually. But where the priest was defeated by his knowledge of evil, the doctor is not. His positive stance is based on a sane and healthy point of view. "All our emotions," he says, "are a tension of opposites. It depends from hour to hour which way the balance swings."[2] Instead of being defeated by circumstances, the individual must liberate himself by the force of his own will and pride. It is his responsibility to transform his state of damnation into a paradise. Just as the priest symbolized in his own character the evils he discussed, so the doctor visibly prefigures what he advocates. It is he, possessing himself as a complete person, who exclaims in response to the Irish setting, "Dear God! This is heaven! Heaven!"[3]

The disappearance of the haunted hero from O'Faolain's writing after 1941 marks an important stage in his development. His discovery of the ambiguous nature of the Irish character, worked out in three historical biographies between 1938 and 1942, brought a more balanced perspective to his stories. Instead of the one-sided formula of the sensitive, intelligent man struggling against insurmountable social conditions, he treats the idea of the ambivalent individual, who is not particularly aware that he lives in sin or in chaos. The rigorous moral tone of the priest in "A Broken World" is replaced by a more humane point of view. The result is a more tolerant and sympathetic observer, well adjusted to the conditions within which the stories occur.

In any case, the suffering characters in *Purse of Coppers* were too closely identified with the writer himself and his concept of a desirable image of life. The romantic appeal of man pitted against the impossible could also be seen with irony and humor. The new perspective is apparent in "The Man Who Invented Sin" (1944), which deals with the evils of clericalism in Irish life after the Civil War. Once again O'Faolain is faced with his vision of sinful chaos, but his treatment of the familiar subject is new and different. His narrator is detached from the events. Unlike his predecessors in *Purse of Coppers*, he is not personally affected

by the change from innocence to guilt; he is not haunted by
memories of happier days; nor does he stand metaphorically
within his own story as a victim of clerical interference. His freedom distinguishes him. It accounts for the dispassionate, objective
tone of his narrative. Instead of brooding on contemporary restrictions, he reflects on the freedoms of his youth. His indictment of
Irish life since the Civil War is of only secondary importance to
him; social commentary is not his main intention. In all of these
he is refreshingly different from his guilt-ridden, socially oriented
forebears.

The opening paragraph, recounting the liberating, unifying,
and hopeful spirit of Irish life at the height of the national resur-
gence in the summer of 1920, is full of the transforming, reju-
venating force of that spirit:

In our youth when we used to pour into the mountains to learn Irish,
places that were lonely and silent for the rest of the year became full
of gaiety during the summer months. Each day there were picnics and
expeditions; every night there were dances, moonlight boating parties,
singsongs in the cottages. The village street became a crowded prom-
enade; its windows never went black before one in the morning; the
pub was never empty. Where once you could have been utterly alone
half a mile off the road, in the bog or up the mountain, you could not
now be sure of privacy anywhere. If you went up the mountain to
bathe naked in some tiny loch you might suddenly see a file of young
students like Alpineers coming laughing down on you over the next
scarp; you might turn the corner of a lonely mountain pass courting
your girl and burst upon a bevy of nuns sedately singing choruses
among the rocks—for every kind of teacher, laymen and women, nuns,
priests, and monks were encouraged in those years to come out into
the hills.

The paragraph is an overture stating the themes that are later
developed and given concrete illustration. Here there is a rich
celebration of naturalness. The first sentence, placing the actions
in youth, gives dramatic force to the transforming spirit that
accompanied the movement to the mountains. Loneliness and
silence change to gaiety. There is an intensification of experience,
a keenness of response, an insistence on the wonder of what took
place ("Each day . . . every night"). All the details express liber-

ation and vitality—picnics, expeditions, dances, boating, singsongs, the crowded street and pub, late nights. The theme of change from loneliness and isolation continues through the last two sentences, where it is enriched by the conjunction of dissimilar pursuits—naked bathing encounters only a laugh, courtship exists side by side with the song of the nuns. There is no sense of incongruity or impropriety, no puritanical note. All those who "pour" into the mountains are joined together by a common goal; all "were encouraged in those years" to participate in that spiritual and cultural regeneration.

After this introductory celebration of a general condition the story progresses quickly to the four main figures, all of whom are lodging in the house where the narrator has also found accommodation. Sister Magdalen is "dainty and gay and spirited," Sister Chrysostom is "a bit of a Miss Prim," Brother Virgilius has "natural ways," and Brother Magellan is "an intelligent, sensitive man" whom the narrator likes "immediately." At first they treat each other with distant formality, but their growing responsiveness to each other is projected in three separate scenes. Their formality of address yields in the first section under the pressure of argument about the proper pronunciation of Irish words. That common interest yields even further intimacy in the next section where in pursuit of an essay on autobiography they exchange memories of childhood. Virgilius and Chrysostom discover they both come from the same part of County Limerick ("she held his arm excitedly"; he speaks "in a huge childish delight"). By the end of this delicately written scene Magellan and Magdalen are standing close together ("She was dabbing her eyes with his big red handkerchief").

The third section shows them as friends, relaxed and happy in innocent, carefree pleasures. They now call each other by shorter, informal names, Jelly, Chrissy, Maggie, and Jilly; they play pitch and toss in the garden; they sing songs together around the piano. But their happiness is overshadowed by the appearance one evening of the local curate. In the upstairs room there is singing, Virgilius is beating time with an empty tankard, Jelly and Maggie are trying to waltz. It is the final moment of natural, unselfcon-

scious pleasure. Into it steps Lispeen, the curate, whose nickname
means "frog." His entry is falsely melodramatic: "The door was
slashed open with a bang that made the piano hum, and there was
our local curate's black barrel of a body blocking the opening."
He confronts them with a suspicious and humiliating interpretation of their actions. His behavior is calculatingly dramatic and
contrasts with the natural, spontaneous, unaffected quality of the
monks and nuns ("he moaned. . . . He let his voice fall solemnly,
even secretively. . . . He roared then. . . . His voice fell again").
"If Martin Luther could only see this," he says, viewing the singing, the dancing, the upraised tankard as evidence of evil. "To
think that this kind of thing has been going on under my nose
for weeks."

The effect of the curate's disapproving, puritanical mind is to
intensify the demands of the religious for greater personal freedom, but now they are secretly affected by the degrading view,
their consciences trouble them. A new transforming force is at
work, countering the invigorating spirit of the opening paragraph.
"The Serpent had come into the garden with the most wily of
temptations. He had said, 'How dare you eat this apple?' And
straightway they began to eat it." Clericalism breeds irresponsibility and the stifled conscience. On the last evening the nuns and
monks "swallowed the last morsel of their apple." Repressing
secret misgivings they join a late boating party, abandoning themselves to the beauty of the scene, the singing, the timeless peace
of the lake, the knowledge that this is their final moment of such
freedom before duty, routine, and city life close in upon them
again. But when the party tries to land Lispeen is before them,
determined to get "the name of every person on that boat!" The
religious disguise themselves, all rush about the priest to give
them time to escape, then all scatter. But the priest sees a nun's
gimp at his feet. But even this and the possibilities it offers him
for denunciation are denied. The narrator fakes a sick call for
the priest and steals the gimp in his absence.

The final episode, showing the effects of Lispeen's actions and
his position of power in the new Ireland, takes place twenty-three
years later. The narrator meets Magellan, on whom the years have

taken a physical toll: "he was greying, and a little stooped; and much thinner." Together they lament the passing of those days in which they all went to the mountains; now the mountains are empty and no one wants to learn the language as they did. But the change in Magellan goes deeper than physical alterations. The intelligent, sensitive monk of former years has become suspicious and uncertain of himself and of others. He no longer approves of those early days; a puritanical outlook colors his memory. "I'm not sure I altogether approve of young people going out to these places. I hope I'm not being puritanical or anything like that, but . . . well you know the sort of thing that goes on here."

Lispeen's froglike mentality has poisoned the monk's mind. Sadly, the narrator watches him "stooping his way back to his monastery in the slum." In that defeated, altered portrait lies the sad results of excessive clerical interference. Almost immediately, he encounters Lispeen, of all places, looking into a bookshop window. The conjunction of these two meetings provides a vivid, unforgettable contrast. Lispeen has come into his own; the serpent has, paradoxically, entered the garden in the likeness of the shepherd and thereby transformed it to a glowing, hellish world. He is prosperous, well-nourished, exuding charm and benevolence, but the satanic overtones are everywhere: "the sunset struck his rosy face and lit the sides of his hat so that they glowed and shone." He is without regret for what he has done; indeed there is no evidence that he realizes the evil he creates. He is unpleasantly cheery—laughs three times and beams at the narrator—as he moves through his kingdom that glows about him: "he bowed benevolently to every respectable salute along the glowing street, and, when he did, his elongated shadow waved behind him like a tail."

The story is written and developed with great clarity of design, structure, and language. Nothing is too elaborate. Progressing steadily from the fine sweep of the opening paragraph, it introduces the characters with a minimum of detail; records their growing response to each other in three varied sections; and then, after the climax of freedom, innocence, and unity of imaginative background, shows Lispeen's disruptive and corrosive effect on human nature. In the final episode the contrast of Magellan's ignoble life and Lispeen's smug insensitivity is quiet and without rancor. The narrator handles this with the same detachment and care that has characterized each separate episode. His well-balanced outlook infuses the story with a light, buoyant atmosphere in which the innocent delight of the characters blends easily with the natural beauty of the setting.

This responsiveness of man and nature is used for effect in each episode. For example, on the evening that the nuns and monks drift gently into reminiscences of childhood, "The mists lifted from the hills, and the sun began to raise gentle wisps of steam from the rocks, and the trout were leaping from a lake as blue as the patches of sky between the dissolving clouds." And on the final evening when they deliberately abandon themselves to the natural freedoms of the setting, the description of the night on the lake is evocative and haunting: "the gray mountain slowly swelled up like a ghost against the spreading moon, and the whole land became black and white . . . the white cottages shone under their tarry roofs . . . Heavy drops of phosphorescence fell from the blades." Each detail is remembered with wonder and delight, just as every incident of the story is filtered through the imagination of the narrator. And Lispeen's jarring entrance into the paradise of innocence is seen as descriptive of man's relationship with nature; they see "his shadow passing across the paling sheen of the lake."

The attraction of the remote, Gaelic-speaking areas of the country is also expressed in "The Silence of the Valley" (1946), which focuses upon the death of an old storyteller as upon the end of a whole way of life. In its poignant sense of the passing of an era of natural innocence and force it is closely related to the narrator's sad knowledge in "The Man Who Invented Sin" that the mountains are empty, that people are no longer encouraged to seek spiritual rejuvenation in those lonely parts of the country where the remnants of Gaelic civilization still survive. "The Silence of the Valley" acknowledges O'Faolain's allegiance to the ancestral heritage. Just as the doctor in "Lady Lucifer" was deeply appreciative of the heavenly beauty of the Irish scene, even when in exile and even while advocating the need for involvement in more complex and more competitive civilizations, so O'Faolain who in editorials has been urging his countrymen to become oriented toward internationalism, now describes the traditional way of life with great feeling and power. The story is a celebration of wonder, a ritual in which the death of the cobbler and story-teller fuses with the larger consummation through which the gradual disintegration of the old way of life is completed. A vital, living contact between old and new has been destroyed, and the sense of loss is magnified by the fact that at best the cobbler's contact with the past was incomplete, since he is virtually the last of his kind, coming at the end of a diminishing line of tradition. Nevertheless, through his stories, his idioms, his richly imaginative view of life, his fantastic mixture of knowledge and ignorance, the ancestral heritage could be sensed.

Through the views and behavior of the seven main characters and their attitudes to the cobbler and his wife, O'Faolain presents a diversified picture of the relationship between the old and the new, the past and the present. But the priest is the most important figure, since he is most conscious of what is involved in the cobbler's death. And behind the overintellectualized confusion of the Celt, the extreme moodiness of the Scots girl, the philosophy of efficiency of the American, the half-peasant quality of Dinny, the undefined character of the inspector, and the gentle sensitivity of the priest, behind all these degrees of awareness, lies the quiet of the valley. In that silence lies the end of a distinctive way of life.

In *The Irish* (1947) O'Faolain argued that the Celt's sense of the Otherworld has dominated his imagination, that he struggles with this domination, attempting to find a synthesis between dream and reality, aspiration and experience, a shrewd knowledge of the world and a strange reluctance to cope with it, and tending always to find the balance not in an intellectual synthesis but in the rhythm of a perpetual emotional oscillation.[4] "The Silence of the Valley" draws close to that sense of the Otherworld. O'Faolain is deliberately reversing the practice of Irish pseudo historians who were euhemerists in their approach to the pagan past. By humanizing and mortalizing the divinities of pagan Ireland, they hoped to eradicate pagan beliefs that still lingered on. His aim is to correct the limited view of the Celtophiles by emphasizing the ribald, satirical, earthy content of the cobbler's speech and his wife's, the rich blend of the spiritual and the physical that characterized the old way of life. He also suggests the antiquity and Otherworld quality of that life by lending to his mortal characters a more than human significance.

The priest is both Christian shepherd and magician who can find historical counterparts in the Celtic Dagda or in Finn MacCumhaill. He cooks the eel, the symbol not only of evil in the Christian tradition but also of the Celtic Otherworld deity, Balar or Aedh. The hotel with its fire and feasting has a resemblance to the dwellings to which Finn is enticed in the *bruidhean* tales. The priest as cook is described as a porpoise, a word that etymologically summarizes his dual aspect—L. *porcus*: a hog, the favorite dish of the Celt and one of the creatures in a fable told by the cobbler; and *piscis*: a fish, the traditional symbol for the Church. Shimmering reflections of the Celtic world abound, as when at the cobbler's funeral the priest, as priest *and* magician, officiates with the help of a diviner. The Romanesque church recalls the blending of the saintly cenobitic life of an ascetic or student in Celtic times; it also recalls magic fables.[5]

The great achievement of this story is that it moves ever closer, with increasing resonance and conviction through each of its five sections, toward the realization of wonder. Seeking to evoke the mystery behind the silence of the valley, it brings together—to the wake, the funeral, and the setting—representatives from the old and the new way of life. But the one man who could interpret between the traditional and the contemporary has died. There can be no voice speaking for the past. That absence is felt through the silence of the valley. Instead of a direct revelation in character, the story works by indirection and suggestion, depending on the reader's ability to derive an imaginative synthesis from the tangential treatment. In no other story has O'Faolain been so daringly nonchalant in his handling of material; the organic pattern of imagery and event is made of loosely assembled elements, brought together in a seemingly careless and casual manner.

Central to this grouping is the emphasis on the unusual, the exciting, and the magical quality of what the valley has sheltered. This idea of the unusual is expressed in many ways in the first section, where the introductory paragraph draws attention to the pervasive silence of the valley at all times of the year, even when the great cataracts slide down the side of the mountain. In the assembling of visitors at the hotel, that immediately follows, the dominant impression is of their relaxed physical postures; they are on vacation, away from their customary routines. The singing tramp has a strange, almost phantastic appearance with his beard, his curls, his billycock hat, his too long raincoat and gnarled stick. But it is the setting that combines and defines them; they are united by a common response to its beauty: "There were five of them, all looking out the door at the lake, the rhododendrons on the hermit's island, the mountain towering beyond it, and the wall of blue air above the mountain line."

Dinny's reference to the cobbler's imminent death transforms the indolent, almost static scene: "The priest whirled. 'Is he bad? Did you see him? Should I go down?'" Lazy pleasure suddenly changes to concern. The rhythm is repeated; the vigorous battle with the eels that follows, a scene full of vitality and exuberance, is juxtaposed with the arrival of the quiet, grief-stricken messenger who announces the actual passing of the cobbler. Again the effect is remarkably powerful, the second clue to a power more important than any hitherto encountered. "The Lord have mercy on him," said the priest as his eyes filled and the others murmured the prayer after him. "The poor old cobbler. I must go and see herself." The section has moved away from all the adventurous activity of the guests to a simple, dignified discussion of the wake that will now take place.

The short section that follows is almost entirely descriptive, as the priest visits the cobbler's cottage, meets the widow, looks at the kitchen, reflects on its silence, and goes to the upper room to pray for his dead friend. Simplicity is the keynote for this traditional world and the vitality of a life informed by inherited customs and instincts. The wrinkled appearance of the old widow is belied by the suggestion of inner power; her voice gives out "a tremendous vitality." The iconographic evidence of the kitchen, also aimed at the dignity of this life, so warmly associated with the dead man, makes the priest keenly conscious of what has now gone. Upstairs the arrangements are classically simple: five wax candles about the cobbler's head, snowy sheets forming a "canopy" about his face, "fluted" folds on the long counterpane. It is formal and reverent and the few remarks of the widow are restrained, her grief muted in resignation. Nevertheless, as the priest cycles back to the hotel he feels the cold wind, the permanent impression of loss.

Section three deepens the sense of wonder. In contrast with the decorum of the preceding scene, the discussion at the hotel supper table is pointless and angry; it deals with the values of efficiency, modernity, and primitivism. The priest rescues his companions from heated argument with talk of the cobbler, his ability as a story-teller, his importance in the area. Then comes the most evocative scene, the cooking of the eels, for which the priest removes his clerical jacket and looks "like a necromancer" in the firelight. The section is thus both dynamic and colorful, moving from the lively discussion at the table to the quietening memory of the cobbler, to the eerie, almost supernatural scene in the firelight, which is accompanied by the merry dance song of the fantastically dressed tramp. The final line is an invitation by the priest, a reminder of the larger purpose or occasion for this scene: "Come, lads," cried the priest, suddenly serious, "it's time for us to visit the poor cobbler."

Part four, dealing with the wake of the cobbler is also indirectly evocative of wonder. The setting has an emotional effect on the visitors; under the full moonlight the mountains look "like the mouth of hell;" the priest feels "as if the dark would come down and claw at them;" the Celt is "wildly excited at the sight of the dark and the light and the creeping lake;" the Scots girl shows her emotion "by cycling madly away by herself." Within the little cottage there is excitement and the old widow entertains the foreign visitors. The climax comes with the laughing command of the priest that they say the rosary. Then as the American goes outside there is a further evocation of magic:

He went out and found more men, all along the causeway and under the hedges, kneeling likewise, so that the mumbling litany of prayers mingled with the tireless baying of the dog. All about them the encircling jags of the mountains were bright and jet, brilliant craters, quarries of blackness, gleaming rocks, gray undergrowth.

In part five, the largest section, comes the most explicit account of the loss caused by the cobbler's death. Again the setting is beautiful: the "morning a blaze of heat," the island "a floating red flower," its rhododendrons "replicated in the smooth lee water." The old "diviner" has a gravity and dignity befitting the simple, timeless nature of the occasion. After their prebreakfast swim in the lake, the younger visitors race about "hooting with pleasure in the comfort of the sun, the blue sky, the smells of the island, and the prospect of trout and bacon and eggs for breakfast." Their exuberance is a tribute to the valley. In the early afternoon the priest enjoys the stillness, "the sparkling lake, the idle shore, the tiny fields, the sleeping hermit's island."

There are recurrent references to the cobbler, his beliefs, his wake, his funeral. These serve all through the story as reminders of what lies behind the silence, behind the gaiety of the visitors, behind the external actions. By now the discussion between the girl and the Celt about religion, birth control, and civilization sounds almost unbearably unimportant in the context of the setting and the mystery it holds. Significantly they are silenced by the arrival of the funeral.

The funeral has a natural grace and beauty. Men carrying the coffin are silhouetted against the sky. A "double file of horsemen descend out of the blue sky." A bell tolls on the ancient hermit's island; the priest stands under the barrel arch of the little Romanesque chapel, "distent in his white surplice, impressive, a magician." The voices saying the *De Profundis* sound "like the buzzing of bees." Thus the present and the past combine in a complex relationship, the present with its own natural beauty of custom and the past remotely represented in land and stone. Christianity and paganism fuse in priest and magician. But the peace of the scene is disturbed as the noise of the coffin lowering into the earth "outraged the silence." For the first time, the widow, hitherto vitally alive and ribald, cries out without restraint. It is the climax of the muted grief, the half-expressed sorrow that has been a constant undercurrent of emotion throughout the story. The prayers sound hollow, the mourners disperse slowly, reluctant to admit the finality of this event. But the silence of the valley has been broken. In a last, quiet exchange the visitors reflect on the autumnal mood of this May day.

Chapter 10

A Design for Confusion

Once he had won detachment from the Irish scene, O'Faolain turned his attention to the exploration of character. He sought to express the presence within the contemporary Irishman of forces that could contradict or alter his public image. It was, in fact, another way of coming to terms with his surroundings, even with the old idea of the individual within a restrictive environment. The important difference lies in the fact that now the central figure is not particularly aware of social issues and may even be indifferent to the whole question of the natural right to a full development of his potential. The new hero is essentially an image for personal confusion or irresponsibility. In analyzing such a contradictory and inconsistent character O'Faolain could take advantage of the subject for comedy or satire, that is, for a detached treatment; at the same time he could draw attention to the forces from the past and from the present that produce the muddled hero.

His detachment was partly the result of his observation that

not all Irishmen had made his particular kind of adjustment to
the romantic dreams of the recent past. While adapting shrewdly
to the commercial aspects of a contemporary civilization, many
retained sentimental bonds with a romanticized past. He saw them
as confused in their allegiances and attitudes. Irishmen in general,
he decided, making a healthy distinction between them and his
own behavior,

were still thinking about themselves, or rather, in their usual way,
double-thinking or squint-thinking about themselves, in terms of
dawns, and *ands*, and *buts*, and *onwards*, and *dew*, and *dusk*, while at
the same time making a lot of good, hard cash to the evocative vocabu-
lary of *tariff, tax, protection, quota, levy, duties* or *subsidies*, meanwhile
carefully compiling a third and wholly different literary style (*pious,
holy, prudent, sterling, gorsoons, lassies, maidens, sacred, traditional,
forefathers, mothers, grandmothers, ancestors, deeprooted, olden,
venerable, traditions, Gaelic, timeworn* and *immemorial*) to dodge more
awkward social, moral and political problems than any country might,
with considerable courage, hope to solve in a century of ruthless
thinking.

His problem was to find a technique capable of rendering that
distinctive combination of realism and romance, hardheadedness
and sentimentality. The stories he now wrote revealed the changing nature of his response to this question. At times he views his
subject as comic, presenting characters who are absurdly irrational
and contradictory. At times he tries to be satirical about their
absurdities, exposing their moral ambivalence and vacillation to
ridicule. Finally, in "Lovers of the Lake," he finds a subject that
enables him to probe deeply into the question of contradictory
forces at work within the Irish character. In this long story he
accepts what he had previously dealt with as comedy and satire
but handles it with sympathy and tolerance. Fittingly enough the
story marks the climax in form and subject of his long analysis of
Irish life in his short stories. Its subtle psychological insight not
only transcends his more recent handling of character but also
prepares for his mature and mellower mood in the following
collection, *I Remember! I Remember!*

Before examining that satisfying story, it is worth seeing it in
the perspective of its preceding, thematically related stories. Sev-

eral of these are devoted to the thesis that Irish character, at least
in the postrevolutionary, transitional period, is fundamentally
chaotic, without clearly definable standards and aims. Perhaps
none show his view of this so much as "One True Friend," which
appeared first in December 1941 under the title "The Lonely
Woman." His portrayal of the main character, Mrs. Moore, illustrates the change in O'Faolain's approach and attitude from this
date. It is one of his most human and most amusing stories.

Central to its success is the way in which characterization, tone,
and action are each evenly balanced between exasperation and
affection. Mrs. Moore is a denial of almost all the standard attitudes that have hitherto prevailed in O'Faolain's work. Devoid of
an intellectual assessment of her own nature, her religion, or her
responsibilities as a member of society, she cannot be made to bear
any burden of nostalgia or frustration in which O'Faolain's own
sense of restriction can find identification. She is a stubborn, self-
pitying, self-centered, vain creature, obdurately living by herself
in a noisy house despite the entreaties of her sons and daughters-
in-law to live with them, Their well-meant plans meet with her
customary suspicion of human motives. She is, as the narrator
says, "A damn nuisance" but at the same time "a good, pious,
kindly, Christian soul." His tone catches the combination of irritation and regard, the tensional relationship that unifies the whole
narrative. The same intermixture is found in her relatives' full
reaction to her refusal. Despite their understandable disappointment at her unwillingness to accept their charity, they can appreciate why she prefers being by herself.

She had company of her own kind. She would sit looking into the
fire in the range, her eyes lost in the great distance of her love for her
dead husband, her dead sisters, or the saints. Her sons had each, at one
time or another, seen her like that, and as they would look about them
at their childhood home picked to the bone, they would find that even
in the middle of the day the busy, hammering house would cease to
exist, and the little city streets would drop away. Looking at her, and
hearing her gentle sigh, how could anyone say to her then, as they so
often said on other occasions, "Mother, why the blazes don't you try
to make some friends?"—not seeing her glance up with a smile at Saint
Francis, and Saint Francis smiling back.

The characterization in this introductory section is confirmed by the action of the story, which deals with her momentary contact with a Mrs. Calvert. Mrs. Calvert has much in common with her; she is a widow, her children have gone from her, she lives alone, she frequents the churches and finds her friends among the saints. Above all they have in common the self-commiserating, falsely humble, irritating way of speaking about themselves and their lot in life:

> "Now, now, Mrs. Moore, you know you're a saint anointed."
> "Ah, Mrs. Calvert, that's all you know. I'm a sinner. A wicked sinner. But when I look at you, I say to myself, 'If there was ever a soul with the mark of salvation on her, it's Mrs. Calvert.' "
> "Now, Mrs. Moore, it's not kind of you to flatter a wicked person. You must pray for me every day. I need it badly."

The happy adventure, however, leads to disappointment. The promise of friendship cannot survive the test of human contact. When a police detective, for example, asks Mrs. Moore to go down to the police station to identify the thief, she agrees only after great persuasion, suspicious of reasons for which Mrs. Calvert gave him her name. Her treatment of the detective is mainly exasperating and his reaction is not tolerant.

But anger alone is an unfair and a typical reaction, however justified in his case and from his limited acquaintance with Mrs. Moore. However stubborn and contradictory she may be, however capricious, she is a fully rendered individual. To a degree unusual in a short story her character is given detailed and complex attention; her actions define her. She is seen as a muddled, annoying, pious, irresponsible creature, but her defects are presented in the light of a kind and wise understanding. The detective is alone in his one-sided judgment.

Because the tenor of the story is favorable to her, it is to some degree a tribute to her. All the elements fuse to bring about an ordered, complex but definite response. By contrast with many of the previous stories, "One True Friend" is unusually complicated in its structure and development. It does not have the poetic orchestration of mood, setting, and conversation found in "A Broken World" or "The Patriot" nor the bright clarity of design, the pure sanity of line and tone to be found in "The Man Who Invented Sin." There is instead a pattern of repetitive situation, repetitive incidents, repetitive attitudes and responses, an achieved fussiness of action, almost a cult of inconsistency. Even the sentences lack O'Faolain's usual directness; they are often full of qualifications, repetitions, evasions. One example should suffice; it deals with Mrs. Moore's explanation of why she can't go to the police station to identify the thief.

"O-o-oh, n-o-o-!" said Mrs. Moore. "I couldn't do *that!*" And she began a long, long rigmarole that went on for half an hour about how she never went out except to go to the church, and how she could never go down there, behind the old-clothes' market, to the Bridewell, where all the drunks are put every night, and how she really never did go anywhere, and how her sons were always at her to go out more and make friends, and what a lonely life she had, and how it would be far better if she did go out, and all about how she used to go out long ago with her husband, and all about her sisters, and her daughters-in-law, and he listened with the endless curiosity of the born detective, and the endless patience of a man whose spirit is broken from dealing with women, and he kept on talking about the motor car, and how she would drive across the city, and be driven back again, until, gradually, his tempting began to win out. She began to see herself in the car. She thought how she would tell her sons about it. She yielded. Off he went, wiping his brow, exhausted but victorious.

But she did not yield in her mind. . . .

In other words the method of the story is subordinated to her, to the portrayal of her kind of behavior. Accepting the limitations of her mental and emotional life, the story infuses them with vitality, irony and stature. She becomes an unforgettable woman, so emphatically herself, winning our affection despite our reservations about her behavior. Whereas former heroes in O'Faolain's work stood within an attractive moral frame, wearing their dissatisfactions and disappointments like badges of integrity, Mrs. Moore refuses to fit into any conventional mold.

Not all of these stories are so considerate of human frailties. A few, seeking to reveal local idiosyncrasies, are frankly satirical. Content to sacrifice universality in the process, they have at best the value of being entertaining. One does not have to believe in the facts they relate to be amused. The best examples are "Unholy

Living and Half Dying" and "Childybawn," which can be read
as companion pieces to "One True Friend," since Mrs. Moore,
as a representative of the older, more simple, more pious way of
life turns up under a different name in each. She is associated
with a sceptical, worldly-wise Irishman whose approach to life is
consciously rational, or so he believes, and opposed to her old-
fashioned piety. There is, therefore, a conjunction in these stories
of two generations with their contrasting attitudes and experiences.

The contrast in "Unholy Living and Half Dying" between
Jacky Cardew and his landlady, Mrs. Canty, illuminates the
ambiguous ironies that arise when the old and the new, the trusting and the sceptical meet. His scorn of her traditional piety and
her fear of death is a sceptical screen upon which memories of
childhood religious lessons occasionally impinge. Jacky, a middle-
aged bachelor bank official, physically well-groomed and well-
preserved, is spiritually negligent and vulnerable. Mrs. Canty, a
poor, lonely widow living in drab surroundings, has little interest
in life's material goods; like Mrs. Moore she finds her most trustworthy friends among the saints. In Jacky's eyes her way of life
is superstitious and typically Irish because based on nothing more
solid than habit, emotional piety, and fear. By contrast, his own
position appears to him as a sensible and civilized rapprochement
between the demands of the next life and the attractions of the
present.

Jacky's rational, man-of-the-world outlook, however, is considerably undermined by the events of the story. On the two occasions
Mrs. Canty is brought to the point of death, or seems to be, his
fearful reactions are every bit as "unenlightened" as hers and
decidedly more ridiculous. His sentimental reflections on the
loneliness of life mock him:

Jacky was left alone in his room. He sank into an armchair by the
open window. The spring night was gentle. The blood of life was
pulsing through everything. Even the three old London planes in the
middle of the square had their little throb and the high Easter moon
was delicately transparent as if with youth. He leaped up and began
to circle the room. He had never seen anything so lovely, it seemed to
him, as those little babies gazing at him out of their big eyes, with their
soft little lips parted. He was looking again over the shining roofs and

the blank chimney pots, and as if a shutter flicked he felt for one moment the intense vacancy and loneliness of his life and saw it, as the years went by, becoming more lonely and more empty. And when he was gone, that moon out there, the old trees below, would still be there, still throbbing. . . .

Jacky's misery brings him to remorse and repentance; remembering his days of sin, he plans the confession he will make. But remorse turns back to indifference in the days that follow. Inappropriately, while the Easter bells of the city and the strengthening sun of a new season announce a resurrection and the presence of a Redeemer, he reverts to the comfortable, self-deception of a life that no longer seems only transitory. He ends as he began, "well-groomed, well-preserved, pomaded, medicated, and self-cosseted." But his precarious retention of scepticism has been well demonstrated.

The idea of hidden resemblances is carried further in "Childybawn." Jacky Cardew's moral chaos and the ironic nature of his self-justification is found also in Benjy Spillane. But here there is the important addition of Benjy's mother, a possessive, sharptongued, pious creature whose deviations from the path of rectitude, although not as spectacular as Benjy's, are at least as frequent. The mutual deception practiced on each other by mother and son is projected in a series of antithetical incidents in which the differences and similarities between the two characters are humorously revealed. Behind the mother's piety and maternal possessiveness lies a habit of secret drinking, betting, and ever increasing debts to the butcher, the grocer, the bookies, and the moneylenders. Behind Benjy's mother-love and respectable position at the bank lies his drinking, his gambling, and above all his affair with Angela; at the age of forty-one he enjoys the inordinate attentions of his mother and his relations with Angela without the responsibilities of the married state. The mother's determination to separate her "boy" from this "Jezebel" is projected in a skillfully regulated campaign in which the rapport between St. Augustine and his mother, St. Monica, is the intended result: "the two of them sitting in the window, and the sun going down over the sea. Hand in hand. Mother and son. Lovely! Ah! Lovely! Lovely!"

Unexpectedly, like Jacky Cardow, Benjy, afflicted by a ruptured ulcer, succumbs to the fear of death and damnation, abandons Angela, makes his peace with God, and enters enthusiastically upon the good life so earnestly prayed for by his mother. Ironically, the answer to her prayers is painfully inconvenient. A pious Benjy, anxious now to repeat the Augustine-Monica situation, soon discovers his mother's secret habits. The result is that her life is made miserable by his piety. Fortunately he relents, returns to Angela in a profane purpose of amendment, and lets his mother have her minor vices. And five years later, when his mother dies, he even marries Angela.

Chapter 11

Lovers of the Lake: A Penitential Journey

In the process of describing the contradictory elements in the Irish character, O'Faolain came to appreciate the power and the value of the various influences on thought and behavior that lie beneath the conscious or rational part of the individual. What had been a subject for detached treatment in comedy and satire gradually gained importance for him as an essential element for any full study of human nature. In "Lovers of the Lake" he found a subject large enough and complex enough to contain and express his mature awareness of some of the profound forces within the psyche.

Its theme, given dramatic form in the characterization and experience of Robert Flannery and Jenny, his mistress, is that "inside ourselves we have no room without a secret door; no solid self that has not a ghost inside it trying to escape." They represent in a more sophisticated and generous manner the contrasts and confusions of Jacky Cardew and Mrs. Canty. Their journey to Saint Patrick's Purgatory draws them in to the lake of the atavistic and the subliminal in which some of their deeper instincts are revealed. Her capricious urge to make the rigorous pilgrimage contrasts with his sceptical indifference to religious matters, so that at first they seem to stand for clearly drawn antitheses: rationalism and emotionalism, agnosticism and Catholicism, male common sense and feminine impulsiveness.

In the course of the story, however, these easily defined contrasts are given a subtle alteration. Jenny wants to choose between Flannery and God, desire and duty, sin and virtue. Her pilgrimage is a desperate reaching out for a solution to a daily experience of conflict between what her heart wants and her conscience counsels. But her quest is doomed to failure; her flight to the medieval rigors results in a messily tearful admission that she cannot renounce the Devil when he appears in the likeness of her lover. For Bobby the whole idea of the journey seems absurd; he feels superior to the spiritual anguish that motivates her. He rests smugly in an agnostic rationalism that sees the Devil only as manifestations of disease or as failure in the operating theater. Ostensibly he follows Jenny to the island of abominable excesses in a spirit of scientific curiosity; he wants to investigate the conditions that produce spiritual changes. Ironically he emerges from the island in an unusually devout mood. Enigmatically refusing to say whether he has been to confession and promised therein to renounce Jenny, he is nevertheless foremost in insisting on the rules of the pilgrimage that forbid eating until midnight, and that night yields to her request for separate rooms. The pilgrimage has had an effect upon him; the sceptic has succumbed to some extent, however momentarily, to what he has previously condemned as superstitious nonsense.

Central to the theme, structure, and development of the story is the contrast between Bobby and Jenny that, changing as the story progresses, reveals unsuspected similarities between them and deepens our understanding of each. The gradual revelation of those hidden resemblances reaches a natural and appropriate climax on the island during the height of the penitential journey. It is entirely fitting that we should see the characters most sharply at the moment when they are experiencing most keenly the spiritual and psychological unmasking brought about by the various ordeals of the island purgatory. The whole trend of their journey, from their customary world of ease and sophistication in Dublin to the unfamiliar world of medieval harshness and searching self-examination in Lough Derg, is an atavistic one. Jenny and Bobby are brought out of the world in order to find their real selves; that is exactly the purpose of the pilgrimage. Only on the island can the pilgrim escape the barriers of pride that surround him on the mainland.

Our initial encounter with the lovers is deceptive. There is very little in the opening scene to indicate they are not husband and wife. They are sipping tea and looking down at tennis players in a suburb; he speaks amiably to her, she pats his cheek, kisses him sedately, and sees him out the door with a loving smile. The fact that he talks to her "from the lazy deeps of her armchair" is the main clue that it is her house and her furniture. The slow pace of the opening scene is maintained in the comic treatment of their contrasting characters. In the light of the story's later intense psychological analysis, the conversation here is deceptively superficial and light. Yet much is subtly being forecast; her impulsive nature is indicated by the suddenness and irrelevancy of her request that he drive her to Lough Derg. His distance from religious interest can be seen at once in his assumption that she means the Lough Derg famous for fishing; it can be seen also in the changing tone of his reactions—from amiability to surprise, to laughter, to incredulity, to ridicule—as he realizes she really wants to go to the "other Lough Derg," for which he has only contempt. As the scientific man he has no respect for "that place with the island where they go around on their bare feet on sharp stones, and starve for days, and sit up all night ologroaning and ologoaning"; he asks "coldly" if she is "going religious" on him. Reluctantly and ungraciously he consents to drive her, warning that her "Holy Joe streak," which he has noticed before, may appear "once too often."

Neither the causes nor the consequences of her religious impulses spoil the happiness he feels as they drive in the morning sunlight—"like any husband and wife off on a motoring holi-

day"—to the River Shannon. The joyous tone of this passage
causes us to see them in a sympathetic light, and even their quarrel only makes them seem compatible lovers, well-accustomed to
differences of opinion. His concern that it is her adulterous relationship with him that makes her want to do penance and seek
forgiveness also shows him in a favorable light, as do his show of
temper, his irritation, and his bafflement. At the same time his
interrogation exposes her weaknesses. She has no rational explanation for doing the pilgrimage or for doing it at this particular
time. His search for reason behind her action is doomed to failure.
In a swift sequence of questions he asks for a "cause," a "reason,"
and thinks her behavior may be a "symptom." All he discovers in
horror is that she is ravenous and faces two more days of fasting.

The climax of this interplay of contrasting attitudes and temperaments, brought on by his well-intentioned investigation,
comes in a frank admission on her part of the muddled nature of
her religious condition; despite her six-year affair with him, she
goes to confession every Easter and Christmas. His reply is that
that was routine. "There's no harm," he tells her loftily, "in going
to church now and again." He does it himself sometimes—on state
occasions or to save friends from being upset. Her firm answer is
honest: religious observance has never been routine with her.
"It's the one thing I have to hang on to in an otherwise meaning-
less existence. No children. A husband I'm not in love with. And
I can't marry you." They have reached an impasse against which
his rational mind is powerless. She accuses herself frankly of moral
ambivalence, not as a defense but as a statement of fact; the truth
as she sees it, blasphemous though it may sound, is that all she
has is Flannery and God. His response to this confession is sympathetic, but he cannot reconcile his present knowledge of her with
her wish to seek out and endure the penances of Lough Derg.
Reason and impulse face each other without any common ground
for understanding.

Their approach to the lake confirms his sceptical view. A mist
falls, the hills are sunless, the rain flays down, the pilgrims' clothes
are ruffled by the wind like the fur of cattle, the lake itself has
"creeping worms of foam." The whole atmosphere depresses him;

the pilgrims are not his kind of people. Even Jenny is disappointed; she had expected a Gougane Barra, the scene of "The Silence of the Valley." Romantically she had thought of "an old island, with old grey ruins, the old holy trees and rhododendrons down to the water, a place where old monks would live." The reality is a complex of tall buildings, one tree, and an appearance of commercialization. Bobby, expressing his views that the pilgrimages are a good financial proposition, looks at her grimly and bids her a sarcastic farewell.

Their arrival at the lake marks the end of one major section of the story. In it the two main figures have been introduced. Their conversation expresses not only their social position and sophistication, but also their easy companionship and mutual love. Imagery, working unobtrusively, sometimes in seemingly casual references, such as those to tennis players who should wear whites, to a dolmen, to a child in a pink pinafore, subtly indicate the childlike and atavistic nature of Jenny's quest. But it is in the description of their arrival at the lake that the imagery plays the most prominent part in creating a mood and in revealing a response. The presence of rain, cloud, mist, lake water, cold light is increasingly felt. Their separation is made to the accompaniment of "gurgles of streams" and "a sound of pervasive drip." Jenny is abandoned to the dreary landscape of the penitential island, while Bobby drives away. Their sunlit morning of happy compatibility has been blotted out by argument and atmosphere. The feeling of submission reaches its fullest significance at the height of the story, when Bobby and Jenny, their public selves eroded by rain and ritual, succumb for a while to the transforming spiritual power of the pilgrimage.

The symbolic presence of water is intensified in the following section in which Jenny is ferried across the dark waters to the island. Individual identity is blotted out as Jenny "without transition became yet another anonymous pilgrim." Her entrance to the purgatorial island is not joyous; atmosphere and mood combine, she feels a sense of shame, she detests the pity and kindness that distinguish human relationships on the island: "she felt the abasement of the doomed. She was among people who had surrendered all personal identity, all pride. It was like being in a concentration camp." Her romantic conception of the pilgrimage receives many shocks, not only the commercialized setting but even the routine. What had seemed like a relatively short period is really an arduous and extended experience: long hours of walking the rounds of stones, praying, kneeling, renouncing her sins, night-long vigils and sleeplessness, and three days of fasting. Her initial antipathy is strengthened by the difficulties; above all she hates the public renunciation of sin with her arms extended, her face to the lake, the rain beating upon her. Her mood is sullen, and "her heart cursed herself for coming so unprepared, for coming at all."

All through the first section dealing with the island she retains the feelings of the mainland, experiences shame, regrets her impul-sive decision, forces herself to participate in the prayers and the rituals. All the time she feels separate from the anonymous mass of pilgrims cheerfully united in fervent prayer. "On all sides, before her, behind her, the same passionate exchange of energy, while all she felt was a crust hardening her heart. . . ." She prays for release, for acceptance, for identification but is carried numbly through the exercises and gets soaked by the rain. Her sudden dis-covery of Bobby as a detached observer of her miserable state infuriates her. By contrast he is calm, is also soaking wet, but maintains a spirit of scientific curiosity. He wants to see exactly what she believes in; he has none of her irritation and shame; he speaks "calmly," "without raising his voice," "softly," "casu-ally," and even smiles and laughs. His detachment is seen in his quiet statement that he thinks she should not have gone to the island, that he knows she has come in a cowardly spirit, hoping to get the "druids" to get rid of him for her; and what's more, he tells her with maddening calm, he's going to ask them to grant her request.

His spirit of scientific inquiry, however, is no longer pure. He is, he explains, not really doing the pilgrimage, at least, not the fasting; he has his pockets stuffed with chocolates and he certainly intends to sleep. Taken in conjunction with his angry denuncia-tion of fasting and sleeplessness, his words are unusually mild and suggest change; he *probably* will not fast and he *might* stay awake. Already he has been reminded of going to midnight Mass with his father as a child or of going to retreats, "when we used to all hold up a lighted candle and renounce the Devil." "It was a queer sensation," he tells her, "standing up there by the lake and saying those words all over again. Do you know, I thought I'd completely forgotten them!"

The scene is subtly done. No major event or statement jars our given image of Bobby, and appropriately he is unaware of the quiet ways in which his public self is being altered. Implicitly, we imagine Bobby for Jenny in the recent account of her experience with rain, sharp stones, mass fervor, and we notice that while she "was a drowned cat," "his hair was streaked down on his forehead as if he had been swimming." Childhood experiences of religion rise to the surface to exert a surprisingly powerful influence. On the island there is an alteration of personality, an unmasking of the self. The section ends without any major change in his characterization; confidently he explains his position in relation to the island. He cannot accept its renunciation of the flesh and the world; nothing can make him believe that her body and his are evil; and she, he asserts, is not going to renounce the world because she is tied to it hand and foot. Her indignant denial meets his sharp rejoinder: "Then why do you go on living with your husband?" . . . "You do it because he's rich, and you like comfort, and you like being a somebody." They part in anger. "His voice cut her like a whip." . . . "He cut at her again." . . . "With a switch of her head she brushed past him." All the appearances, therefore, make Bobby the victor: he is cool-headed, rational, and objective. Jenny suffers a succession of defeats, physical defeat by the weather and the penances, moral defeat by Bobby.

The climax to this interplay of contrasting attitudes comes during the long, sleepless vigil following the first long day of travel, fasting, penance, and prayer. Jenny transcends her antipathy, her sense of alienation; during the mass prayer in the church, she sinks ecstatically into communion with her fellow pilgrims, joined with them in spiritual devotion. It is the most perfect moment of the pilgrimage for her, as she escapes into the lake of forgetfulness and is released from worldly attachments. The description of this experience emphasizes its hypnotic quality.

The night world turned imperceptibly. In the church, for hour after hour, the voices obstinately beat back the responses. She sank under the hum of the prayer wheel, the lust for sleep, her own despairs. Was he among the crowd? Or asleep in a corner of the boatshed? She saw his flatly domed fingers, a surgeon's hand, so strong, so sensitive. She gasped at the sensual image she had evoked.

The moon touched a black window with color. After an age it had stolen to another. Heads drooped. Neighbors poked one another awake with a smile. Many of them had risen from the benches in order to keep themselves awake and were circling the aisles in a loose procession of slurring feet, responding as they moved. Exhaustion began to work on her mind. Objects began to disconnect, become isolated each within its own outline—now it was the pulpit, now a statue, now a crucifix. Each object took on the vividness of hallucination. The crucifix detached itself from the wall and leaned towards her, and for a long while she saw nothing but the heavy pendant body, the staring eyes, so that when the old man at her side let his head sink over on her shoulder and then woke up with a start she felt him no more than if they were two fishes touching in the sea. Bit by bit the incantations drew her in; sounds came from her mouth; prayers flowed between her and those troubled eyes that fixed hers. She swam into an ecstasy as rare as one of those perfect dances of her youth when she used to swing in a whirl of music, a swirl of bodies; a circling of lights, floated out of her mortal frame, alone in the arms that embraced her.

Jenny is isolated where the normal measurements of time and place forfeit their comforting regularity; the individual's responses become uncertain and fragmentary. The passing of time is told vaguely and imperceptibly by the slow passage of the moon from one window to another. Initially the pilgrim struggles against the sense of dissociation ("voices obstinately beat back the responses"), but it is a vain test of endurance ("hour after hour"). Many rhythmical movements combine to absorb him, to take him out of his separate identity. Jenny "sank under the hum of the prayer wheel," her mind drifts into questions about Bobby. But inevitably she is caught by the trancelike atmosphere, the distant, dilatory moon, circling people, slurring feet, voices in unison.

Exhaustion undermines her control; objects appear to lose their reassuring fixity. Hallucinatory experiences draw her still further away from the world of fact and reason. The whole sequence has the nightmarish quality of taking place under water; it is the climax to the imaginal pattern of mist, rain, and water. Here verbs and adjectives support the sense of submersion: Jenny "sank," people rise and circle about like fish in a bowl, objects seem suspended or floating in a state of weightlessness, heads "sink," bodily contact has no more force than that of "two fishes touching in the sea"; Jenny no longer controls her actions; in the final sentence "She swam into an ecstacy . . . floated out of her mortal frame. . . ." She has become totally absorbed, disjunct, caught up in the mesmeric experience. When she is released she is happy; she shares in the island's mood of kindness, can grin, joke, and laugh. In this mood she seeks Bobby.

Bobby's participation in the vigil, although not unexpected from his earlier remarks about childhood memories, is evidence of a further weakening of his rational defenses. On the surface he is still objective, still the man of science analyzing experience; he speaks "smugly" and "eagerly," feeling that his theories have been confirmed; the ordeals of the pilgrimage, he argues, the rituals, the sleeplessness, the exhaustion do not renounce the flesh at all; they use the flesh to achieve a trancelike, visionary condition. His explanation, so close to the truth, spoils Jenny's newly found peace. Feeling guilty of irrationality, she turns from him in fury and tries thereafter to mean and feel each word of the prayers. In the morning she is calm from exhaustion, unaware of her companions, of Bobby, or of herself. "She no more thought of God than a slave thinks of his master."

The decline in Bobby's position reaches its lowest point in their next encounter. Both are sleepy, both reduced to contentment by sheer fatigue. And Bobby, as he now openly admits, is actually doing the pilgrimage, the prayers, the rituals, even the fasting; he has thrown the chocolates into the lake. His main accomplishment is to reveal to her how much he loves her and thereby negate her whole purpose in going through the ordeals. He is, she realizes, in an accurate assessment that cuts beneath all his pretenses, doing the pilgrimage "stupidly, just like a man; skeptically, just like a man; and not at all for the only reason that she knew was his real reason: because she was doing it, which meant that he loved her." On three separate occasions in this one section, she has thought of him with love, even at the very time when she was trying to make a decision to give him up: at the beginning of the vigil, during her meeting with him, and at the end. The strength of her love is unmistakeably evident; her pilgrimage is a failure.

Under the pressure of the island's spiritual forces Bobby's smothered religious feelings have come to light to contradict his public veneer of agnosticism. Not that he himself is aware of the unmasking; the rational man does not see what the impulsive woman sees. In contradiction of the initial impression we have of her, Jenny emerges as more logical than Bobby because more honest. She has not tried to hide her moral vacillation, and now in the clear light of her inability to renounce Bobby she seeks to explain her impulsive need for repentance. It has never been a superficial feeling and illogicality is of its essence. Her moral confusion can only end when there is an end to their love, but as the island has shown that is not yet. She is therefore unavoidably caught in the conflict between her love for Bobby and her need to repent. Both needs are as deeply felt; their presence intensifies her story and, in contrast with Bobby's complacent self-deception, gives her greater integrity. Her tearful admission produces no answering self-criticism in Bobby, nor indeed any real understanding. His main contribution to their conversation is that he has no intention of going to confession and does not want to "get into the same mess" that she is in. By now, however, his confidently announced intentions ring somewhat hollow; what he proposes to do and what he actually may do are liable to be two different things.

Jenny's anguished state of moral confusion is placed in larger perspective in her encounter with two fellow pilgrims, Goat's Eyes, a girl from Connemara with an insatiable sexual appetite, and an anonymous Englishman who has been making the pilgrimage for twenty-two years. For the former, confession is but a momentary stay against confusion and unhappiness, since her physical desires constantly overcome her spiritual intentions. The two women, joined in their common predicament, see the water surrounding the island as "a lake of human unhappiness," and Jenny's understanding of the human condition is widened and deepened. The Englishman's noble concept of love brings her into contact with a demanding ideal. To love, he says, is to make another happy; "it is something godly to love another human being. . . . What does 'godly' mean if it doesn't mean giving up everything for another?" To love, he says is "a divine folly, beyond all reason, all limits." The chance encounter strips Jenny of her central illusion, the idea that all she has in life is Bobby and God. Bobby's earlier accusation that she can never renounce the world is true, nor can she renounce Bobby. With rigorous honesty she faces this final revelation about her own nature, "overcome by the thought that inside ourselves we have no room without a secret door; no solid self that has not a ghost inside it trying to escape."

Dante's journey led into ever deeper awareness of the possibilities of evil in human nature and into a regenerative spiritual progress through the various levels of the purgatorial process to his final all-encompassing vision of Truth. O'Faolain's lovers are led to another kind of truth; their withdrawal from the underworld does not signal a turning toward salvation. No major spiritual alteration has taken place. They return "by the road they had come" to their customary state of compromise and self-deception. But the pilgrimage has not been totally devoid of grace; intimations of the spiritual accompany them, and they now have a clearer understanding of their condition and a better understanding of what the lake signifies.

That significance pursues them. It lies behind Jenny's opening question, has he been to confession: "had he, after all his years of silence, of rebellion, of disbelief, made his peace with God at the price of a compact against her?" It lies behind his refusal to answer. And behind that lies the contrast between "the impenetrable wall of identity that segregates every human being in a private world of self," his condition in the world, and the experience of the island where "the barriers of self break down." Seeing that contrast in his evasion, Jenny sees the validity of the Englishman's argument that self only surpasses self when "love desires nothing but renunciation, total surrender." Sadly she accepts Bobby's flat assertion that people in love do not give up everything for each other; in other words she will not sacrifice the comforts of home and position for love.

Bobby's reaction to the island is not so clear. In an almost total reversal of roles, she has pursued the lesson of her pilgrimage with merciless logic, facing up sadly but frankly to her moral condition. Bobby is now guilty of the kind of self-deception and evasion that earlier was found in her. Unlike her, he will not say whether he has experienced her conflict through confession and the conflicting demands of amendment and desire. In ironic contrast with his angry condemnation of fasting on the journey toward Lough Derg, he now intends to fast until midnight in accordance with the rules of the pilgrimage. The whole account of these adulterous lovers maintaining an allegiance to a spiritual experience for this one day out of loyalty to formal rules is amusingly revealing of human nature. Planning the luxurious meal that will reward their virtue, they drive by the longest route possible; when he catches salmon trout, they roast them over an open fire. (" 'I nearly ate them raw,' he said. 'Let's cook them and eat them,' she said fiercely.") Despite such need, both, in an unconscious imitation of Diarmaid and Grainne, the medieval lovers who left untasted fish as a sign of sexual continence, fling their fish back into the fire. Having tea later, he orders "lots of hot buttered toast." But neither will eat them and neither will even put milk in their tea, and both are angry with each other for their foolish behavior. Trying to wear away the long, hungry day to midnight, they go to the movies and watch the slapstick of *Charley's Aunt* "gloomily." Around them the west of Ireland countryside is beautiful; their desire for each other grows as the day advances into night. The climax of this parallel development of spiritual observance and physical need ends with their arrival in Galway, where they will spend the night. Happiness comes with the certainty of that rewarding meal, and when he pats her knee her whole body vibrates in response.

The tone of this homeward journey has been ironic and light. In a short descriptive passage their individual plight is merged with the familiar experience of returning pilgrims, ravenous for food. "Revelry is the reward of penance." The hotel porter welcomes them like "heroes returned from a war," assures them of bodily comforts and satisfactions. They indulge themselves in the dimly lit bar, mix convivially with the crowd, consume the ritual dinner, return to the bar, become aware of "a soft strumming and drumming near at hand," and dance until three o'clock in the morning. Their story concludes in a short enigmatic scene. Happy, gently tipsy, and gently tired, they stand with their arms about each other watching the moon on Galway Bay. The moment of decision has come. Bobby thinks he might do the pilgrimage properly next year; desire floods over them in the romantic setting, and he invites her "gently, ever so gently, with a gentleness that terrified her" to go into their hotel. She pleads for one night of continence:

He looked down at her, and drew his arms about her. They kissed passionately. She knew what that kiss implied. Their mouths parted. . . . Hand in hand they walked slowly back to the hotel, to their separate rooms.

"Lovers of the Lake" reveals much about the generous and intelligent manner in which O'Faolain approaches his work. Against a background of religious belief and practice, he poses the human story of lovers caught in the mesh of desire. That both are middle-aged adds to the poignancy of their autumnal passion. Sophisticated and intelligent, successful surgeon and socially prominent mistress, theirs is no casual relationship but a genuine love maintained in the sight of God. The world, the flesh, and the devil, renounced in the otherworld environment of the island, are reinvoked in the everyday world as inescapable elements of life. Instead of an effort at complete renunciation, the lovers give a token acknowledgment for one long day and perhaps for one night—there is no certainty about this nor does there have to be—and then continue to pluck their apple from a tree in which the winter of age and the fading of desire already appear. They are in the final scene, as all through the story, lovers of the spiritual power of the lake, but O'Faolain's sensitivity to the presence of secret rooms within the self, hidden instincts and feelings, causes him to view his story with the widest sympathy and understanding. His position is detached but definite: the lovers are gently and carefully presented; after a lifetime of creative endeavor and technical advancement, he moves confidently through all the phases of the story, holding the balance between Bobby and Jenny at all stages in a steady and precise focus; the judgment is clear but not harsh. The island is not the world; it can command a rigorous self-examination and can unmask the external self; "it is a brief, harsh Utopia of equality in nakedness." The world of human activity is more like that represented in the muddled, well-meaning, complicated, amusing state of the lovers.

Chapter 12

Some Bright Destination

His work now shows his achievement of an inner harmony in the face of external circumstances. Many stories in *I Remember! I Remember!* (1961) show a concordance between the subject and the temperament of the author.[1] They are the work of a mature, complex, and extraordinarily subtle personality. In manner and development, in delicacy of mood and feeling, in their wise understanding of human nature, they represent further refinement of feeling in O'Faolain and a more sophisticated control of emotion. To match this subtlety he has worked out a new technique. Depending on understatement and on meaning achieved through an interrelation of elements within the story, a resonance of moods, images, and incidents, they are the result of an exact and deliberate kind of writing. Every good short story, he has written in his perceptive and germinal commentaries in *Short Stories, A Study in Pleasure* (1961), has some bright destination, and every step into the story must lead towards its point of illumination.

These later stories are linked thematically with "Lovers of the

Lake" and the preceding satires and comedies. O'Faolain's growing respect for the deeper psychological experiences of his characters causes him to concentrate now on the universal themes of
time and change, the impermanence of youth and age, and the
accommodations of middle age. He leads his characters to a realization of the transitory quality of life and measures the value
of individual endeavor within the perspective of man's littleness
in an immense world. There is a sad awareness of the price paid
for growth, for the individual's response to the challenge of life,
his submission to the fate within his own character. One of the
characters in "One Night in Turin" reflects on this complex idea:

> "We make happiness easily when we are young, because we are full
> of dreams, and ideals, and visions, and courage. We make our own
> world that pushes away the other world. . . . But you know what
> happens to us. That little flame in us that could burn up the world
> when we're young—we sell a bit of it here, and a bit of it there, until,
> in the end, we haven't as much of it left in us as would light a ciga-
> rette." "And yet," she said, frowning through him, "it is there, to the
> end. You always feel you might blow on it, make it big again, go on
> to the very end, without giving up, find the thing, discover the thing,
> invent the thing, call it anything you like, that you'd always been
> wanting."

The sadness comes from the idea that merely to live is to suffer or
to cause suffering in others. All progress is made at the expense
of loss either in one's self or in others, and it is the recognition of
that truth that is at the heart of these stories.

One of the most valuable achievements of *I Remember! I
Remember!* is the creation of a distinctive and perfectly suited
voice through which the stories move to their moment of sad
truth. It is comfortingly friendly and open, moving along the surface of the story in a deceptively artless and casual manner. Even
the style seems uncontrived and flowing; it appeals to the ear.
Upon examination, however, it shows deliberate craft in its balance of elements within the sentence and the paragraph. But it
suits the narrator in its unhurried pace, its pausing for small and
apparently irrelevant ideas and feelings; essentially it is his con-
versational manner, so that style and character are one.

The new voice makes for flexibility of approach; it brings in the omniscient author under the disguise of the trustworthy voice that deals maturely and tolerantly, in a gentle and wise manner, with its subject. We are made happily aware that it will make no uncomfortable demands upon us. There is no trace of the haunted, compulsive manner, the reforming zeal, or the apocalyptic tone. We feel relaxed, soothed by the voice. It is a fine achievement, because once we have submitted to its grace and friendliness, its exquisite courtesy, we are in its power. The opening paragraph of "A Touch of Autumn" illustrates some of these comments on style and manner:

It was, of all people, Daniel Cashen of Roscommon who first made me realize that the fragments of any experience that remain in a man's memory, like bits and scraps of a ruined temple, are preserved from time not at random but by the inmost desires of his personality.

The relaxation in mood and manner is partly the result of O'Faolain's detachment, almost an indifference, from the Irish scene. But he is still interested in the subject of frustration. "I am concerned," he has said recently, "about the freedom of the individual in an environment which is very often constricting to him. I'm interested in the growth of the personality within the individual creature."[2] Each of the stories in *I Remember! I Remember!* is a reflection of that concern. The approach is different but the subject is essentially the same as in his earlier books. His characters are no longer caught within the web of social, political, or religious conflicts; they are not usually struggling either to overcome the particular deficiencies of a particular society nor revealing in the ambivalent, contradictory manner of their lives the unsettled state of Irish society. The restricting factors now are internal and an inescapable part of every man. Individuals are seen now as the victims of their own nature. The stories gain in universality by being released from the local pressures of an Irish setting. But there is a loss in amplification; the stories no longer express a whole generation and a whole society. They forfeit this distinctive intensity of dilation. The context of human endeavor is defined now in the light of the limitations of opportunity and choice that attend any man's growth. It is the realization of these limitations, as it strikes various characters, that they seek to present.

The basic technique used to bring about this realization is contrast; by reflecting on past events and becoming aware of change, characters gain insight into their own lives and their own natures. The general philosophical truths that emerge come from the exploration of small, seemingly trivial incidents. By analogy and association one is led to consider universal aspects of human existence. Such a result is a tribute to the craft of these stories as well as to the validity of their content. The short story justifies itself as a distinctive genre because of its ability to derive insights of this nature from limited material.

What usually happens is that the situation explodes or dissolves, as a result of some simple trigger-incident, when out of human tension between those two or three people, the main character breaks through to some sort of truth-to-self, or truth-about-self, which had up to then been hidden from him, or which he had weakly or stupidly dodged.[3]

"A Touch of Autumn in the Air" is a good example of O'Faolain's methods. There is the casual manner and the device of the engaging narrator. There is the surprise in having the basic truth revealed unconsciously by Daniel Cashen. That truth is that the things we remember are indicative of the inmost desires of the personality. In his old age Daniel Cashen finds himself remembering incidents from an autumn vacation spent as a boy on a farm with Kitty Bergin, his sweetheart cousin. The images that have remained are ones that gave him in the past a feeling of human littleness. Now they return to undermine his confidence and cause him to question the value of his life as a businessman. It is the manner in which these effects are created that gives this story its vitality. Little is explicitly stated but much is suggested and implied. Through contrasts in images, incidents, situations, and characters the central effect is achieved. In isolation no single image, or incident, or character would cause the moment of realization.

In the manner of a character in a novel by Conrad and for a similar psychological reason Daniel Cashen does not go directly to the main memory. Nevertheless all relates to the emergent idea that he had as a boy an intuitive recognition of his own small-ness. He remembers an afternoon when he watched a river flowing and a time when he saw men standing in a river, ducking a pro-testing boy and laughing at his screams. In both cases the flow of time is present in the water and the sense of human generations passing while natural objects remain. Attendant images support the general effect: soft, surrounding fields, clouds moving slowly, and the silence of the countryside. Space and silence, the vastness of the land, the mysterious forces of nature, all speak to the small boy. In his major memory Daniel Cashen describes going with Kitty Bergin from his aunt's warm cottage "one sunny, mistified October morning" to the men in the fields. Again there is the vast, level plain, the flat river basin, and two men shrunken under a vast sky.

As well as being haunted by such sensory impressions of his lost boyhood, Daniel Cashen's memory also contains the idea of growth and separation. This time it is an incident that becomes suggestive. The children bring two letters to the men in the fields. Two sons have left home; one works in the mines at Castlecomer, the other is studying for the priesthood in Dublin. When the father reads their letters it is clear that the sons have gone beyond his experience of life. That estrangement and loss, which affects both the children and the parents, is present also in the account the son in Dublin gives of visiting a convent to see a local girl: "Saint Joachim's has nice grounds, but the trams pass outside the wall and she said that for the first couple of weeks she could hardly sleep at all." Her loneliness in the unfamiliar city is made more sad by the impression that the men never cared much for the girl anyway and so have little sympathy or understanding of her situation now.

Loneliness, separation, growth and change, the drift from the rural background, the individual response to life, all reflect on Daniel Cashen's own life. The feelings and ideas evoked by the account of the men's reponse to the letters are similar to our understanding of and response to his present state; they express his condition. Now as an old man he remembers the warm, sensory pleasures of that morning, its sense of security and peace, its evidence of a traditional way of life, and at the same time he remembers the feeling of disruption and change that the morning brought. Its moments of joy and its promise of love and happiness are further indications of this complex effect. Kitty Bergin was his girl, they shared the pleasures of that vacation, she wrestled with him in the field, she also pretended to be a nun and he felt the touch of impending loss. But they jogged home together in the cart, and even then the migratory geese and the autumn moon provided an overtone of sadness:

As they ambled along so, slowly, chatting and chewing, the donkey's hooves whispering through the fallen beech leaves, they heard high above the bare arches of the trees the faint honking of the wild geese called down from the north by the October moon.

It is a beautiful story. Daniel Cashen's discovery of what he has sacrificed comes gradually and tangentially through these lucid and luminous impressions. Self-made, rich, hardheaded, and surrounded by concrete evidence of his success as a businessman, he is perplexed by a few images of a youthful time, a girl he never married, and a peaceful, patriarchal way of life. He is teased into the idea that perhaps he has bartered too much of that warm, simple life for worldly success. His last, revealingly pathetic act is to leave his money to his cousins on that childhood farm.

The title story is also concerned with memory and with the concept of loss as inseparable from growth. It announces its theme in the first sentence: "I believe that in every decisive moment of our lives the spur to action comes from that part of the memory where desire lies dozing, awaiting the call to arms." The setting is the little Irish town of Ardagh, where Sarah Cotter lives. She is a plain, kindly, innocent creature who has been confined to an invalid chair since the age of eleven. She is distinguished by a phenomenally retentive memory but has to depend on what others tell her and on what she reads for her information. Twice a year her sister Mary comes, a lively, travelled, and experienced girl who is married to a Continental buyer for a New York store. She and her husband alternate between New York and Switzerland, where they have a small house and where their children go to school. Mary, however, has never told Sarah she passes through

Shannon Airport about six times a year. Sarah thinks she goes to Europe twice and visits Ardagh each time. At the end of the story Mary lies even more and tells Sarah her husband is sick, that she will not be travelling back and forth to Europe, but that she will come to visit Sarah "lots of times."

Told in that blunt way it is a cruel story in which Mary's abandonment of Sarah seems selfish and thoughtless. But it is not presented in such a harsh manner. Mary leaves to protect herself from the blinding accuracy of Sarah's memory. What Sarah remembers is the factual record of what Mary or someone else has told her. There is no feeling in it, no life. It is a contradiction and a denial of memory as Mary experiences it. Incidents remembered from the past and told to Sarah by Mary have a warm romantic glow about them. But when Sarah speaks of the same incidents the glow of feeling is lost. The result is a distortion, as Mary complains:

"I told her the bones and all she has of anything now is the bones. I can't remember the bones. All I have is the feeling I had at the time. Or else I can't remember at all."

Sarah's indelibly factual recollection is therefore an assault on Mary's own remembrance of things past, and in the conflict between fact and feeling, fact invariably triumphs. It is to escape the defeat of her own memories that Mary is forced to leave Sarah and to discontinue her visits. Sarah's memory is a vault in which the happiness of youth, her girlish escapades, her glorified memory of a man friend are all immured.

Furthermore, after twelve years of marriage Mary needs her memories and cannot afford to have them taken away or exposed as inaccurate. There are many hints of personal troubles: her husband does not love and admire her as he did; she has suffered because of another man; she has had to leave the gentle, unhurried way of life in Ardagh for the elegance, the sophistication, and the acquired pleasures of America and Europe. With the passing of time her sense of estrangement is stronger. All she has are the feelings recaptured from her youth. If she cannot be allowed their consoling warmth she is diminished. Therefore, against her deepest instincts, she decides to leave; it is an inevitable decision to

which everything in the story leads. The separation of the sisters
has been apparent in many small ways: in the earlier lies about
Mary's life in Europe; in the thrust and parry of their conversation in which Mary tries to protect herself from Sarah's sharp
memory; and in the simple fact that Mary finds it increasingly
difficult to keep up with Sarah's conversation about local people
and local issues. But it is a decision made and revealed in the
story in the light of many extenuating and explanatory circumstances. Central to it is the fact that to possess herself Mary has to
keep her memory intact and that to survive she has to hurt Sarah.
That abandonment is saved from cruelty by our awareness of her
attachment to the scenes of her childhood, her need for their
warm, deceiving comfort. Again it is not a matter of direct
statement but of inference:

> The Franciscan belfry was reflected in an islanded pool among
> the gravel at the bend of the river, and in the pool a sweep of yellow
> from the far hills that rose to the farthest mountains over whose
> rounded backs the sailing clouds had long ago seemed so often to call
> her to come away. Today the clouds were one solid, frozen mass, tomb-
> like, and she could not tell if they moved at all.

Such indirect effects are not dominant in O'Faolain's collection, *The Heat of the Sun, Stories and Tales* (1966). They
play a smaller part, because the tale, the main genre in this book,
allows more time and space for character development, for a
succession and variety of incidents, for descriptive passages, for
reflections, for many moods, and even for plot. Since effects are
created on a broad scale, there is less reliance on compression
and suggestibility.

Fluctuations of emotion and decision form the rhythmic pattern
of these stories. And whereas in the previous collection O'Faolain
had been sadly, sometimes subjectively, often tenderly, concerned
with man's liability to err, to suffer, and to be self-deceived, he is
now mainly amused. Ironic contrasts and reversals reveal complications and lead to insight. But the way is luminous and the tone
is dry.*

* See "Epilogue to the Short Stories," page 187.

PART III

Revolution and Dislocation

Chapter 13

The Misfit Hero

O'Faolain's novels also are concerned with the fate of the individual caught within an inhibiting environment. His interest lies in revealing the ways in which men can be affected by their surroundings, and his whole approach to the art of the novelist, as will be seen in Chapter XIII in an examination of his articles on the problems and aims of the novelist, is essentially sociological and moral. The important consideration in this examination of the novels themselves is that they are traditional in manner. They do not come within the range of the more modern or more experimental kind of novel; O'Faolain is, in practice, primarily outside of the contemporary concern with aesthetic principles as applied to the novel form. Each of his novels—*A Nest of Simple Folk* (1934), *Bird Alone* (1936), and *Come Back to Erin* (1940)—can best be examined in terms of its social implications.

They belong to the period in his life when he was least detached from the problems of the restrictive environment; it is the period of *Purse of Coppers,* when moral and sociopolitical concerns were uppermost in his mind; it is the period of *Countess Markievicz, King of the Beggars, De Valera,* and numerous articles of social commentary. It is not surprising to find history and social forces playing important roles in these novels; in fact, the characters have importance mainly insofar as they exemplify such forces. Each novel has the world of the lower middle class as its predominant setting, and in each a central figure at first abides by the strong canons of respectability that distinguish his class but then rebels in favor of more liberal ways. This rebellion affects all of his subsequent career; it cuts him off from the familiar patterns of his childhood and adolescence and propels him in quest of a more congenial and more satisfying adult existence.

But it is the peculiar fate of the O'Faolain hero to be forever denied a happy conclusion to his search for fulfillment. For closely similar reasons he becomes an *étranger* like Stendhal's misfits. Like them he is at odds with a muddled society. Emerging at a time when the passionate individual cannot readily identify with any particular group, he remains in basic discord with society. Left to work out his destiny in a chaotic world, he has to rely on his own character and will, his own intense demand for a rich and varied existence. That he is doomed to failure is not completely his fault. He is strongly influenced by his sense of the past greatness of his country and strongly dissatisfied with its present condition. Caught between the memory of a strong past and his awareness of a weak present he can only work for a better future.

In each novel the past is represented by at least one remarkable character. For Denis Hussey, the boy in *A Nest of Simple Folk* who rebels against the values of his father's house, the past is seen most forcefully in his uncle, Leo Donnell. Leo's contact with Irish life reaches back to the eighteenth century and even further: an uncle has been a hedge-schoolmaster; a great-uncle had known the Gaelic poets of the eighteenth century; his memory, linked with theirs, "reached back so far that in that one decaying brain one might see though tangled beyond all hope of unravelling, the story (as well as the picture) of his country's decay." An uncle in Limerick was local President of the Tenant's Right League; in that city he met men who had suffered for the national cause.[1]

His nationalism has been nurtured by these contacts and by hearing that his great-uncle had been flogged during the rebellion of the United Irishmen in 1798, or that his mother's relatives of the landlord class had starved the peasants during the Famine of 1845–1847. An encounter with James Stephens, the Fenian leader, ignites his imagination. He enters upon a lifelong career as an extremist revolutionary, is jailed twice, but remains loyal to his beliefs. His final act in this long novel is to set out from Cork to take part in the 1916 Rising in Dublin. By that time he is seventy-six years of age and has met Denis Hussey, age eighteen. Leo himself, strongly influenced by a heritage of racial oppression, becomes for Denis a representative of national frustration. His contact with Denis is intended to bring past and present into a dynamic relationship.

Leo is an embodiment of the best principles of the Fenian movement. He has the tough individualism and the integrity that characterized men like Tom Clarke and the John O'Leary whom Yeats admired. Like them he stands as a symbol for durability of will and character. Like them he survived the humiliation of the British jails, the tortures, the starvations, the loneliness, and the isolation. Even as a free man he remained loyal to the cause, ready as before to risk life and liberty. It is as the summation of Irish nationalism that he lives his final years in Cork, a constant reminder to Denis that men cannot live by bread alone.

There is a similar figure in *Bird Alone*. In this novel the past is represented by Philip Crone, a dedicated supporter of Parnell, whose influence on his grandson, Corney, the narrator of the story, is compelling. Corney's close association with the old man introduces him at an early, impressionable age to the proud loyalties of Irish nationalism, its litany of heroes faithfully recalled in innumerable pubs, its hatred of British rule, and its inherent anti-clericalism. Philip's principles are vigorously demonstrated in such actions as galloping about the countryside every third Sunday of the month to decorate the graves of the Fenian dead, in buying only Irish-made goods, and in strongly vocalized contempt for middle-class piety and respectability. But what Corney also learns early is that the conflict between Fenianism and the Church imposes a burden of guilt on the individual Fenian. A man's nationalism may be held with fervor and great personal dignity, but it inevitably imposes on the Catholic the strain of a possible everlasting price. When Philip's Fenian friend Arthur Tinsley dies, Philip takes it upon himself to arrange for his burial, and it is then that the anguish of the conflict between integrity and fear becomes clear. His desire to see Arthur buried in a Catholic cemetery is complicated by his awareness of clerical opposition to the Fenians, as his argument with the caretaker of the cemetery illustrates:

> The man drew out a sail of a handkerchief and blew his nose.
> "Write down R. C.," he ordered, like a pope.
> "NO!" said my grander and he flung down the pen in a fury. "The church never said yiss aye or no to Arthur Tinsley. But you know and I know and everybody knows that no Fenian could get absolution in confession or the sacrament from the altar unless he retracted his oath to live and die for his country. And . . ."
> "Mister Crone . . ."
> "And . . ."
> "Excuse me, one moment, mister . . ."
> "AND if Arthur Tinsley was asked here and now whether he would retract that oath . . ."
> "There's nobody asking him . . ."
> ". . . whether, to obtain burial in this bloody cemetery, he would bow the knee to the church, and the first question they'd put to him would be, Do you admit that oath was a sin?—what would he say? What would he say?"
> The man walked away to the door.
> "What would he say?" roared my grander. "He'd say 'I wo' NOT!' And what would they say?" he bellowed, with a great sweep of his hand through the air. "They'd say 'Then we'll have nothing to do with yeh, and yeh can go to hell!' "
> "This cemetery," said the caretaker loftily, "is a Catholic cemetery."
> "Then," sobbed my grander, "where will I bury him?"[2]

The defense of principle and the refusal has its price and it is now Corney notices that his grandfather's face has the "damned look of another Faust."

Corney's education, however, is not limited to nationalism. The arrival of his Aunt Virginia from London provides him with another example of individuality. At a special party in her honor, to which the Crones have invited their useful connections in the city, the subject of Parnell's divorce arises. Virginia declares her admiration for the man no matter what his private life and protests feelingly against the sly insinuations of the company. In the violent discussion that follows, her own life as a prostitute is brought to light, the Crones suffer that disgrace, and Virginia makes ready to leave for London, tired of Cork's pettiness. Of all those present only Philip continues to treat her with kindness. In contrast to the swift reversal of attitudes of Corney's parents, he has known her sad story from the beginning but has never been discourteous to her.

He has the courage also to persist in a conviction. When Parnell's death a year later throws Irish politics into disorder and sours Corney, Philip's behavior demonstrates an abiding lesson: Corney sees that for the sake of principle one must transcend difficulties of chance and circumstance.

Immediately I thought of my grander I stopped. I realized that life does not entirely stamp men with a dead hand. . . . he was become again, incorrigibly, one of the fiercest and most conscientious Parnellites in the city, an all-night committee man, a three-newspaper man, a speechifier, a tender of graves. Life, apparently, was a challenge. That is a great thought.

In the story of Leo Donnell and of Philip Crone there is a similar concentration on passion, will, and integrity. Their nationalism brings out greatness of character and gives direction to their personality. It is closely connected with behavior; both men resist the restrictions placed on their lives by society, politics, and religion. Both strike out for a full life in terms of their physical and emotional needs. Both face the consequences—the disapproval of the respectable, the condemnation of the clergy, and/or imprisonment—without self-pity and without losing their self-respect. In their relationship to and their effect upon the boy-figures, Denis Hussey and Corney Crone, they stand as hypnotic embodiments of an almost heroic way of life. In the third novel this relationship is not as dynamic, mainly because Frankie Hannafey, the rebel, is almost middle-aged and has been active as a revolutionary for about twenty years.

The past is represented most tangibly for Frankie in the person of his Aunt Nell, who lives on a small farm in County Limerick. In her presence, away from the urban background of his immediate family, he comes closest to the mysterious impact of Irish tradition. When he discovers that she is about to die of cancer, he voices the sense of loss the news of her imminent death occasions in himself.

"It's queer," he said bitterly, "but if there's one person in the world who put me where I am this minute it's that old woman. I can't think of her being snuffed out. The way she talks of the Famine, and Dan O'Connell, and Emancipation, and '98, or the way the landlords ground them to bits—it's all as if she was two hundred. One thing is as near to her as another. These people don't know where their own memory stops and their grandfather's begins. Somehow when she goes everything goes. For me anyway."[3]

In this case the evidence from the past is not dramatized in action as it was in the long account of Leo's career or in the compressed turbulence of Philip's later life; it is simply stated. Aunt Nell's memory includes what they experienced; it reaches back as did theirs, and it is like theirs a memory with a distinctive pattern and bias. In each case the heritage of oppression is keenly expressed, even visibly rendered, and the younger figures are drawn to the service of a people who have suffered too much frustration. Like Daniel O'Connell and Hugh O'Neill in O'Faolain's account, the young rebel is driven into action by the "memory of the lost generations of his tribe, the ineradicable *pietas* of all submerged peoples."[4]

The contrast in these novels between the unselfish and impassioned response of the older rebels to the feeling that the country's genius was being denied and the selfish and calculating outlook of the present generation is highly effective. The younger rebels, Denis, Corney, and Frankie, are caught in the conflict between their awareness of the practical values of middle-class self-interest and their feeling for the impractical, idealistic nature of the legendary and symbolic lives of the older rebels. There is never any question of a reconciliation between the two concepts of life; no compromise or synthesis is possible between positions so mutually antagonistic. The young men have to choose and once the decision is made there is no turning back. For better or worse they have cast themselves into the restless and ultimately unsatisfying quest for a way of life more in keeping with their deeply felt but unformulated needs as men and as Irishmen.

That choice is occasioned by the nature of the middle class to which their families belong. When the Husseys, the typical example, move to Cork they surround themselves with the alien furnishings of their acquired status, gold-framed pictures, plush-covered chairs, tasteless ornaments. The cultural loss is great; two incidents give it particular emphasis. Leo Donnell grew up in contact with men whose minds transcended the cultural catastrophe of the Famine. Denis Hussey is reared in accordance with the imperfectly assimilated values of the urban middle class. At his birth a policeman ignorantly displays his knowledge of the stars. But when a child was born to Nicholas O'Donnell in 1854, Leo listened to his uncle and his great-uncle recite one of Horace's odes. In this case there is an affinity with classical, aristocratic culture and a response to poetry and beauty. In the other case there is a vulgarization of learning and no imaginative response.

Behind the Husseys lies the diminished heritage that Leo Donnell fought to sustain in his own way. Ahead of them lies the new Ireland that will emerge slowly as a small capitalistic state. They look to that future, preparing themselves and their children, working hard to satisfy an ambition whose limits and standards are reflected in the father's nightly prayer:

For all Johnny's pleasure was in his ambitions for his two children. All he ever thought of was to bring them up respecting the law, and to make them look up to the respectable merchants of the city—his boundless world and their battle-field. He tried, above all, to instill into them the love and fear of the good God who made them, and at night he would kneel by his bed with them, one on each side, his braces a bifurcated tail sweeping the floor, his regulation woollen blue shirt rolled to his elbows, his hands clasped and raised at the level of his eyes towards the bright day in the dormer window. He would pray in a loud voice, that could be heard downstairs echoing through the landing and the lobbies:

"O dear, kind, and loving Jesus," he would intone—his voice falling and rising in supplication—"give all thy help to my poor wife, Bid, and give thy help to these my two poor little sons, Denis and Robert, that they may grow up in love and regard for Thee, dear sweet loving Jesus, and give them thy help to raise themselves in the world, and to be good boys and good men. And have pity, O sweet Jesus, on me a sinner. Have mercy on my poor mother that is gone before me, and my poor father, and my brother Phil, and my sister Kate. . . ."

The new values are respectability, position, and worldly success. Denis grows in a world carefully hedged about with parental injunctions as to what is socially acceptable and advantageous. Its gods are the successful merchants and professional men of the city, its demons, the poor, uneducated Irish with whom he is forbidden to associate. Like his father he looks toward the British Empire, inspired by the thought of the age and glory of England. He thrills to the sight of "the Sherwood Foresters on parade, their flag before them, their band playing, the colonel and his staff reviewing them." His first sight of Irish Volunteers sickens him:

. . . when he saw them clearly he burned with shame to find them dressed in comical scraps of military uniform, a brown empty holster on a blue belt, a wide hat that came down on a man's eyes and stuck out his ears, a cheap trouser-belt wound outside an overcoat, tight as a corset, and one who had not even a belt or a hat wore his cap back to front, like a coalheaver's shoulder apron.
"God!" Denis groaned to Manus, as he looked at the absurd costumes. "They're disgracing us to the world."
. . . With a groan, almost of pain, Denis turned and ran home grimacing like a person who has seen something mean or humiliating.

Denis seems to have accepted his father's attitudes, but in the long run they burden his young spirit. The excessive restrictions placed on him cause him to question their validity. One incident serves to illustrate the psychological effect of so much parental authority. A teacher slashes his essay so cruelly with blue crayon that Denis removes the pages lest his father see them. Next day the teacher notices what he has done, punishes him, makes him rewrite the essay as it was, keeps him in after school hours to do this, and then marks it as before. Denis is late in getting home, his parents have become worried, he tries to hide the real reason for his delay but his father goes to the school to find out. The result is a traumatic scene, absurd in its magnification of a trivial incident yet illustrative of the tensions of the home:

Then he was standing before his mother, and she was weeping up at him, and his father was sitting in a corner crying like a child between his palms. And before they had done with him he too was crying, even while he knew how comical the three of them were there crying for one another. That evening, as he stood weeping before them, he promised them all sorts of things if they would only let him go to the college as they had planned; he promised them everything they asked, and that night he worked without raising his eyes even once from his books. But in his heart he knew his promises would come to nothing, because they had wrung his pride dry, like water from a dishcloth. They had shared, too, in his debasement; his mother's lamentations went on all through the night, while his father insisted on going tediously over his essay and asking him endless questions about his work, and he said Brother Carty was "a most awfully highly educated and cultured gentleman," and said that that was a very poor essay indeed, as anybody could see, and even his mother could do better, and explained how if he worked hard and passed the Civil Service he would be in with the highest of the land, and know secrets of "the financial affairs of the empire."

From that night he worked hard—but only to get away from his mother's tears, and his father's endless encouragement, and his cheap clothes, and his Sunday bowler hat that made the bare-footed newsboys call out rude names at him in the street while he passed on, red to the ears but with unturned head.

Gradually Denis draws apart from the rigid codes of his parents. His earlier disgust with the nationalists gives way to a feeling of pride. Unconsciously he has been molded by chance remarks and contacts, by references to oppression and to men who suffered for the cause. Above all he is influenced by contact with Leo, symbol of endurance and the dignity of national pride. Suddenly he is swept up, as Leo was, by a power he cannot control and whose source of energy he but dimly perceives.

From some hidden well of memory all the stored hate of centuries jetted into his mind—words fallen from his mother, spoken even by his father, by the monks, by his school companions, read in his history, they fountained in him like the blood that surges to the head and blinds the eyes with rage.

In the tense and violent exchanges that take place between father and son, the pseudo piety of that middle-class world, its debasement of religion and human dignity, and its ignorant misuse of education are all exposed and rejected. Denis has chosen Leo and what he represents in preference to the timidity, hypocrisy, and self-interest of his father.

In *Bird Alone* Corney Crone grows up in a home circumscribed by values similar to those encountered by Denis. The Crones are small building contractors with ambitions. For them respectability and piety are aids to social acceptance and position. His grandfather, Philip, is the dominant force in the boy's life. Corney is drawn to the old man, to his wild ways, to his reputation as a lecher and an atheist—both exaggerated by local gossip—and by his vital air of independence of thought and action. By contrast his parents' timidity and caution do not excite his interest.

The effect of his grandfather's influence and of his parents' hypocrisy and deceit comes out in Corney's love affair with Elsie Sherlock, the climax of his narrative for which everything in the novel has prepared him. Elsie comes from a home vastly different from Corney's. Her brothers and sisters are either clergy or on their way to becoming clergy. Her home is devoid of the bitter differences of opinion and attitudes that are in his. Where his innocence is already tarnished by contact with Philip, hers has been preserved by a life filled with respect for religion and an unquestioning submission to the teachings of the Church. The love affair that develops between them forms the core of the novel. On one side is Corney's emergent disbelief and bitterness as religion and politics come into conflict during the Parnell divorce case and as he rebels against the insincerity of his parents' religion. On the other side is Elsie's piety, her fear of sexual sin, her shame at· the thought of bringing dishonor to her family or of hurting her father by her behavior. Inevitably their love leads to a war between their contrasting attitudes and values. Corney's Fenian associations causes her family to forbid her to see him. This, coupled with Parnell's death, drives Corney in upon himself and sours him.

I hated her cowardice. I hated the way she let her family crucify her, bully her with gentleness, shape her whole life by a look or a sigh. By lonely wandering and brooding I increased in bitterness. My contempt spread to so many people that I felt what had happened to me as an image of the far worse that had happened to Christy, to his friends, to the Fenians, to the Land League, to Parnell.

In Corney's search for self-definition Elsie becomes the sounding board for his ideas. He is the small-town intellectual drawn to rationalize his sense of isolation and alienation and forced to have Elsie as a disciple as he is to have her as a lover. Philip's abuse of the boy's innocence is repeated in Corney's treatment of the girl. Persuasion has to precede seduction, since she is so secured in the simple faith of her family. To feed his pride in the rightness of his position he has to prey on the girl he loves. "I left her, priding in my own intelligence, and in the satisfaction that comes to a man when he is gradually moulding another mind to his own image and desire." But his sexual triumph over Elsie only makes him feel like a murderer. Remorse and guilt overwhelm him, and he identifies once again with the national paralysis:

I realized suddenly that in those dead years in which I lived, the years after Parnell, the shore of Ireland was empty, too, and would remain empty for a long time, and that I was merely one of many left stranded after the storm. I began, fevered by that thought, to walk on and on. For it was the first bit of wisdom that I ever really held firm in my hand. It made me realize what life can do to men, stamping them out like tin cans. When I thought of it, I felt so indifferent to myself, so freed of my conscience, that I wanted to rush home to my grandfather, to write it to Elsie. Immediately I thought of my grandfather I stopped. I realized that life does not entirely stamp men with a dead hand. . . . Life, apparently, was a challenge. That is a great thought.

It is Corney's great lesson from the long education by his grandfather: men must exist forcefully, by the light of their own character and will. They must define their own mode of life, must resist predeterminism in their environment, and must be true to themselves. Corney has to be true to his own sins and therefore cannot grant Elsie the freedom to confess their love as sinful. Now a satellite of his mind, she cannot hope for forgiveness in confession, since she cannot alone put an end to their sin. He has forced her into his own condition of possible damnation.

The results are tragic and, for the aged narrator, haunting. For months they try to keep her pregnancy secret, and her spirit gradually breaks under the tension, the shame, and the guilt. In their frozen immobility there is a sad reflection on the inadequacies of their backgrounds. Elsie's terror of discovery is a pathetic and moving comment on her home, which is so religious and so innocent that it excludes the sort of trust and understanding she needs. Corney's stubborn refusal to release her from her terror of sin by admitting their passion has led to evil in the sight of God, is a comment on the warped pride that his grandfather has given him. Between the two ways of life there is a common failure of human love and interchange. The result is that both must endure the full and final agony; nothing in their environment speaks of a warm, inclusive charity of mind and heart. Of the obvious solution, escape to England, O'Faolain makes no mention. Instead, Elsie must seek release in suicide, and Corney must hold on to a barren freedom of action.

They are lost souls. A love affair that under better conditions could have easily been enriching is doomed to terror. Their youth and immaturity bring pathos to their story, which rises slowly to the crisis of her attempted suicide, her rescue from the waves, her premature delivery, and her death before the priest arrives, with Corney's desperate efforts to recite an Act of Contrition into her ear. The lyrical intensity of their story appears in the description of the rescue:

Madly I ran into the surge shouting as I ran, but she could hear nothing with that bellow of waves and wind in her ears and she kept on and on. A little way out and the foam was beating my face. The moon sank away and the beam with its gentle sweep. It was a slow descent but the waves were high and if she fell I knew she might not rise again. I saw her again in the moon and she stopped. In a nightmare one's legs become leaden. It was like that, slow, slow, through the wind and waves, and the beam that I wanted so madly seemed to move slower and slower like a clock running down. When I howled at her a wave filled my throat. When I was still ten yards away the lighthouse finger struck her and she fell. I was now swimming and

the moon blazed full on the sea, and when her body was swept suddenly against me I held her dress. Turning, I floated her, flung along by
the waves, her hair over her face, red as blood, and by degrees, more
heavily when she lifted out of the water and her gravity increased,
I managed to drag her yard by yard until a breaker flung us on the
sand. She was neither stunned nor fainted and when she saw me she
clung to me and screamed my name and all the time I dragged her
inward, walking inward, she just screamed and screamed that soli-
tary word.

This passage is revealing of the tone of the whole novel. Its
agitation is typical of the general atmosphere of desperation and
compression that threatens to destroy Corney. The most constant
mood is one of headlong precipitation. The narrator is obsessed
by memory. Like a Greek tragedy the story is already familiar to
him, and the reader in second reading is content to watch the
story unfold rapidly and inevitably to its foreseen conclusion.
There is no time for digression, as in the first novel, no time for
long, nostalgic evocation; the horror and the anguish grip the narrator. He must reveal all swiftly, must relive the drama. But he
cannot exorcise it. There is, as he insists from the beginning, no
rest and no sleep. His revolt has brought neither peace nor fulfillment. Possessed by memory he has to tell his all-important story,
has to resuffer, and has to accept the nonredemptive finality of
his conclusion. All he can do is assert his freedom and point the
finger of accusation at the life that made his condition and her
death necessary. Their story is a judgment on Irish life; the consequences are blamed not on these misguided and bewildered
children but on society that has not given them a better heritage
and a more congenial environment.

For a while Corney wilts under the pressure of the anguish he
has experienced. Faced with the horror of her death, he succumbs
for a while to the idea of sin and the need for redemption:

I told myself I was Faust, who had sold his child for his lusts—for
now I confessed that our love was a sin, was evil, was bestial: I would
gladly have died to make it be that the priest had come to her on time.

He is evicted from his home and shunned by society because of
what he has done, but gradually his sense of guilt changes to one

of hate for the people and their values. He recovers his integrity; "All my lust was in my pride that returned to me, and my solitariness that required it, and my hate that supported it." The remedy for his unhappiness and for his isolation is obvious—marriage, money, and a position of respectability in the middle class. These he rejects as all pretense and hypocrisy:

"I get no fun out of that sort of thing." I said. "They're all at the same game in this city—they're all out to get money and be rich and respectable. They think of nothing else but what's going to be thought and said of them. It's all pretense and sham and fear and cowardice. They have no guts. Look at the way they treated everyone we know— they've always bit the hand that fed them. Look at the way they're bullied by the priests."

He is strongly tempted to make his peace with humanity, to yield up everything that divides him from his own people. He refuses in a last and final decision: "It was not that I did not believe in men, but that I could not believe in what men believed." He is faithful to himself and to his grandfather.

The present in *Come Back to Erin* is explicitly contemporary. This novel is set against the increased prosperity of the middle class in the thirties. The social revolution dimly predicted in the two earlier novels has become a reality. The Husseys and the Crones have found the stability they wanted; they have no intention of endangering it. As a result it is a bad time for the old type of Republican who still wants the kind of independent Ireland he can be proud of. The old separatist ideal of complete self-sufficiency is still a possibility to him, and he cannot tolerate an economic policy ultimately controlled by the British banks. The idea of a possible British hold on Ireland through the threat of financial retaliation is repugnant to him. By 1936, however, when the action of the novel takes place, that old idealistic Republican is out of place. De Valera has consolidated his position and has a large majority at the polls. The central trend of the novel is the realization by Frankie Hannafey that his brand of Republicanism is out of place. For him, as for Denis Hussey and Corney Crone, these are dead years in Irish history, when the quality of life is diminished.

Like them Frankie has little in common with his immediate family. The Hogan-Hannafeys—his mother had married a second time—have the usual grouping of relatives in the country. Like the Husseys and the Crones they have secured a foothold in the lower reaches of the middle class at the cost of the customary privations and hardships. When the story opens Frankie is a mature man with a history of revolutionary involvement behind him. He has fought against the Black and Tans as a boy, has been on hunger strike, has been through the Civil War and, afterwards, when the Free State hunted extremists, he did not abandon his cause. An idealist, a separatist, a man beaten into a sharp stubborn integrity through years on his keeping, he is also a man whose understanding of life has been severely limited by his experiences as a rebel. His family have grown wearily accustomed to his ways and increasingly intolerant of them. And their weariness and impatience is symptomatic of a general public indifference to him and his cause.

He is in fact surrounded by difficulties. His family in Cork lead the kind of compressed life O'Faolain usually associates with the middle class in that city. His mother is periodically insane because her late husband was unfaithful to her and because she worries constantly about Frankie, fearing for his life and his health. His eldest brother, Michael, has been driven to drink and prostitutes as a release from the economic and emotional problems connected with supporting the family when the father dies. Another brother, St. John, went to America, where he became a successful businessman but at the cost of spiritual guilt and emotional torment; during the novel he returns on a sentimental pilgrimage in search of the innocence and purity he has lost. Another brother, Leonard, ran off to America as a priest in order to escape his home; he has become a bitter hard person. Frankie's sisters are unmarried, impoverished, and worried for his safety.

In addition to his sense of family suffering Frankie recognizes the futility of continuing a revolution at a time when the public has lost interest. Josephine Hogan, a girl who loves him, sums up his years of increasingly hopeless activity: "He's doing it for obstinacy, and for courage, and for the folly of man. For what sense is there to it if nobody hears or heeds him?" What he specifically

wants and cannot hope to get in a country that has satisfied with its share of prosperity and its share of peace after year
of unrest, is a social revolution with a broader base than the one
encouraged by De Valera. He is frustrated by the inertia of the
public. "I want the people to fight," he says. . . . "To fill the
country with factories and machines and money and . . . To work
like blazes, To get rich. To be strong. To be an up-to-date modern
live, fighting, working country."

The indifference of the people is partly responsible for his feeling of futility and his growing realization that he is wasting his
time. In America he explains another cause for dissatisfaction
Ireland, he points out to groups of Irish exiles, is financially
dependent on British banks, and there is a new bourgeois class
exploiting the workers and the farmers. The solution he favors i
a social revolution leading to cooperative ownership by the people and cooperative distribution under state direction. The plan
he feels is a desirable one; the only problem is that it needs the
support of the people to become a reality. And that is something
Frankie simply cannot get. Inspired as he is by memories of oppression under British rule, he is fighting to remove another kind of
oppression by the native middle classes but he fights in vain.

The feeling that the future may not free the misfit hero from
his predicament is present in all three novels. Denis Hussey and
Corney Crone are also uncertain about what is to come. They have
their principles and ideals, they respect the integrity and passion
of the past and reject the hypocrisy and timidity of the present, but
what they themselves will do for Irish life or what Irish life will
do for them is not clear. Despite their rejection of the particular
values in their environment, they find no positive or fulfilling
alternative. Expelled from a certain kind of society, they suffer
thereafter from a sense of loss, and this becomes, in effect, a reflection on the success of their rebellion and a judgment on the composition of a society in which they can discover neither pattern
nor destination.

Of the three, Denis faces the future with most confidence. It is
partly a matter of his youth; the world is still before him and his
optimism has yet to be tempered by experience. The later rebels

Corney and Frankie, are older and wiser men who have had time to reflect on the events that propelled them into isolation and to measure their own success as creative spirits in a muddled age. They speak more soberly and more reflectively than Denis. Yet even he is not without a sense of loss. In his case it is expressed in terms of his changing attitudes toward Cork. In his childhood it is a city of "endless summer daylight," full of delight and wonder for him. But when his parents move to a bigger house, take in boarders, and begin their struggle upward in society, "all his daylit memories of Cork seemed to cloud and fade."[6] Eventually he almost loses his pleasure in the city completely. His growing dissatisfaction with his home, his suffering under the strain of parental ambitions for him, his traumatic experiences with the teacher, and his gradual discovery of what Leo Donnell represents all affect his relationship with the city:

In that way, as when a bright day falls, the city he had known builded of light and loveliness sank before his eyes as into a pit. Dark and tawdry he saw it now, old and deformed, crutched with piles, scabrous, bulged as with a goitre, empty, dark, and, as if to torment him, he found, flickering in the recesses of his mind, bright images of the beauty he had lost, a torch walking with him through the dim, dusty streets of Cork.

He feels estranged from what he has known best and loved most. He has lost his sense of its beauty; he has lost the imaginative background to which he has been accustomed. At the same time he has to live where he has always lived. Despite the spiritual exile he has still to find himself. If his rebellion is to be successful it must lead him into a new and satisfying relationship with the city so unhappily transformed. He is faced with the problem at the heart of O'Faolain's writing: how does one live creatively within a society that is restrictive and unattractive?

The same problem has faced most Irish writers, but only Joyce has made it into the finely wrought statement of *A Portrait of the Artist as a Young Man,* and none has pursued it in quite the same manner. O'Faolain is remarkably close to Joyce in his awareness of the difficulties, but he is fundamentally opposed to the particular solution offered in the *Portrait.* Commenting on this in *The*

Vanishing Hero he wrote, ". . . in rejecting his native city and all it stood for he rejected his one fated field of life wherein he might have read the signatures of mortal things and made them tolerable, intelligible, meaningful." O'Faolain argues also that the writer pays a price for such rejection. By a too total rejection, Joyce, he feels, created an impasse. "That impasse was that he rejected intellectually everything in which he was involved emotionally."[7] A writer has to come to terms with his world if he is to come to terms with himself. O'Faolain has always rejected the Joycean solution of total revolt, and his work is an interesting example of how an artist stays and faces up to home, fatherland, and church. His greatness comes from his stance; it is the fundamental ingredient of his work that so frequently allegorizes the progress of his battle. Like Joyce he had experienced familiar Irish pressures. His list is eloquent of his sympathetic understanding of what Joyce encountered:

. . . the meanness of Edwardian Dublin, the stupidities of the Irish Church, the puritanism of its priests, the total intellectual poverty of his teachers, the misery of his own poor home, the bitter loneliness of his ravaged youth in that little, remote, untutored, inexperienced, conquered, timid and emotionally besotted island on the rim of the world.[8]

Unlike Joyce, O'Faolain stayed and his novels testify to his involvement with his world.

How does the misfit hero survive in such a world? The answer for Denis Hussey resembles that offered by Stephen Dedalus. Denis tries to write a poem, "murmuring to his unborn child that it, too, must be with beauty still." In art he hopes to counteract the decay that lies about him, and although this first attempt is not successful, he remains loyal to art as to the power able to resurrect him from the dead world into which he has fallen. His unborn child is the yet to be created art that will imaginatively transform and transcend the loss of beauty in his life.

Such a position anticipates a whole range of attitudes worked out in *A Purse of Coppers* and elsewhere. It leads also to the predicament expressed through Corney Crone's confessional narration in *Bird Alone*. Corney, a builder by trade, is another alle gorical figure for the artist trying to make experience conform to his needs. In him, however, the optimism has faded. As the haunted narrator he admits failure; he rejected the city and set out to find fulfillment on his own terms but the result is barrenness. He has held on to his beliefs with courage and integrity, but without a satisfying imaginative background his revolt has not been fruitful:

> For I am become an old man and my friends are few, and that faith I set out to find I never did find, and because I have sinned all my life long against men, that whisper of God's reproof, who made men, has been my punishment. I have denied life, by defying life, and life has denied me. I have kept my barren freedom, but only *sicut homo sine adjutorio inter mortuous liber*—a freeman among the dead. They call me Crone the Builder and that is all they think of me—as if I were no more than one of the ancient red bricks I put in their houses.

The misfit hero it seems is doomed to frustration. In a country as small as Ireland, where each town and city produces the same mental attitudes and the same limitations, it is not possible to find fulfillment simply by moving from one city, such as Corney has done. It is significant that even though he leaves Cork with the intention of making a better life for himself elsewhere and even though he makes a number of references to Dublin, where he has been, yet he has returned to Cork. It is still the center of what has most strongly affected him, and like Denis he is still tormented by memories and associations of a more happy time in his youth. O'Faolain's own comment on Joyce's exile applies here with equal validity: "His past haunts him like a succubus. He can talk of nothing else. The flight and the chase are unending, so that his work has no ending except the recurrent denial, the recurrent flight. . . . In the splendid effort to cast away everything old and to create something utterly new he left himself with only one thing to write of, himself, child of Adam."[9] All of this applies to Corney. His revolt is the strongest act of his life, but by its very strength, by its very conclusiveness, by its very integrity, it makes it impossible for him to be creatively at ease with his world.

In his meeting with an English artist, Stella, Corney had sensed alternatives to his own condition. To his dog-eat-dog philosophy she expresses the idea of man's common humanity. She looks for "a spark of soul in everybody," and tries to reveal it in her paintings. She makes him aware of another kind of life, free and adult, full of imaginative and intellectual excitement, and above all, at ease with the world. She discourages his search for absolutes and makes a valid judgment on Corney and what he represents in Irish life:

"I don't think I could live here. It's all wrong. You all remind me of flies a bold boy would put under a glass, all beating against it. Even my old men down the quays—they talked to me like that. And, then, poor Parnell. No, no! Come to the roundabouts."

"But, good God, do you want us to be slaves for ever and ever?"

"There are some prisons you can never break. You Irish don't know, and you never will know, the ones you can break and the ones you can't break. I believe you don't want to know. You remind me of Dante's people in Hell who 'lived wilfully in sadness!' Come to the roundabouts."

I thumped the sea-wall.

"But which can we break?"

"I don't know," she cried. "But I do know that you, Cornelius, don't and never will know, because your mind is a core on core of prisons. It's an onion of them. Come to the roundabouts."

Her contention "People are you, you are people" makes a strong impression on Corney, and the balanced, sane outlook of Stella, indicated here in the recurrence of her invitation "Come to the roundabouts," contrasts favorably with his narrow, self-centered outlook. In her is found the tolerance and the inclusive sympathy he lacks. She represents a way of living he dimly perceived as valid and worthwhile, but it is beyond his reach. He has been made by different forces, and he cannot fully escape their consequences: "life stamps us all out like tin cans, and we can't help what we do."

Corney cannot awaken from his particular nightmare of history and remains, like the early Stephen Dedalus, in bondage to a personal past. Like Stephen he would have to come to realize that he cannot cut himself off from his environment. To have a successful rebellion he must face up to it and to his own responses to it. The latter he is not prepared to do. His final position is as irrevocable as it was when he first decided on it. There has been no change in his attitude on the major issue. He has made a judgment, and until society changes he condemns himself to his isolation and his estrangement. There is no question here, as there is in *Ulysses*, of a man being brought to a less extreme position, to a less inhibiting stance. That is simply the action of another novel, with a different purpose and a different emphasis. *Bird Alone* successfully demonstrates what happens to the misfit hero caught between the attractiveness of a past that is vigorous and the unattractiveness of a present that is weak.

In its moral growth and social alienation the novel resembles the typical pattern of European society. Mr. S. L. Goldberg has drawn attention to this in his discussion of the *Portrait*:

The individual grows to consciousness within a specific social environment and is partly moulded by its pressures; but as he grows, he increasingly finds his society too fragmented, too materialistic, and too restrictive to sustain him. It offers him neither spiritual nourishment nor a usable culture, yet it is too powerful to be resisted or easily changed. If the individual is an artist his problem is especially acute. Just because of his greater sensitivity, he is forced apart from his society; just because of his alienation, he comes to represent its general condition in the clearest possible form.[10]

Almost all of this can be applied to O'Faolain and to his heroes. But there is one very important difference. It is not that Irish society is too powerful to resist; Irish society is fatally easy to resist. A man of courage and integrity can do it, as Corney does. But the ease of the victory does not make this society correspondingly easy to change. It is the very incompleteness of Irish society, its amorphous, undefined, thinly composed quality that protects it from change. By its very nature it tends to defeat the rebel who is creatively inclined and wants a social revolution. It is so adolescent in its habits of self-appraisal, so lacking in hardheaded self-analysis, so imperfectly projected that it defies attack and is not amenable to change. Faced with such a confusing problem the rebel is at a loss. Rigid isolationism is one solution and it is Corney's.

But for the artist it is an untenable position. By virtue of his work he has to be in a creative relationship with his material. He has to keep a steady focus on his society and on the state of his relationship with it. O'Faolain has succeeded through the years in maintaining a definite and flexible outlook and in *Bird Alone* has revealed the limitations and dangers of the isolationist position. Corney's integrity is admirable in many ways and it is the logical result of the novel's progress. Nevertheless it is a barren solution. It corresponds to those stories in *A Purse of Coppers* that also lead to an impasse. By the time he wrote his third novel, O'Faolain had found a way beyond. In Frankie Hannafey we have his final portrait of the misfit hero and a final judgment on the value of his rebellion.

Come Back to Erin deals with the condition of the misfit hero about seventeen years after his separation from his social environment. It tries to follow through with the act of rebellion and to see what its consequences are. It tries to discover what lies between the optimism of Denis Hussey and the despair of Corney Crone.

Frankie Hannafey experiences the sense of loss and misdirection that characterized the earlier rebels. He has become separated from his immediate family and knows little of its financial or emotional problems. He has come to recognize that the revolution is a failure. While he has remained loyal to its initial aims, others have adjusted to the new conditions. When he seeks refuge from the rising decision that these facts are forcing him to make he goes back into the rural background from which so much of his inspiration has come. But there too he meets with defeat. His Aunt Nell, the personification of his faith, is dying. Fleeing from the glimpse of a normal life beyond his own that he has caught in the arrival of Bea Hannafey, his American sister-in-law, he goes to the home of another aunt. Her little cottage is a repository of traditional life in its unchanging and unchangeable aspects: "In the place of honour, on a doily in the middle of the table, lay an enormous family album which concentrated what the whole room contained—the slow vibration of a human drama, indeed many such, pulsing yet quiescent, invisible, alive, never to come to life until the trumpet of Judgement." The unassailable simplicity of heart in this cottage and its remoteness from ambition force him to recognize once more and with greater clarity how futile his hopes are. His aunt hardly understands what Republican means; her whole concept of politics has been formed in the days of the

Land League. "It was the validity and importance of their lives to them and its meaninglessness to him, that oppressed him." Life, he realizes, rots away behind everyman. What had pleased him and inspired him in the past is now remote and uninspiring. One cannot go back into one's past and expect to find it unchanged.

There must be progression, and because he cannot bring about a creative renewal in Irish life Frankie goes to America. He wants to escape the life of his aunt's cottage; he wants to get outside the aimless condition of Irish society. He seeks the intellectual stimulus and the emotional nourishment of a more developed, more complex civilization. To St. John's sentimental observation that Ireland is a "grand country," he replies furiously, "Is It? Well, I've had enough of it. It's all down on top of you. Like a load of hay. There's no space here. No scope. It's too small. Three million people—you can't do anything with them."

Ironically it is in America that he experiences his greatest defeat. Here the one-sided quality of his life, his immaturity, his idealism, his blind involvement in abstract nationalism are revealed as inadequate. Seeing his career as a rebel from this distance and seeing himself objectively for the first time he realizes, at the age of thirty-three, "that of all those he had always known, he had never known anyone." At first he experiences a great release; he enjoys the freedom from anxiety, the liberty of movement. But other freedoms and satisfactions follow rapidly. His starved imagination revels in books, in plays, in concerts. His critical faculties come alive. He reads Ibsen with pleasure:

the man who had grown up in a small, puritanical, ineffectually bourgeois society, who was attracted by nationalism and romanticism. . . .

Significantly, he does not see the other side of Ibsen, the author of *Brand,* "a figure driven out of the body of the world by a hysterically idealistic insistence on honesty from himself. . . ." He reads *Exiles* and responds to the dark passion of some of its scenes; he has not hitherto given rein to his emotions.

On all sides he discovers and delights in undeveloped aspects of his own nature. Each discovery and release draws him further and further from the absolute dedication that had kept him loyal to a cause in spite of failure and disappointments. He is also under-mined intellectually in conversations with his brother Leonard, the priest. Leonard makes him see how careless he has been in relation to his own family, how indifferent to their financial and emotional burdens; he argues that Frankie ought to fulfill him-self as a man by accepting the responsibility of family life. Even more severe on Frankie's self-respect is Leonard's attack on his anticlericalism and his failure to practice his religion. Leonard points out that he cannot attack a universal truth simply because of his own particular experiences. He cannot condemn the Church because he has been treated harshly as a Republican by Irish bishops. Fenian anticlericalism cannot be logically advanced as an attack on Catholicism. Furthermore the misfit rebel cannot reject his religion because it has complicated his nationalism. He can rightly reject or resist episcopal interference on the local level, but he need not and should not reject or resist God because of that interference.

Frankie's discussion with Leonard is not concerned only with the familiar predicament of the Irish Republican. Behind his words lies his need for direction in an immediate personal problem. He has let himself get involved in an affair with his sister-in-law, Bea Hannafey. It is here that his immaturity and inexperience appear most pitifully. He is at the mercy of a shallow, sophisticated, worldly wise woman, who epitomizes all the temptations and delight of his new world. To seduce him she has to overcome his natural shyness, his sexual inexperience, his moral prejudices, his nostalgic attachments to Ireland, and a host of complexities. In his half-reluctant advance to her arms the weakness of Irish life, in its protective and simplifying treatment of the individual, is condemned.

The result of his American visit, as Professor John V. Kelleher has observed, is a breakdown of his defenses:

In America, safe from the tensions of the hunt, he drops his defences bit by bit, tastes with a distrustful tongue the gentler pleasures—poetry, music, the theater, unconstrained talk—and suddenly realizing the fact of his dependent humanity, lets go every restraint and wallows inno-cently in his soul's food.[11]

But America is not the solution to the predicament of the misfit hero. Instead of salvation, Frankie has found confusion. Instead of direction, he has found greater futility: "I thought I knew exactly the sort of life I believed in and I don't think I know any longer." For reasons he cannot really understand or justify Frankie has to return home. "When all is said and done," he tells Bea Hannafey, who has offered him a life with her in America, "there's something warm and soft about Ireland. Like rain on a Sunday morning." The elemental explanation is that the Irishman has to grow from his own roots; he has to survive at home, if he is to be a whole man. Whatever the deficiencies and the disadvantages he belongs to a particular place.

In the context of the novel Frankie Hannafey's return is aesthetically unsatisfactory. Nothing has been solved since he is so changed; he is no longer a man of passion and of purpose. The whole important question of how the misfit hero is to survive is not answered. Corney Crone's inhibiting integrity has far more logic to it and much more nobility. Frankie can enjoy the pleasures of Irish life, the easy-going tempo, the kindliness, the humor, the conversation. On the level of *l'homme moyen sensuel* he has much to look forward to; the warm feeling is there. But if he asks for more, he cannot have it. The sort of creative renewal he had so passionately sought, the magnificent goal that had unified his life for almost twenty years, is lost to him now. The new Frankie is a decent, timid, good-natured man who takes a job as a warble-fly inspector.

It is a pitiful conclusion. In three novels O'Faolain has sought in vain within the simplicity of the Irish world for a way of life that satisfied the whole man. Clearly his failure is not due to lack of talent, or of intelligence, or of sensitivity. His short stories, biographies, and commentaries give convincing evidence of his abilities. The simple explanation seems to be that in his time there has been no clear design. The directions of Irish life have been so hidden in the postrevolutionary period that the misfit hero cannot affirm his belief in a better future nor demonstrate how a better future might be realized.

Chapter 14

Character and Personality

O'Faolain has been influenced in his novels, as in his short stories, by the Irish and European literary traditions. He emerges at a time in Irish literary history when the subjective, romantic attitudes of the Literary Revival were being replaced by a more realistic and more analytical approach. In the Abbey Theater the work of the younger dramatists, such as Padraic Colum, T. C. Murray, and Lennox Robinson, had become more influential than the poetic plays of W. B. Yeats, the founder of the theater. Their interests lay in presenting Irish life, and particularly rural life, as they knew it from experience; their characters lacked the heroic mold that he sought for his plays on Irish mythological themes. Their work in the theater had been paralleled by the gradual emergence of a realistic prose tradition. George Moore and James Joyce laid the foundations of this movement in *The Untilled Field, The Lake,* and *Dubliners.* O'Faolain's generation of prose realists were, therefore, the inheritors of this prose realism.

But although they shared in that revolt against the romanticism of the Revival, their revolt was complicated by their youthful participation in the Revolution. All of them, and particularly the important ones, O'Flaherty, O'Connor, and O'Faolain, had been deeply affected by romantic nationalism, by the guerilla war against the Black and Tans, by the excitement of the founding of the Free State, and by the shock and humiliation of the Civil War. It was almost inevitable that their final disillusion should make them analytical and critical in their approach to life. So much had happened to them; they had moved so rapidly from youthful idealism to adult despair that they had to find reasons and answers. By necessity they became social commentators and questioners, searchers after personal and national identity.

They were not realists by nature or by choice. The conflict in *Midsummer Night Madness* between romance and realism is more than one man's problem; disillusion and bitterness run as an emotional undercurrent through all these writers. And it is this emotional conflict that separates O'Faolain from Moore or Joyce. Their experiences did not embrace the romantic nationalism of 1916 and after or the disaster of the Civil War. Their literary influences of nationalism, a European orientation, and a penchant for social criticism were not affected, as were O'Faolain's, by a superabundance of idealistic patriotism. Moore and Joyce had always had a measure of detachment from the Irish scene, and their work dealing with the scene expresses that attitude. In particular, Joyce's mode of rejection corresponded closely to O'Faolain's earlier feelings, as he responded to the Civil War and awakened to insufficiencies in Irish life, but where the older writer could reveal paralysis as a national condition and something to be shunned, O'Faolain by nature and experience could not reject what he had fought to establish. He would always fall short of total rejection, but his love-hate relationship with his own country and his own people was hard to endure and harder still to resolve in his work.

One of the most disquieting aspects of his relationship with Ireland is his early lack of sympathy. He felt his provincialism, his mental timidity, his self-consciousness. He felt inadequate to the task of portraying his own period because he was unsympathetic to some of it. In a long article in the *Yale Review* (1936), he debated the consequences of such a state for the writer. It is, he said, an admission of weakness when a writer feels obliged to select and reject from his experiences. His own generation had been adversely affected by the revolution: "They lived their most vital years at the peak of the excitement and they fell after that into the pit of disillusion."[2] Because of that intense involvement he had not been able to examine the meaning of revolution, nor had he been aware of the values and meanings of life. He feared that he could not achieve an inclusive and generous relationship with his environment because experience had soured him to certain aspects of Irish life. Therefore his integrity as an artist would be impaired: "I think it is almost inevitable that the integrity of the Irish writer should be impaired. Attacked on every side by political prejudices, national enthusiasm, pietistic evangelism, he has to fight tooth and nail for his vision of life."[3] *Bird Alone* is a demonstration of this truth; Corney's chances of achieving a full life are negated by the ingrained prejudices and values of his society. Denis Hussey was more hopeful but less experienced, as was O'Faolain himself in his enthusiastic and hopeful articles in the twenties. In the article in the *Yale Review* he goes on to point out some of the basic problems that his work actually handles. A realistic interpreter of Irish life, he wrote, would be concerned with expressing the whole range of the new society emerging in the thirties. But he would have to ensure that his bitterness did not affect that side of the creative process in which "the pure creative genius at work ignores morals, politics, time, the social order, place, even people."[4]

O'Faolain's clear-eyed analysis of his own condition paralleled his objective treatment of Irish society in his many social commentaries. Writing in 1942 after he had completed his three novels, he made some valid and illuminating distinctions between his own generation and Yeats. Yeats was aristocratic by birth, Protestant, Anglo-Irish, and European. He felt free to pursue esoteric beliefs, to exploit mythology, and to use nationalism as a literary asset. His successors in O'Faolain's time were not so fortunate nor so free:

They were faced with problems far more insistent; social, political, and even religious problems. They had grown up in a period of revolution, were knitted with common life, and could not evade its appeal. As time went on those problems became savagely acute. For one thing, the younger generation were nearly all Catholics, either by conviction or atavism, and the Catholic Church in the new Ireland was making life impossible for them. The Censorship alone illustrates this, but behind the Censorship lay a general asceticism, or Puritanism, or Jansenism of a quite uncultivated popular feeling, combined with a long social tradition of penury which knew little about the luxuries of mind and body, and which developed in recompense, a suspicion of everything that savoured of that intellectual independence which comes with centuries of social and economic independence. So, on the one hand the younger writers had their deep-rooted longing for intellectual detachment, independence of thought, converse with the world, varieties of opinion, the whole search for what men call Truth. Their problem was to find some synthesis between the gifts of their race, and their own personal integrity, and that had to be, has to be, arrived at objectively, conceived almost in social terms, since they are chiefly novelists, dramatists, fashioning a criticism of life out of their observation of man in relation to society. . . . That synthesis has to be an honestly objective one, a philosophical and moral definition of life as it is lived.[5]

The misfit rebels embody the conflicts expressed here. All of them experienced revolution in one form or another; all are Catholics by birth or by atavism and all suffer from the restrictions of Irish Catholicism. At least three of them, Leo, Corney, and Frankie, drift away or feel driven away from the Church. The references to an uncultivated popular feeling, to years of poverty, and to narrow, suspicious attitudes can be related to the experiences of the rebels with their societies; they are ostracized by people who have no way of knowing or of appreciating the values they stand for. The rest of this passage with its assertion of the need for a synthesis between past and present is also related to the predicament of the misfit hero and his hopes for a more creative life. In the light of this article it is possible to say these rebels not only serve as allegorical figures for the artist in relation to his society but they also indicate O'Faolain's position within the Irish literary tradition and express a wider dissatisfaction and uncertainty.

Their condition of isolation and frustration is not limited to their position in a muddled period of Irish history. Their search for identity and a desirable image of life is part of a widespread anxiety. In a series of lectures delivered at Princeton in 1953, later published under the title of *The Vanishing Hero* (1956), O'Faolain called attention to the prevalance of estrangement and dislocation in novelists whose work had appeared in the twenties and afterwards. Taking as his examples some English, American, and Irish writers, he developed the theme that the central assumption of the novel since the twenties has been the virtual disappearance of the focal character of the classical novel, the conceptual Hero. This figure had traditionally represented a socially approved norm: "The Hero was on the side of the long arm of the law, the Sûreté, the church, the kirk, the headmaster and the head of the family."[6] In conjunction with his opposite number, the Villain, he represented conflicts that were more or less clearly defined and which novelists accepted as expressions of majority opinion as to what constitutes a good or wholesome life. But when traditional beliefs lost their appeal it was automatic, O'Faolain maintained, that the Hero as their personification would also have to become less and less sure of his position. Novelists in the twenties were affected by this gradual disintegration of the Hero. In his place there emerged what O'Faolain has classified as the anti-Hero:

He is a much less neat and tidy concept, since he is always presented as groping, puzzled, crass, mocking, frustrated and isolated, manfully or blunderingly hoping to establish his own personal, supra-social codes. . . . he is never able to see any Pattern in life and rarely its Destination.

The new type of Hero expresses the dissatisfaction of the young with the old and their search for a better pattern of living than they had inherited. They wanted a more attractive destination than their fathers had provided.

O'Faolain's own work places him in the same category as the novelists he discusses: Evelyn Waugh, Graham Greene, Aldous Huxley, Ernest Hemingway, William Faulkner, Virginia Woolf, James Joyce, and Elizabeth Bowen. The dissatisfaction and frustration of his rebels belong to a more than local irritation, to a wider disruption of social, moral, and philosophical values. His achievement as a writer has to be measured not only against the disruptions of Irish life in his time but against a general disquiet. It was not only in Ireland that the traditional order had fallen apart, not only in Ireland that the artist was faced with fragmentation in social, moral, and political values. Proust and Valery, Mann, Rilke and Kafka, as well as Yeats and Joyce, were engaged in creating a literary coherence at a time when incoherence was universal. When O'Faolain turned to the European literary tradition for help in facing up to the problems of the Irish writer, he found that conditions in Europe tended to mirror conditions at home.

It is well to remember his identification with the general uncertainty when considering his response to the influence of the European literary tradition. If he was divided from Joyce, Moore, and Yeats because of the nature of his involvement in the national movement, he was also separated from the traditional European novelist by his experience of the general disintegration of his particular time. At first he had looked to the Russian writers. His first novel acknowledges Turgenev's *A Nest of Gentle Folk*, and Turgenev was Daniel Corkery's favorite novelist. Frank O'Connor and Liam O'Flaherty had also looked to the Russian writers; it was by then an established habit among Irish writers. George Moore had tried to emulate Turgenev's *A Sportsman's Notebook* in *An Untilled Field*. Joyce was closer to Flaubert, whose *Un Coeur Simple* is very similar to many stories in *Dubliners*. On the whole, O'Faolain's generation was more in sympathy with the Russian writers. There was a feeling that Irish and Russian temperaments were alike, and both countries were conscious of national identity. O'Connor and O'Faolain set out deliberately to replace the subjective, romantic heritage of the Revival with one based on the Russian novelists.[8] To turn the parochial into the universal they went to the European models.[9]

Experience was to show serious drawbacks in such plans. It is significant that whereas *A Nest of Simple Folk* is in keeping with those plans, *Bird Alone* is indebted to Joyce. The first novel accepts the European tradition, the second withdraws to the local scene. The tone of the first is nostalgic, the style mainly romantic, and the pace leisurely; the tone of the second is haunted, the style compressed, and the pace is fast. Corney Crone is without illusions. Between 1934 and 1936 O'Faolain had come to see the limitations of the Russian models for his own particular needs.

In a superficial way O'Faolain and Turgenev have much in common. Both are full of sympathy for the land and the people; both are gifted with a poetic and sensitive response to nature and the countryside. Whole sections of *A Nest of Simple Folk* express the same kind of nostalgic delight in rural life that pervades *A Sportsman's Notebook* and *A Nest of Gentle Folk*. Although there are these similarities between O'Faolain and Turgenev, the differences outnumber them and reflect O'Faolain's abilities and opportunities as a novelist. The fact most apparent to both O'Connor and O'Faolain was that there are enormous dissimilarities in the structure of the Irish and Russian societies. Turgenev, Tolstoy, Dostoevsky, and Chekhov handled all levels and classes of society in an inclusive and generous manner, but the Irishman had no corresponding variety of experience or inclusive sympathy. The Civil War and its aftermath had impaired or at least endangered their sympathy, but even more fundamental was the composition of Irish society. "In Ireland," Frank O'Connor sadly explained, "the moment a writer raises his eyes from the slums and the cabins, he finds nothing but a vicious and ignorant middle-class, and for aristocracy the remnants of an English garrison, alien in religion and education."[10] Yeats had Coole Park and the patronage of Lady Gregory, but revolution had gutted the Big House and left a broken world. The difficulties for the novelist were increased by this breakdown in the structure of Irish society. His Russian models could not solve this particular problem for him; their greatness was in some measure due to their having a hierarchical, traditional, well-defined society. "To make a personage, you have to possess an established tradition of living, a convention to define him, a formal society to support him, and that is what we have not and cannot have, until the unfinished revolutionary period is over."[11]

The intellectual climate as well as the social structure were against the Irish writer. Turgenev not only could work within a hierarchical order but also could achieve social significance by making his leading characters representative of successive phases taken by the Russian intellectual. For O'Faolain there was hardly any intellectual tradition. His rebels represent successive phases taken by the Irish revolutionaries, but it is always the same kind of gesture. Not one of his rebels can give an intellectual account of his actions. Their instincts propel them into wild, unthinking, idealistic behavior, but they never formulate an intellectual basis for their responses. Frankie Hannafey's socialism is a series of clichés from the thirties, and when he tries to explain his reasons for being a rebel he can only point to Aunt Nell and her long memory of oppression. It is a good reason, of course, and a valid reason; *pietas* for these heirs of national frustration is a virtue. However, for the novelist interested in complexity of motive and richness of characterization it is a limiting explanation.

The restrictions in intellectual climate and in the composition of society affected the free play of the naturalistic novel. O'Faolain's novels belong to this type; each stresses the influence of heredity and environment and tends to submit the misfit hero to a deterministic mystique of racialism. Nevertheless he is not satisfied with the naturalistic approach. Moore and Joyce had found it useful, although Joyce combined it with symbolistic techniques as early as *Dubliners*. On the other hand, writers like Yeats, Synge, and O'Flaherty had written work that was essentially heroic and expressive of free will. As an inherent romantic O'Faolain preferred the heroic concept to Zola's scientific view of man. Joyce, too, had sought to present Stephen Dedalus in a heroic posture in the *Portrait* and for Bloom had provided Homeric analogies. The Russian novelists had determined movement and growth in their stories by personality and temperament. O'Faolain had examples within both the Irish and the European traditions, and although his novels clearly belong to the naturalistic type, they also reveal a deliberate attempt to surmount what he regarded as its limitations.

As early as 1934 O'Faolain was voicing his dissatisfaction with the naturalistic novel as handed on by his European models. What he particularly objected to was the lengthy analysis of character and the use of "ordinary" characters and incidents. He wished for a kind of novel in which an exaltation of mood would transcend the merely familiar, the trivial, and the incidental and in which character would achieve timelessness.[12] In a later article he drew attention to the disintegration of the moral and intellectual health of the novel. With the disappearance of a central ethic came an almost passive indifference to moral questions. Instead there was irony, satire, and bitterness.[13] In another article the same year (1935) he reverted again to the absence of magnificence in the modern novel. All its present forms, he felt—the Flaubertian novel, the psychological novel, and the proletarian novel—levelled human action to a position where all actions are made equally defensible by a full understanding of exonerating circumstances. Human action could not be significant when denied a significant end. He pointed to the example of the Russian novelists who did not forgive everything simply because they might know all the circumstances.[14] A possible solution lay with the Catholic novelist who could write out of a body of beliefs and a community of faith. Only a transcendental concept of life could restore an ethical foundation to the novel, and a Catholic naturalist, he observed drily, ought to be a contradiction in terms.[15]

Whatever one may feel about the validity or subtlety of his views, they are important here insofar as they throw light on his own work. His dissatisfaction with the seedy view of many of his contemporaries that life is chronically incurable leads him to try to defeat the mechanistic view of man found in the psychological novel and in much of the naturalist heritage. *Bird Alone* gains in interest and integrity because the issues are firmly related to theological concepts of good and evil. The framework is Christian; in fact specifically Catholic. Corney and Elsie are contrasted in the light of their individual response to religious principles. The tragic nature of their story is only realized in terms of an orthodox judgment. And his final state of barren damnation is a burden of guilt that only the Christian could suffer. The pathetic local variations in Irish Catholicism are rendered in innumerable incidents, in the pious hypocrisy of the parents, in the anticlericalism of the Fenians, in the reactions to the Parnell split, in

Elsie's fingering her rosary beads while she walks with Corney, in her numbing horror of sexual sin, and over and over in the over-protected, prelapsarian doll's house that is her home. The novel is fundamentally opposed, in spirit, in tone, and in treatment, to the kind of novel O'Faolain attacks in these articles. People were dissatisfied with the heritage of naturalism, he declared in 1937, because of its inherent pessimism, its destructivism, its distaste for what it handles, its bitterness, its aimless objectivity, and its accurate description of insignificant details. But what really affected them was the lack of philosophical values in such a novel.[16]

The negative response to prevailing literary trends was only one side of O'Faolain's total response. He found an answer to the disintegration of human certainties and the unsatisfactory nature of the contemporary novel in a Yeatsian concept. Yeats had also been uncomfortably aware of a break in the western tradition; he too had sought for a unity of being and a personal synthesis. He had admired the man brought into unity by a mood as against static unity. The former revealed personality, the latter, character. The artist, O'Faolain reasoned, who would try for unity of being must find some traditional subject in which he could counter the disintegrating separateness of the overintellectualised artist, and restore the old breadth and stability and harmony to the novel. Yeats had found such a subject in Ireland, in its magic, its folk-lore, its ancient memory, its mysticism, its passionate love of life, and its nonintellectual simplicity.[17] O'Faolain had found histori-cal biography; *King of the Beggars* and *The Great O'Neill* are magnificent embodiments of his faith in man, his refusal to sub-mit him to mechanistic theories or techniques. They are set in certain distinctive times; their heroes prefigure clearly defined values and attitudes, and at their climactic moments they shine forth, not as characters composed of details and produced by ascertainable forces, but as personalities unified with their people in a deep communion of feelings and instincts, hopes and passions.

His novels also become more understandable in the light of these comments. O'Faolain would like to integrate the two sides of his heritage, the naturalist-realist tradition of Moore and Joyce, derived from the European novel, and the romantic-heroic tradition of Yeats. His heroes or antiheroes, his muddled misfits, have to be seen against the background of his declared literary creed:

> For I know no other art but this; the art of a man who writes out of his naked nucleus of self, his original, primal core of being, with and about those associations of thought, habit, opinion, desire that common life or traditional life wraps about each one of us. These accretions are mostly alien, habits and sanctions by chance of time and place and training; but a few are inherited wisdom, and all are bits of life as it is lived. We cannot go into a tower away from these things. They are our language with which we work on men's minds, symbols to hate or symbols to admire, the stuff of argument, the stuff of poetry and prose—cancer or coitus; communism or Catholicism; that love is divine or that love is the Devil; that all fathers are fools, like Lear and Old Goriot; that Nature hears and sorrows with us; or that nature is a stone—what is any literary movement but this opposition and alliance of naked self and caparisoned self?[18]

In this passage he propounds the concept that underlies and defines his treatment of character and his stress on the importance of personality. Leo, Denis, Corney, and Frankie illustrate the conflict mentioned in the final sentence. Ostensibly molded by a particularized environment, ostensibly representative figures in definable social context, they suddenly rebel against the forms of that caparisoned self and assert primal factors in the inner self. The opposition of the outward "character" and the inward "personality" forms the core of their unexpected and contradictory revolt. Of course the passage refers to much more than this; it is a definition of a stance held by O'Faolain through the years and the essence of his wisdom as a man and his greatness as a writer. But the opposition of the two selves is his way of overcoming the restrictions of the naturalist heritage. Joyce and Yeats had implemented a similar intention with the aid of mythology, but O'Faolain has never relied on epic analogy or heroic parallels.

His achievement as a novelist can best be measured in *Bird Alone*. It excels the other two principally in its compact structure and the integrity of its design. *A Nest of Simple Folk* undertakes too much to be unified. The long, leisurely paced and overdetailed account of the history of the Husseys and their ancestors for over two generations is not sustained either through the characterization or the action. Book One best illustrates the tension arising between violence and self-interest in the compressed account of Judith Foxe's marriage, her opposition to her husband, and her plans for Leo. The action is then paced to the development of Leo, his background, upbringing, associations, influences, and wild behavior. The conflict between mother and son, her hopes and his instincts, rises to the climax of his attack on the local police barracks, and descends to the quietness of his ten years in jail, his mother's death, and his subdued return. Book Two, despite the great beauty of its account of life in Rathkeale and its gentle, sensitive treatment of Bid and Johnny Hussey's love, lacks the passion and the growth in character that distinguishes Book One. Leo now plots secretly, no longer a disturbance to the sleepy locality. He no longer grows as a character and is supplanted by the Husseys, who lack his variety of action, his deviations from local customs, and his inherent force. Their ambitions are narrow and quietly achieved. The climax to such action as there is comes when Johnny succeeds in having Leo jailed again. But the progression has not been steady; too much peripheral detail has been included—in particular, the long account of the return of Leo's colorful, illegitimate son Johno. Book Three shifts the setting to Cork. There the memory of betrayal lingers in Leo's mind, and he plans for vengeance on Johnny Hussey. But again his methods are so sly and unobtrusive that they lack dramatic effect. The main interest of this book, and one of the finest achievements of the whole novel, is the perceptive rendering of life in the Hussey home. Denis's growth is as carefully presented as was Leo's; the main forces that go into his molding are visible. The chief weakness of this Book is that the connection between Leo and Denis, so important to the action, is not made real. Leo is passive and overburdened with significance. He is intended to serve as a symbol of nationalist integrity, as he does if one has had the opportunity to follow his career, but how his symbolic presence affects Denis is not made sufficiently clear. They hardly ever meet and there are few conversations in which Denis can hear about Leo's past. Yet in the final pages Denis's rebellion is overtly caused by his attraction to Leo and what he represents. In the bitter quarrel between Denis and his father that climaxes the novel, Leo's memory serves as the culminating thrust:

"That's a good one," he mocked. "Save us from starvation! And what did they do to my own grandmother, that had to sweat and tear on a rack-rented farm for her ten children? To your own mother, and my mother here, that had a hard and cruel life in Limerick when she was young? Who did that?"

He thrust his face down into his father's face. "Who did it? Who but the English landlords? What did they do to Leo Donnell, but throw him into jail three times because he dared to rise against them?"

His father staggered to his feet, pale with rage.

"Leo Donnell is a common criminal and nothing else, and he'll suffer for it. I put him into jail before, and I'll put him into jail again."

The children were shrinking, all pale, to the sides of the kitchen. A dim rattle of rifle fire echoed in a distant street.

"You put him into jail?"

"Denis! Johnny! Denis!"

"So that's what Johno meant by calling me the son of a spy? You put him into jail, and you're proud of it. You spy on your own uncle?"

"Silence, boy!" his father cried.

"And now he's fighting up there in Dublin."

His father struck him across the face. Then the red smear on his bandage began to spread, and he staggered. The boy held his hand to his face; tears of rage came into his eyes.

"You spy!" he choked. "You spy on your own people." His father sank weakly on the lounge.

"Get out!" he commanded. "Get out!"

In his second novel O'Faolain avoids the structural weaknesses of the first. In *Bird Alone* the action is compressed and controlled. The theme of the influence of the past upon the present is illustrated in the account of Corney Crone's growth in the presence of his grandfather. Essentially it is a repetition of the relationship between Denis and Leo, but instead of the vaguely presented symbolic quality of Leo, Philip is fully realized and projected as a character closely associated with the boy Corney. The novel gains in intensity from its explicit thesis that Corney's development has been forced by his guilt-ridden Grandfather. Structurally it is carefully related to that development. Corney's extending consciousness is affected by the changing influences of his life, his

parents, his grandfather, his Aunt Virginia, Elsie, and the artist
Stella. Each introduces him to a mode of thought and action, a
way of life, a philosophy of behavior, an attitude toward the world
that determines the composition of his final resolution. Middle-
class values, the compressed life of Cork, submissive piety, liberty
of personal action, intellectual independence, all are manifested
in actual persons and incidents. Each person he encounters leads
him beyond what he has known. Each sequence of the novel follows the organic pattern of discovery, understanding, and decision
until finally Corney stands as a bird alone, his final position fully
understandable because of what has gone before.

Bird Alone is very successful from the technical standpoint;
its structural pattern is an organic expression of the growth and
development of the main character. It is also a tribute to O'Faolain's retention of a balance between judgment and understanding, intelligence and sympathy. He can reveal the good as well
as the bad in his characters: the harsh, petty-minded father; the
soft, pleasure-loving mother; the gentle, pious Elsie; the forthright
Stella; the gay, irrepressible Virginia. All are firmly and objectively rendered. They embody different points of view and contrasting affinities. Corney, the rebel, who reacts strongly to his
surroundings and carries the burden of accusation against them,
is also given a final position in which he has as much compassionate understanding of his people as he has contempt for them.
O'Faolain has overcome some basic personal prejudices, and the
novel must be regarded as an important step in his struggle to
deal sympathetically with aspects of Irish life that offend him
emotionally and intellectually. Despite the strong anticlericalism
in Philip and Corney, such aspects as Elsie and her family, the
love affair, her death, the section dealing with Corney's desire
for communion with the faithful are all quiet, sensitive statements
of the value and depth of Catholic teaching in the Irish character.
The moral problem of the lovers is made clear on their terms, and
Corney's final position is a gamble on salvation but a gamble not
taken wildly; it postulates an infinite mercy and a supra-human
judgment.

Come Back to Erin lacks the force, the unity, and the integrity of *Bird Alone*. Although it is full of mature, effective writing, the central break between Frankie in Ireland and Frankie in America cannot be overlooked. His change of character leads him away from what he represents. It is unfortunate that the novel is marred in this way because it contains some of O'Faolain's most impressive and most sustained writing. The sensitivity and skill, so apparent in the stories in *Teresa* and afterwards, are apparent here. In the first section successive panels of carefully contrived incident combine to give an overall impression of compressed living. And even in the second section O'Faolain handles the American scene with an understanding and subtlety remarkable in a foreigner. But it is here that he digresses most; the material is not always pertinent. In particular the extended account of the love-affair and of St. John's marital problems have too little to do with Frankie's original problem. They lead him further and further away from the issue of how the man of passion and dissatisfied longings for a better life survives in the Ireland so finely rendered in the first section.

Chapter 15

Man's Most Ingenious Invention

'Man,' O'Faolain has declared, 'is not a roll of wallpaper. He is not homogeneous. He is a multitude of particles, full of contradictions, inconsistencies and incompatibilities that are our efforts to adapt to change, to chance, to fate, to unforeseen experiences, to new discoveries and to our manifold mistakes'. His later fiction, comprising one novel, *And Again?* (1979) and three collections of short stories, *The Heat of the Sun* (1966), *The Talking Trees* (1971), and *Foreign Affairs* (1976) embodies this complex point of view.

The idea of the infinite variety of human nature is central to *And Again?* in which the narrator, Robert Younger, is given the opportunity to live his life over again so that the gods may discover if experience teaches him anything. But the plan is impossible, since, as he realises almost at once, nobody can live the same life over again unless the same world lives with him. As for experience teaching him anything, since no comparison can be made between the Robert Younger of his first life and the Robert Younger of his second, it is impossible to measure what he has learned. The gods remind him that while there is a pattern of repetition in human affairs, it is not one of exact repetition. 'Exact repetition,' they explain, 'would eliminate everything that makes life life — challenge, free will, ignorance, chance, choice, the unforeseen'. Therefore they have severely curtailed his memory of the first sixty-five years of his life so that the next sixty-five may be full of similar but not identical challenges. They have also arranged for him to grow younger, not older, and remind him that every single life from the beginning of time is linked with every other life.

The pattern of repetition is most vividly illustrated in the women he loves — Ana, Anador, Nana, Christabel. He idealises each in turn as goddess, viking, ikon, heroine, and sees each as a dynamic union of contradictory elements, multiple yet one. All are variations of the same woman. Their names emphasise their similarities and differences. So do their volatile personalities. Anador is her mother, Ana's, 'matching antithesis'. Ana was a realist in search of romance, Anador is a romantic 'with a sixth sense of reality' but without her mother's toughness and genius for living. Nana is almost a reincarnation of Ana; she has her grandmother's 'mastering desire . . . for life-involvement'; 'idealist in mind, realist in body', she is highly intelligent and unromantic. Christabel has Nana's love of freedom. Even though she is 'a chit of a girl' Robert turns her into a heroine and endows her with splendid, conflicting qualities. His repetitive behaviour is seen in these love-affairs with women who resemble one another but are also different and individual, in his transformation of each into an ideal and in his recurrent romantic substitution of new loves for old. In the process his character emerges: he is finally shown ironically to be an ordinary mortal.

Robert's successive love affairs are a major manifestation of the pattern of repetition, but it is also present in the parallel attempts to unravel the past made by him, his grandson, Anador, Amy Poinsett and other, lesser characters. It reveals itself in other ways: just as Ana sent Anador to boarding school so Anador sends her daughter, Nana, and Nana in turn sends her daughter, Ana. Robert's grandson even sends his daughter to one university and his grandfather, Robert (by then a young man) to another. Just as Fr. Des Moran does not have the pleasure of watching his daughter grow, so Robert does not see his daughter grow. Just as Robert and his grandson once faced each other with the image of Nana, whom they both loved, between them, so Robert faces Bill Meister with the image of Christabel, whom they both loved, between them. In London Anador wants to buy a zip-fastener and Robert a tea-infuser; in Rome years later Nana wants to buy a zip-fastener and Robert a tea-infuser. Ana married a gynaecologist, so will her namesake. When she lost Robert in 1930, her glow of happiness faded; when she dies, Reggie's interest in life declines. She and Robert met twice by chance at the fountain in Trafalgar Square. In his first life Robert fell in love with Christabel when they were both very young; in his second life he falls in love with her great-grand-daughter, Christabel, when they are both very young.

Family names are repeated to the point of confusion; it takes considerable concentration to keep the names, their relationships and the generations apart. The gods contribute to the confusion by giving Robert a false identity to begin with. So does O'Faolain in the repetition of names and in the complications of the genealogies. At times the results are comic, as when Nana asks him 'Did you know that your father was once in love with my grandmother?' Who would know better? He has devoted the first part of his narrative to that five year rapture. And when he is suddenly confronted with his grandson, bearing his name and determined to find *his* ancestors, he has to act swiftly to divert suspicion from his own longevity. 'I was frightened,' he admits, 'by the results of my own imaginings. I had turned myself into my own father, rediscovered myself as my own son, and here was my real grandson'!

The more we piece together the connections between actions and characters within one generation and between one generation and the next, the more we agree with the gods that all human lives are linked through time. The narrator's occasional observations on other literary works reinforce that truth. Behind Christabel Lee, his first love and Christabel Younger, his last, lie not only their mirroring reflections in Ana, Anador and Nana, but Coleridge's mysterious 'Christabel' and Poe's hauntingly romantic 'Annabel Lee'. Behind the tutoring presence of Bill Meister lies Goethe's Wilhelm Meister. Behind Robert's deception by Christabel Younger lies Prevost's Manon Lescaut. Behind the multiple perspectives and the interchangeable characters of *And Again?* we may detect the self-evident sham of Flann O'Brien's *At Swim Two Birds* and similar works. Robert's love letters to Anador some of which he uses again for Nana, with suitable modifications, have been borrowed from love letters by Victor Hugo and other writers. The book's interest in the nature of truth, reality, love, time, memory, free-will and so on echoes a complex of recurrent philosophical arguments, as do the discussions of monism and dualism. All are lightly evoked. The book gestures towards them, suggesting their relevance and indicating that its concerns have a timeless and universal interest.

Although Robert Younger is a careful man, his life is affected by ignorance, chance and the unforeseen. He does not know, for example, that his letters to Nana are being intercepted by her father, or that Des Moran was more than 'fond' of Anador whom he claims to be his daughter, that Christabel Younger two-times him, that Amy Poinsett is on their trail when they go to Europe, that Ana may have deceived him, that Nana does. While he is perceptive about Ana he is much less perceptive about her husband, Reggie, whom she despises but who, it turns out, loved her deeply and could not live without her. Part of the reason for his failure is that he has accepted Ana's view of Reggie. As it turns out her deception of Reggie was less complete than she or Robert thought. So too her deception of Robert may have been more successful than he cares to imagine or find out. His view of Ana is affected by love and must be modified by the views of others. But Robert is not always able to accept this truth. He demands visible proof of her infidelity by challenging her son-in-law, Les Longfield, to kiss her. When he does, Robert condemns *his* unfaithfulness, not Ana's. Then he himself kisses Anador, Les's wife, and consciously deceives her.

There are mysteries on all sides, in all personal relationships, in the narrator's origins, in the nature of his relationship with his dead wife, in the question of who is the father of Ana's baby, Anador — her impotent husband, Les Longfield who later marries Anador, Des Moran who later becomes a priest, someone never revealed, or Robert himself? Only Ana knows and she never tells and Robert respects her reticence. On every side in this subtle and complex account of human nature truth is divisible, reality qualified, love never absolute. Yet man aspires to the ideal, wants certainty, enlarges the significance of the beloved.

The human image is always enmeshed in those circumstances the gods mention. Ignorance in the shape of lack of understanding, or knowledge, or self-awareness, in limited perception, in self-deception attend Robert Younger at all times. So does chance, the ultimate proof of free-will. By chance Robert and Ana met each time by the fountain in Trafalgar Square, by cruel chance they lost each other again in Nice. By chance he lives next door to Les and Anador Longfield when he begins his new life and that leads to his meeting with Ana ffrench whom he has loved for thirty years in his first life and will now love for the last five years of her life and the first five of his. By chance Les Longfield meets James Younger in Philadelphia and that leads to the return of James's son, Robert Bernard to Ireland. By chance Robert meets Robert Bernard years later in New York and that leads to his affair with Christabel Younger. Chance, repetition, ignorance, the unforeseen are present in virtually every situation in the book.

Despite their restrictive presence, Robert is not defeated. He rises to the challenges of his second life, pursues the scant evidence of his past, faces the difficulties that arise in his relationships with each woman, leaves Nana in order not to embarrass their daughter by his youthfulness and faces the loneliness of life by himself in America. He has to resort to disguise, evasion and lies in order to hide his amazing survival. It is fundamental to the imaginative vision of the book that human nature is courageous. Des Moran has come through battle and endures the secrecy of his being as he believes, the father of Anador. Reggie lives with the knowledge of Ana's infidelities. Anador survives the disgrace of her husband's dishonesty. Ana faces death on her own terms, just as she faced life when she loved and lost Robert. Humans are not flawless. Des Moran can be ruthless and unjust, as when he tries to turn Anador against Robert. Reggie maintains his social and professional position at virtually any cost. Ana and Anador keep a 'base', staying with husbands they no longer love. Robert Bernard Younger manipulates the lives of others. Compromise, evasion, deception are present in most lives. So are truth and honesty, love and loss, folly and pride. The human image is many-sided. Robert may idealise his several loves, but O'Faolain, the author behind his author-narrator, sees things on a larger, more balanced scale. His ironic, discriminating understanding encompas-

ses and controls the book at all stages. It is articulated by Robert:
'There is no such person as I . . . . Everyone of you, of us, is a plural-
ity, shimmering with variety, endlessly changing, as honeycombed
and tangled as the back of a telephone switchboard, as mobile as a
ballet, or a circus. All life is . . . .Our multiplicity of mind saves us
from the madness of the idea of a homogeneous reality. In variety
and changeability is freedom'. This is Robert's 'faith' — and O'Faolain's. Experience may teach us little, but life itself is good, full of
challenge, as Nana's last musings state. She, too, commenting in her
philosophical way on Robert's story echoes O'Faolain's point of view
almost word for word: 'Man is not a roll of wall-paper . . . not
homogeneous . . .' and so on.

The uncertainties and ambiguities that permeate *And Again?*
include its author-narrator in two main ways: as a writer faced with
the problems of writing an autobiography and as a human being,
who happens to be a fiction. On the one hand he sees his task in a
relatively straightforward way: he writes 'to clear his mind' and he
points out that this is different from writing 'a little harmless mystery
to tease or amuse the reader'. Ironically, *And Again?* is a mystery and
concerns itself with the mysteries of existence. Robert's search for
identity involves him in genealogical detective work; he is a fictive
archaeologist motivated by what he somewhat expansively calls 'a
preternatural eagerness to lay bare in layers the composition of one's
present by excavating one's past'. This naive understanding of the
task gives way however to more complex considerations as he
becomes more deeply involved in the special problems of autobiographical writing. 'It is,' he tells us 'of the essence of the modern novel
that the writer is an interpreter not a recorder — anybody may
record — and we who attend to him are collaborators in his guessing
and hinting game. I who am neither author nor audience, who am
the main character, who was so to speak, there, I know'. This notion
of himself as protagonist in immediate, uncomplicated and truthful
contact with his material is not valid. Autobiography is a special
blend of fact and fiction, imposing a pattern on a life in order to
create a coherent image of its subject — the man at its centre. Robert
also inevitably selects and shapes his material for aesthetic purposes.
His memory is faulty, he idealises, and his facts can be wrong.
'Everything he has in his manuscript', Nana observes, 'is a warning

against the futility of trying to write a wholly truthful autobiography
. . . if he were to live not twice but six times he would still be compos-
ing rather than recording, still groping in dissatisfaction for those
many pieces of his jigsaw . . . .'

Truth being subjective and therefore limited, it is inevitable that
Robert Younger's manuscript will give only a partial account of the
events and characters he chooses to write about. Relativity affects
the individual point of view and understanding. So do strong feelings
and Robert is recurrently influenced by his love for the women who
are the subjects of much of his autobiography. 'How could bare
words cope', he asks, 'with what had ultimately become for me a
symbol of a love beyond definition?' and right away he abandons
those bare words from which records are made and tries impressionistic metaphors. When he tries to revive his memories of
Ana, he admits that he has 'no hope of recording the overwhelming
variety of impressions that she made on him'. The reality of his five
years with her have been clouded, time has disembodied her and he
has elevated her to a star. The touching sentiment is pointedly
juxtaposed with his admission that he is writing this memoir on the
morning after the night he became Anador's lover. Far from being a
simple recording, his memoir is by his own admission an attempt to
'record even in an approximate way' and to 're-evoke her'. Time,
change, idealisation, fiction and even a new love affect his memoir.

Memory, a notoriously defective instrument, is essential to the
creative writer. There are different kinds of memory: Ana's total
recall, old Stephen's fantasies, Anador's vibrant recollections,
Nana's blunter reassessments and there is that 'dark memory' from
the unconscious that Robert learns to trust more than public records.
Memory tends to idealise and since true feeling, as Nana says
quoting Stendhal, leaves no memory, emotion cannot be recollected,
only reconstituted. Robert feels that if he could find out why Des
Moran remembers one thing and not another he would understand
him. Similarly the only way we can understand Robert is to see him
through these memoirs, in their personal pattern. It is in keeping
with their poetic truth that they mirror him in a complex, multiple
manner so that we can never see a total picture. Five women have
loved him, or thought they did, or he thought they did. He was
devious, but had to be, at least some of the time, honourable about

some matters, not about others, loved well, if not always honestly or wisely, and in his own fashion, was alert or tried to be, could be clear and factual in his writing, could also be vague and impressionistic. He loved certain kinds of women, idealised them, often consciously, could be absurdly romantic and shiningly honest. Like anyone else, like Everyman, he is beset by ignorance of his own self and learns almost nothing from experience. There is, as Nana says, quoting Sartre, 'no recognisable Self, we can know ourselves only by observing the effect we make on others, who in turn only know themselves by the effect . . .'

II

In broad terms O'Faolain's three collections of stories have the same psychological emphasis as the novel. Within their smaller compass he investigates the multiple nature of a variety of characters all of whom are enmeshed in the existential circumstances that prevailed in the novel. The settings are international: Ireland, France, England, Italy, America. The narrator is often articulate, intelligent, perceptive and worldly-wise; the characters are usually middle-class, often middle-aged and generally capable of learning from experience, even if not all of them do. O'Faolain's mind is enriched with experience of people, countries, arts and ideas. The greater range of flexibility of this work make it necessary for him to use the more expansive form of the tale in addition to the compact form of the short story. The tale, as he explains in the preface to *The Heat of the Sun* has 'time and space for more complex characterization, more changes of mood, more incidents and scenes, even more plot'. In both kinds of stories he leads characters through a process of discovery, bringing them towards unsuspected truths about themselves, or others, or about the nature of man. These moments of insight are found in short stories like "Feed My Lambs", "The Planets of the Years" and "The Talking Trees" or in tales like "Hymeneal", "Falling Rocks, Narrowing Road, Cul-de-Sac, Stop" and "In the Bosom of the Country". Stylistically, there are two kinds of stories and tales, the realistic and the non-representational. In the latter, as for example, in "Hymneal" or "Falling Rocks, Narrowing Road, Cul-de-Sac, Stop", characters tend towards caricature, their reactions are over-stated, the situations are exaggerated and the language is at times flamboyant.

Stereotypes are natural subjects for character investigation: the alcoholic artist, the frustrated civil servant, the crackpot intellectual, bachelors, sentimental Italians, romantic Frenchmen, idealists, realists, cynics. O'Faolain delights in showing them to be less stereotypical than they seem to be and to be capable of a greater range of feeling or of a profounder insight than one might expect. For the same reasons he likes to bring people from different countries together — the French diplomat and the Irish wife in "The Faithless Wife", the Italian count and vacationing Irishwoman in "Liars", the Protestant English major and the Catholic Irishwoman in "In the Bosom of the Country', the young people in "Before the Daystar" — so that he can reveal their contrasting attitudes, values and patterns of behaviour. Through these encounters he illustrates national traits, confirming their existence but also demonstrating that human nature is too unpredictable and varied to be easily categorised.

In "The Faithless Wife", the diplomat, a romantic Frenchman, pursues the Irish wife only to discover that she is sexually direct and enthusiastic and impatient with his prolonged campaign. In a comic reversal of roles she is quite content to play a romantic game but he urges her to seek a divorce and begin a new life with him. She has no intention of giving up her satisfying life in Dublin. Furthermore, when her husband becomes ugly and cretinous after a stroke she nurses him devotedly. The Frenchman, transferred to Los Angeles, but no wiser from this experience takes up with yet another Irish woman.

A similar comic oscillation runs through "In the Bosom of the Country" where the somewhat stupid Englishman has an affair with an Irish woman, reluctantly marries her when her husband dies, even becoming a Catholic at her insistence, only to discover that Catholicism is not really important to her. So why did she urge him to become a Catholic and why is she indignant when he tells her their love has been sinful? O'Faolain plays with these issues with skill and ingenuity.

Complexities are also revealed through a variety of incidents. In "Something, Everything, Anything, Nothing" the rational American reporter limns the history of modern Italy as he journeys south to Sicily and, in a series of seemingly haphazard encounters, suggests the mixture of myth and reality that characterises the Latin temperament. Old men dream nostalgically for things past, a young man dreams in vain of a great future, another scoffs at the old sentimentalists and rails against the Catholic Church but rushes off to pray at the shrine of the weeping Madonna when his wife has a baby. Even the hard-headed reporter succumbs to 'the intensity of the human feeling circling the altar like a whirlpool of air, or bees in a swarm, or butterflies over a wave, or fallen leaves whispering in a dry wind'.

O'Faolain approaches his subjects with an equal measure of insight and irreverence, compassion and mockery. Men seek love, freedom, opportunity and are fascinated by the unusual in others. They are drawn, in his words, by whatever is 'alien or private or elusive in the person loved'. The narrator in "Our Fearful Innocence" is haunted by his memories of Jill Jennings whom he loved but has never been able to understand. The little boy in "The Talking Trees" has a vision of beauty when he sees the naked girl and runs away with metaphors bursting in his head — 'Like Birds. Like Stars. Like Music'. The vivacious wife in "The Dead Cert" is married to her one true love yet paradoxically yearns occasionally for a change of lovers: 'she has what she wanted, wants what she cannot have, is not satisfied with what she has got'. Men also try to protect themselves from the painful realities of life and love, as the eccentric bachelors do in "Falling Rocks, Narrowing Road, Cul-de-Sac, Stop", the young men in "One Man, One Boat, One Girl", or the old woman in "The Planets of the Years".

'We are not one person', the writer observes in 'Dividends'. 'We change, die and live again'. This seems to be a simple story about a foolish, penurious old woman, but becomes a story in which each of the main characters, the successful stockbroker, the experienced writer and the old woman, is shown to be a victim of illusions and limited understanding. Clearly Anna Whelan cannot understand, nor will she be induced to understand, that — as Mel Meldrum says — he who does not speculate cannot accumulate. She bought shares with a small legacy, then sells them and stubbornly maintains that she should continue to get her dividends. The problem could be solved easily and charitably if the stockbroker would agree to pretend to give her the dividends and allow her nephew, the writer, to repay him. Mel, an intelligent, decent man, is adamantly opposed to this pretense; it offends his sense of integrity and his view of himself as a realist. But his view of himself is less realistic than he imagines: he gives charity through the Saint Vincent de Paul Society but will not be charitable to Anna Whelan. His major illusion is that he can continue his passion-filled romance with his young house-keeper, Sheila, indefinitely. The writer makes him see that he should be realistic and marry her, but he is afraid — 'if I married her, I might be unhappy all my life'. He cannot see that in love, as in finance, he who does not speculate cannot accumulate. The writer who is supposed to be knowledgeable about human nature is also found wanting. He does not realise that his Aunty Anna's years of service with the grand ladies of the Curragh have given her a yearn-ing to imitate them. She uses most of her reclaimed legacy to buy a mink coat. Similarly, and pointedly, Sheila buys a mink hat. The writer's education is complete when he thinks how tactless he has been. 'I had probed, I had interfered, I had uncovered his most secret dream and destroyed it by forcing him to bring it to the test of reality'.

No one has a monopoly on truth. O'Faolain's view of human nature has not changed greatly since he wrote about the intricacies of the Irish mind. It has been confirmed and extended in the realisa-tion that men are inextricably linked through similarities of behaviour. The human image of O'Faolain's later fiction is multiple and inexhaustibly varied. Finding complexities, contradictions and mysteries in all men, whatever their nationality, he writes about them with undiminished zest and skill. As far as his imaginative faith is concerned man's most ingenious invention is man. There is no finer subject.

Chapter 16

The Growth of a Writer

In locating the time and place of his birth as an artist, O'Faolain likes to recall the January of 1915 when he went as usual to the Cork Opera House and saw two plays, George Bernard Shaw's *John Bull's Other Island* and Lennox Robinson's *Patriots*. The Shavian wit that had cut through the overblown atmosphere of the London theater had reached Cork, where O'Faolain had been accustomed to seeing such theatrical favorites as *Eliza Comes to Stay, Mrs. Wiggs of the Cabbage Patch, A Girl in a Taxi, The Bells, East Lynne, Bella Donna,* and others of the same kind. But it was Robinson's play, his first encounter with the Abbey Theater, that was decisive. Here for the first time it dawned upon him that literature could impinge upon the realities of life. Hitherto his imagination had been fed on romance, on the proud patriotism of Empire as found in G. A. Henty, on the life of adventure as found in R. M. Ballantyne and R. L. Stevenson. In his untutored mind he had formed idealizing notions of the world; he lived in a dream. *Patriots* dispersed that dream.

Now he discovered that literature is not dissociated from life, from the social context in which the writer lives. He got his first inkling of the complex relation of art, artist, and society.

To his surprise he saw on stage the parlor of a house in an Irish country town, his uncle, people talking as naturally as if they were in his aunt's kitchen in Rathkeale or in any number of cottages he knew of. It was reality itself "tenderly, delightfully, recognizably familiar: a geranium pot in the window, a chenille cloth covering the table, pictures of Robert Emmet and Pius X on the walls, the lace curtains, the old, padded furniture."[1] Not only the setting, the dialogue, and the characterization but even the action was familiar. The patriot was an old Fenian who returned from jail, still burning with nationalistic ideals, and the young men to whom he spoke were not much older than O'Faolain himself. "The fantastic thought burst on me that in Rathkeale, even in Cork that night, there might be other real, living, exhaling-inhaling old men with these same noble, gallant, hopeless ideas."[2]

Not that he began to write immediately of the common life around him; it was over ten years before he wrote "Fugue" and in between was much juvenilia of a romantic kind. However, in time he came to appreciate that literature not only holds the mirror up to reality but does much more, when the writer sees reality with heightened emotions, when his experience of life is enlarged. Then he penetrates the outward circumstances of his place and time to the eternal truths about men and the world they live in. Through the transforming power of the imagination, as O'Faolain himself has observed, the writer attains that "emotionalized reality which is the father of the truly creative imagination—life-based, life-transforming, what Berenson so often loved to call 'life-enhancing.'"[3]

Of all the realities encountered by O'Faolain after he had seen Robinson's play, the revolution was by far the most influential on his early work. Coming as a climax to the various alienating and disturbing incidents and conditions in his own life and then compounding them with further difficulties of a political and religious nature, it propelled him beyond the familiar realities of

family and church, even of society, with such finality that in order
to find himself afterwards he had to examine it to discover its
meanings in his own life and in the life of his country. It appeared
in *Midsummer Night Madness* as an exciting, anarchical, and
liberating experience. The idealistic young rebel was driven in
bewilderment and joy from one unusual experience to another,
from Henn's lechery to Bella Browne's sacriligious seduction of
him in a Trappist monastery, from Stevey Long's amorality to the
demoralizing confinement of the bombshop, and finally, through
these and other encounters, to the transcending choice of permanence in "The Patriot." He moved toward domesticity with a
farewell look at the lawless exuberance of a disturbed and disturbing period. In marked contrast with his irresponsible companions, he went beyond anarchy to order, to the security of his
dark-haired girl.

A Nest of Simple Folk encompassed Irish history from the time
of Daniel O'Connell to the Rising of 1916. Looking at the story
of his own family, a typical account of unexciting, wearying struggle from a rack-rented little farm in the country to impoverished
respectability in the city, O'Faolain saw their lives as "a slow tale
of pathetic endeavour," constantly torn between opposing forces,
"the instinct to strive violently, to erupt volcanically on the idealistic plane, the instinct, as deep and as terrible, of self-preservation."[4] The tensional relationship thus created, first experienced
in his own home, served as an integrating factor on the action of
the novel, providing a dramatic interplay between opposing passions and values. It explained the recurrent disappointments
through the generations as parents and children responded to one
or other of the mutually exclusive and equally obsessive forces.
Both Leo Donnell and Denis Hussey were driven apart from their
families, both affected by the powerful thrust of the racial heritage.
At the climax of its influence they acted less from individual will
than from uncontrollable impulse, and in each the revolt was
inextricably joined with the need for personal freedom of behavior. Inevitably they acted thereafter in some bewilderment and
searched back into their lives and into the lives of their people
for the sources of such passion.

The novel ends with the climactic rejection of the father and through him of what he had come to represent: respectability, righteousness, law, frugality, the Catholic Church, the British Empire. But the objective conclusion was only part of its achievement. Whole sections were evocatively sensitive to the small joys and the gentle happiness of simple, uneventful lives; others, like the ending, were clear-eyed accounts of warping toil and passion. At every stage of its development it was firmly and affectionately rooted in ordinary life.

A similar insistence on fact distinguished *Constance Markievicz*. Dismissing her as a typical, thoughtless rebel, O'Faolain stressed the social, political, and literary forces that led to rebellion. He replaced his avatar, Leo Donnell, with the stocky, dynamic figure of James Connolly, who had a definable social program. Seeing the facts had become a necessary part of his life as a writer, and throughout the thirties he combined the writing of articles of social analysis with his fiction and historical biographies. After *Constance Markievicz* he entered on the greatest phase of his career. In a period of about ten years he wrote his best novel, his two great historical biographies, most of his finest stories, and a host of intelligent commentaries on Irish life and letters. His development was intense and varied as he worked out his views on Irish society, sought for ways of handling it in novels and stories, and turned back to the whole range of Irish history in quest of continuity.

It was by any standards a man-sized job, and his reputation rests securely on what he wrote at this time. It is in the range and intensity of that work, its intellectual vigor and imaginative power, its passionate devotion to Irish life, its achieved control of form and manner, that he emerges as the most important writer of his generation. In its totality it is by far the most complex and valuable response to Irish life in the generation that lived through the revolution into the realities of independence. It was, as has been seen in studying its manifestations in the three main forms, and achieved success, a working toward detachment, a hard-won victory over the enemies of promise in himself and in his surroundings.

He began his journey toward that success, toward, for example, the controlled intensity of *The Great O'Neill* or the dispassionate intellection of some of the editorials in *The Bell* in a mood of depression. The landscape of *Bird Alone* and of the early stories in *A Purse of Coppers* was peopled with artist-rebels defeated by the lack of vitality in their surroundings. These spiritual heirs of Leo Donnell were stranded after the tides of revolution. *Bird Alone* and the disillusion of the post-Parnellite period as its temporal background; Corney's sexual and religious liberation came at the height of Parnell's defeat, and he identified personal calamity with national disaster. Implicit in that identification was the analogous political and social realities of O'Faolain's own life after the Civil War and after DeValera's failure to bring about social reforms. The new Ireland was tinged with the same pressures Corney encountered, and in between the passionate individualism of Philip Crone, the old Fenian, and the boy-hero growing up in daily association with him was the dull rectitude of the boy's pious, middle-class father. The middle generation thus represented corresponded to the new middle class of the thirties—pious, materialistic, unadventurous, out of sympathy with the dreams and needs of rebellious youth. Although past and present were joined in the old rebel and his young disciple, there was one major difference. After Parnell, as after independence, there was no longer any large cause to which a dissatisfied youth could attach himself in half-forgetful dedication. He and his lonely compatriots in *Purse of Coppers* were birds alone, sadly separated by pride and principle from the common humanity about them.

Corney's strongest loyalties were to the past, to the heritage so fiercely and so passionately felt in the older rebel. Old Philip was presented as a parasitic figure feeding on the boy's innocence, corrupting him intentionally, bringing him into his own condition of social and religious alienation. There is some obscurity and confusion in Corney's account of this conscious abuse, but he has an intense conviction that he was made in the image of his master, not through any natural and gradual process of normal growth, but prematurely and so totally that he was broken away from his own people in an irreparable displacement. As the com-

pulsive narrator of the novel he experiences again the dark
confusions of his growth and displays his barren freedom as a
judgment on the society he cannot accept. He shares his loneliness
with many characters in *Purse of Coppers* similarly affected by
inadequacies within their environment. All seek in vain for
imaginative richness, and until society changes they cannot even
hope for contentment.

The two major historical biographies were powerful and successful strategies for examining conditions around these lonely
figures. It was typical of the rhythm of O'Faolain's output that
he moved back and forth between short story, novel, and biography to find adequate ways of dealing with Irish life. Faced with
social insufficiency, he could best express his criticism of life
within the framework of a previous time and through the persona
of a historical figure whose creative energy and representative
value were unmatched in the postrevolutionary period. In O'Connell and O'Neill he depicted the forceful reformer he so much
wanted in his own time, men joined in a unity of being with
their people, absorbed in projecting the deepest feeling of the
country. The lessons and principles they embodied served as
enduring and valuable parables for his own time. They satisfied
his needs as a man and gave him as a writer the kind of full
challenge he needed.

He moved in these ten years from an oppressive feeling about
Irish life, from didacticism, from a too personal involvement, to
detachment, a calm objectivity, a poetic gentleness. This progress,
so evident in the stories, was apparent also in the contrast between
the romantic gusto of the O'Connell work, its mythic glorifica-
tion of the hero, its hard-hitting moral asides, and the realistic,
factual, and disciplined portrayal of O'Neill and his more reasoned and even reluctant approach to the problems of his time.
O'Faolain reached his maturity as a writer in these years of intense
intellectual and imaginative effort. He never rested on any plateau
of achievement and, after the war continued his search for ways
in which to channel and reveal, in all its complexity, his understanding of the human condition.

He has exemplified in his own life the principle of European alignment that he so consistently advocated as more fruitful and more healthy than introverted nationalism. He had looked to European models for his own writing and had hoped to see Irish studies made part of European life and thought. His historical biographies, particularly the O'Neill study, stressed the generative association with intellectual movements outside Ireland. In editorials in *The Bell,* entitled "One World" and appearing occasionally from January 1944 to July 1945, he had urged Ireland to forget isolationism and be responsive to trends toward economic and intellectual unity in Europe and elsewhere. In practice he had himself become cosmopolitan, writing two travel books about Italy, a series of articles on American cities in *Holiday,* a biography of Cardinal Newman, and an autobiography.

He has achieved in his own life and ways of thinking a fruitful rapprochement between his attraction to all in Ireland that was deeply and richly rooted in his nature and all in Europe and America that stimulated and trained his intellect. His travel books on Italy constantly refer back to rural, Catholic Ireland, and to his own involvement with both countries. In Sicily, for example, he was passionately excited by the reclamation scheme in Calabria, by the giving of land at last to the peasants, and by the generosity of the United States pouring dollars into that vast wasteland so that the poor might not be landless. His study of the novelists was particularly valuable for the light it threw on his own work and on the work of his generation of Irish novelists. His biography of Cardinal Newman, a study of the man's growth, mentality, and conversion to Catholicism, a highly personal document in many ways, was an unusually subtle and perceptive study of a man who was himself endlessly complex. O'Faolain was interested in his blending of meticulous intellectual accuracy with a delicate perception of the subtleties of the mind and argued that he oscillated all his life "between the intellectual, expressible thing, which emerges from man as law or morality and the irrational, inexpressible thing which enters into man as faith or mysticism."[5] The biography revealed the mature nature of O'Faolain's own character in its ability to follow the ramifications of Newman's mind and in its perceptive response to the reservations and subtleties behind the external pronouncements. It was closely related in its appreciation of emotional and mental complexities to the treatment of Jacky Cardew, Benjy Spillane, and Robert Flannery in the stories. Man's capacity for self-deception was treated initially as matter for comedy and satire, but in "Lovers of the Lake" it was given respectful attention as an important part of human nature. Finally, in the better stories in *I Remember! I Remember!* the internal, half-buried self, the heritage of childhood that every-man carries within, was resurrected for delicate, affectionate analysis. In recent years O'Faolain has turned back more and more, in mellow mood, upon memories of childhood and youth. Settings and incidents from his novels and early stories appear again in his autobiography, where they are treated with the same blend of poetic sensitivity and realistic observation that characterises the stories in *I Remember! I Remember!* At the same time those retrospective impulses are only one side of his later achievement. In *The Heat of the Sun* his imagination delights in man's capacity for confusion.

"There is," O'Faolain wrote in *South to Sicily,* "only one admirable form of the imagination—the imagination that is so intense that it creates a new reality, that it makes things happen, whether it be a political thing, or a social thing, or a work of art."[6] All his life as a writer, as this study has sought to demonstrate, he has been loyal to his belief in the re-creative quality of the imagination. It has not been possible to show the full range of that loyalty nor even to reveal all of its qualities within any one particular work. However, he has admired its operation in historical figures, has looked for it within the society of his own time, and, above all, has written much that is memorable and enduring under the spell of its influence.

The opening story of *The Heat of the Sun,* "In the Bosom of the Country," deals with the perplexities and tribulations of a decent, but dull-witted and self-deceiving Major who undergoes the ordeals of a conversion to Catholicism so that he can marry his mistress, Anna, whom he no longer loves. Her reasons for wanting to get married are social: she wants to be accepted by her former husband's friends. His reasons are mainly honorable: he feels that it is the right thing to do for her.

They are amusingly opposite in character and temperament. She is volatile, clever, superficial, cruel, and a nominal Catholic. He is steady, dull, loyal, considerate, and rather serious. They are not saved from mockery by the profound spiritual and emotional issues that involved the adulterous lovers in "Lovers of the Lake." Those were granted the dignity of real religious conflict, and the eternal background was never wholly forgotten. Their love for each other was mature, fully satisfying, and vibrant. Anna and the Major, however, are not spared the absurdities of their situation; and of the two it is the weakly compliant, self-deceiving, and sentimental Major who is most keenly mocked.

Lying with her in bed, as the story begins, he is aware of age and the death of their love. Unexpectedly at that moment of truth she receives news of her husband's death. Dutifully, foolishly, feeling trapped by events, he returns later with a proposal of marriage. To his surprise his gallantry is deflected as Anna counsels delay because of the danger of gossip and because she wants to be married in a Catholic ceremony.

Reluctantly, even distastefully, he makes his way to the parish priest, who turns out to be a genial Monsignor, formerly a chaplain in the first world war. The Major's long-standing oppositions to Catholic beliefs and practices crumble before the Monsignor's persuasive manner.

The Major's victorious progress faces one great obstacle: his sin of adultery. To achieve conversion he must reassess his love and judge it as evil. His battle with this demand is complicated by Anna's refusal to admit that their love was sinful. His dogged insistence even causes her to regret her request that he become a Catholic.

But the Major becomes a Catholic, and Anna's predictions come true: because he has been converted, her old friends gather round and they are both happy. Their idyllic days are, however, darkened by quarrels, as the Major clearly sees that Anna is really indifferent to religious matters. In misery and outrage at this discovery, he seeks the old Monsignor, who only counsels him to pray for miracles but not to expect them.

Ironically, a miracle does take place. One April morning he has a transforming vision of the unity of all things: everything in the world has been created by the one God. That insight grants him the peace and the harmony for which he has longed, in himself and in his relationship with Anna. But in a final reversal he no longer lives up to his religious beliefs.

O'Faolain's exuberant treatment of the adulterous lovers is beautifully sustained. Despite the lengthier quality of the narrative and despite its complications of incident and attitude, the pace is evenly maintained. The details of setting, situation, and character, and the verbal skill in the dialogue that reveals the varying moods and feelings of the characters, are all handled with sensitivity and precision.

The Heat of the Sun has a youthful vigor and freshness. Not only has O'Faolain chosen a new form, but that form clearly satisfies his sense of joy in the complexity of life. Once again he has achieved in a number of these pieces a happy fusion of form and content. Once again a particular sensibility has found a subject uniquely suited to itself.

Appendix

When the Irish bishops considered the proposals of the Mother and Child Scheme, as it came to be called, they decided these were in direct opposition to the rights of the family and of the individual, and were liable to abuse if adopted because they would constitute a ready-made instrument for totalitarian aggression. The bishops pointed out that the right to provide for the health of the children belongs to the parents, not to the state; that the state may not deprive 90 per cent of parents of their rights because of 10 per cent needy or negligent parents. They maintained that it was not a sound policy to impose a state medical service on the whole community on the pretext of relieving the needy 10 per cent from the so-called indignity of a means test. They maintained also that since education in regard to motherhood includes instruction concerning sex relations, chastity, and marriage, the state had no competence to give such instruction and local medical officers were unsuited for the task. They feared that gynecological care might be interpreted to include provision for birth limitation and abortion and expressed concern at the absence of a guarantee that state officials would respect Catholic principles on these matters. They maintained that the proposed services destroyed confidential relations between doctor and patient since it viewed all cases of illness as matters for public records. These were the main objections forwarded by the hierarchy to Mr. Costello and Dr. Browne on October 10, 1950.

In reply, Dr. Browne pointed out that there would be no compulsion with the Mother and Child Scheme since it was an entirely voluntary program. He argued that the powers taken by the Bill were not in direct opposition to the rights of the family and the individual and were not liable to abuse. He made reference to the existence of medical charities and a Public Assistance system of medical relief for the poorer classes of the community, which provided comprehensive maternity and child health service, and about which no complaint was ever made in regard to the invasion of the rights of the individual or the family. He pointed out that the only fundamental difference between these existing schemes and his proposed Bill was that there was a means test for the former and none for the latter. He presumed that the hierarchy did not object to the absence of a means test. He commented also that since the scheme was voluntary, merely placing means for providing health services for the family at the disposal of parents, it did not infringe upon the right of parents to provide for the health of their children. He maintained that the scheme was not an imposition; that there was no pretext of relieving the necessitous 10 per cent but the intention was to provide a good medical service for all because of the high mortality rate among mothers and children; that the necessitous 10 per cent was really 30 per cent if based on the numbers using Public Assistance already but that many more people needed aid.

Furthermore the omission of a means test was not a new principle, since it was part of the existing service to treat infectious diseases. He pointed out that education for motherhood included instruction about correct diet, the avoidance of certain forms of

work and social habits. It was this kind of education that the
Scheme provided, and care would be taken to see that nothing
objectionable would enter. In any case, since the medical profession was predominantly Catholic and the doctors would be those
already in local appointments, and since only those trained in
appropriate medical schools, where Catholic teaching prevailed,
would be appointed, and since the people could exercise choice,
there was a reasonable guarantee that no objectionable instruction
would be given. In addition, the confidential relationship of doctor and patient would not be damaged; local medical officers
always kept records and no violation of confidence had occurred.
Was the proposed scheme contrary to Catholic teaching? This
was the substance of a memorandum sent by Dr. Browne to the
hierarchy.

The bishops considered it and announced that they could not
approve of any scheme that in general tendency must foster undue
control by the state in a sphere so delicate and so intimately concerned with morals as that which deals with gynecology or obstet-
rics and with the relation between doctor and patient. They
considered the proposed scheme to be contrary to Catholic social
teaching because the state intended to arrogate to itself a function
and control in respect of education, more especially in the very
intimate matters of chastity, individual and conjugal; because the
state intended to arrogate to itself a function and control in respect
of health services that ought to and could be secured by individual initiative and by lawful associations; because the state must
enter unduly and very intimately into the lives of patients, both
parents and children; because the state must levy tax on the whole
community independently of the necessity or desire of the citizens
to use the facilities being provided; because the state would by
taxation indirectly compel the people to avail of the services;
because the scheme would damage the self-reliance of parents who
could pay for medical treatments; and because the state would
have to rely on ministerial regulations as distinct from legislative
enactments of the Oireachtas (or Parliament).

Because of the objections of the hierarchy, the Scheme was withdrawn by Mr. Costello and Dr. Browne was dismissed. The rift between these two men is illustrative of O'Faolain's ideas on how the individual should behave in the face of ecclesiastical opposition. Where one was prepared to challenge the arguments of the bishops, the other was prepared to meet those arguments without opposition. Browne clearly recognized the authority of the Church and obeyed when the bishops enunciated their opinion that his Scheme was contrary to Catholic social teaching. "As a Catholic I accept the rulings of Their Lordships without question." Communications between Browne and Costello show the latter stressing the serious implications involved in a potential defiance of the bishops and conflict with them on proposals affecting moral questions. Browne, on the other hand, was not convinced that his Scheme was opposed to Catholic teaching and showed himself prepared to stand over it until such time as the bishops would explicitly condemn it for that reason. In a series of letters between Browne and Costello, the uncritical submission of the latter contrasts with the more argumentative approach of the former. Reference to "many occasions" in which Costello had private interviews with the Archbishop of Dublin (letter from Costello to Browne, March 28, 1951) indicated that the Minister for Health was being abandoned because of clerical opposition. The failure of Costello to transmit Browne's defense as contained in the memorandum to the bishops immediately not only embarrassed Browne but proved to him later that even during those months, from October, 1950 to March, 1951, in which he had acted on the belief that he was carrying out an approved government policy, Costello had been secretly opposed to it. Furthermore, because the hierarchy, as he thought, had not made any reply to his memorandum he was under the impression that they were satisfied with his explanations and assurances. He had, in any case, expressed these orally when called to an interview by the Archbishop of Dublin on October 11, 1950. (*Irish Times,* April 12 and 13, 1951)

Notes

Introduction

[1] *Vive Moi!*, p. 72.*
[2] *Ibid.*, p. 117.
[3] *Ibid.*, p. 119.
[4] *Ibid.*, p. 11.
[5] *Ibid.*
[6] *Ibid.*, p. 78.
[7] *Ibid.*, p. 57.
[8] *Ibid.*, p. 130.
[9] *Ibid.*, p. 131.
[10] *Ibid.*, p. 132.
[11] *Ibid.*, pp. 140–41.
[12] *Ibid.*, p. 155.
[13] *Ibid.*, p. 173.
[14] "Principles and Propaganda," *The Bell,* 10, 3 (June, 1945), 200.
[15] *Ibid.*, p. 185.
[16] *Ibid.*, p. 186.
[17] *Ibid.*, p. 221.
[18] *Ibid.*, p. 311.

[19] *Ibid.,* p. 317.

* Complete publication information for books followed by an asterisk is given in the Bibliography.

Chapter 1

[1] *King of the Beggars,* p. 138.*
[2] "Sean O'Faolain," *Atlantic Monthly,* 199 (May, 1957), 69.
[3] "The Gaelic Corpse," *Leader,* 76, 24 (August 20, 1938), 566.
[4] This idea is discussed in Chapter XIII, "Character and Personality."
[5] "Eamon De Valera," *The Bell,* 10, 1 (April, 1945), 8–10.
[6] *King of the Beggars,* pp. 58–60.
[7] *Ibid.,* pp. 62–63.
[8] *Ibid.,* p. 29.
[9] *Ibid.,* p. 77.
[10] *Ibid.,* p. 69.
[11] *Ibid.,* p. 77.
[12] *Ibid.,* p. 87.
[13] *Ibid.,* p. 214.
[14] *Ibid.,* pp. 267–68.

"My dear O'Hara, I do most anxiously wish to confer with Lords Meath and Cloncurry on the present awful position of public affairs, and the possibility of calming the public mind. I would wish that this desire of mine should be communicated to their lordships. . . .

I have had a communication from a person in the confidence of the ministry, in England, but whose name I cannot disclose, who states distinctly that all the ministry desire is to postpone the union question until those of Reform, abolition of corporate monopoly, and reformation of Church abuses are disposed of, thus leaving the 'Union' for the last.

I think this may be done by Lord Cloncurry and Lord Meath in such a manner as to carry with them the public mind, preserving only just so much, or rather so little, of popular agitation as would *continue* the confidence of the people in the prospect of legitimate redress: such mode being in my mind the only mode of preventing violence and outrage and preventing *probable* rebellion. . . ."

[15] *Ibid.,* p. 253.
[16] *Ibid.,* p. 254.
[17] Michael Tierney, ed., *Daniel O'Connell, Nine Centenary Essays.*
[18] Review of above, *The Month,* 2, 5 (November, 1949), 342.
[19] *King of the Beggars,* p. 214.
[20] *Ibid.,* p. 29.
[21] *Ibid.,* p. 330.

[22] *Ibid.,* pp. 154–82.

[23] *Ibid.,* p. 304.

[24] *The New Ireland,* 25 (Winter, 1936), 320–29.

[25] *King of the Beggars,* p. 274.

[26] *Ibid.,* p. 105. O'Faolain's admiration for O'Connell at this point fails to consider that he was also speaking as an Irish Catholic lawyer out of office.

[27] "Revolution and Counter-Revolution," *Nine Centenary Essays,* p. 87.

[28] *King of the Beggars,* p. 107.

[29] W. D. Killen, *History of Congregations of the Presbyterian Church in Ireland and Biographical Notices of Eminent Presbyterian Ministers and Laymen,* pp. 7–8, 270.*

[30] T. W. Moody, *Thomas Davis, 1814–1845, A Critical Address,* pp. 41–42.*

[31] *King of the Beggars,* p. 318.

[32] R. Dudley Edwards, "The Contribution of Young Ireland to the Development of the Irish National Idea," *Feilscribhinn Torna,* ed. Seamus Pender, p. 131.*

[33] Reynolds, *Catholic Emancipation,* p. 17.*

[34] *King of the Beggars,* p. 120.

[35] *Ibid.,* p. 120.

[36] *Ibid.,* p. 183.

[37] *Ibid.,* p. 188.

[38] "The Dail and the Bishops," *The Bell,* 17, 3 (June, 1951), 5.

[39] *Ibid.,* 8.

[40] *Ibid.,* 9.

[41] *Ibid.*

[42] *Ibid.,* 10.

[43] O'Faolain is correct in assessing the role of O'Connell as protector of the independence of the Church, but it is possible that he was not really in sympathy with the religious indifference of the secular liberal. He did minimize the religious aspects of Emancipation. But he can also be seen as the Catholic liberal who found a way out of the impasse created by cisalpinism by discarding the unorthodox elements of the revolutionary creed and retaining what was reconcilable with the Church's teaching. (See Roche, "Revolution and Counter-Revolution," *Nine Centenary Essays,* p. 79).

[44] Daniel A. Binchy, comment on "Daniel O'Connell and the Gaelic Past," by Michael Tierney, *Studies,* 27 (September, 1938), 369.

[45] *Ibid.,* 372.

[46] *King of the Beggars,* p. 213.

Chapter 2

[1] *The Great O'Neill, A Biography of Hugh O'Neill, Earl of Tyrone, 1550–1616,* p. 15.*

[2] *Ibid.,* p. 86.

[3] The idea that there was no national spirit in Tudor Ireland has been challenged by Thomas L. Coonan in *The Irish Catholic Confederacy and the Puritan Revolution,* pp. 23–24.* He argues that the orders of the bards and the brehons were national in organization.

[4] *The Great O'Neill,* p. 279.

[5] *Ibid.,* p. 43.

[6] *Ibid.,* p. 129.

[7] *Ibid.,* p. 276.

[8] *Ibid.,* p. 265.

[9] *Ibid.,* p. 206.

[10] *The Vanishing Hero,* p. 152.*

[11] *The Great O'Neill,* p. 175.

[12] *King of the Beggars,* p. 249.

[13] *Ibid.,* p. 186.

[14] *The Great O'Neill,* p. 31.

[15] *King of the Beggars,* p. 213.

[16] Charles Neider, ed., *The Stature of Thomas Mann,* p. 222.*

[17] O'Faolain has relied heavily for factual information on J. K. Graham's unpublished thesis, "An Historical Study of Hugh O'Neill."* But the psychological delineation is mainly his own.

[18] *King of the Beggars,* p. 144.

[19] *Ibid.,* p. 147.

[20] *Ibid.,* p. 232.

[21] *Ibid.,* p. 51.

Chapter 3

[1] "Eamon De Valera," *The Bell,* 10, 1 (April, 1945), 1.

[2] "Principles and Propaganda," *The Bell,* 10, 3 (June, 1945), 200.

[3] Letter to the editor, *Commonweal,* 15, 10 (January 6, 1932), 273.

[4] O'Faolain doubted whether De Valera would be able to make any practical contribution to the development of a genuinely Irish civilization (see "Celts and Irishmen," *New Statesman and Nation,* 4, 77 (August 13, 1932). His caution arose from his difficulty in determining De Valera's actual political aims. Ultranationalist ideas, he felt, might take precedence over more pressing and fundamental economic and social problems. De Valera, he argued, wavered between the role of reformer and rebel, effective as the latter but unproven as the former (see "Mr. De Valera—Rebel or Reformer?"

New Statesman and Nation, 4, 77 (August 13, 1932), 173).

5 "Principles and Propaganda," 197.

6 "The Irish Year," *New Statesman and Nation,* 6 (December 9, 1933) 734.

7 "Revamping Ireland," *Commonweal,* 22, 18 (August 30, 1933), 418.

8 "The New Ireland, A Letter from any Irishman to any Englishman," *Yale Review,* 25 (Winter, 1936), 325–27.

9 *De Valera,* pp. 68–69.*

10 *Ibid.,* pp. 49–69.

11 *Ibid.,* pp. 67–68.

12 *Ibid.,* p. 116.

13 *Ibid.,* p. 123.

14 *Ibid.,* p. 71.

15 *Constitution of the Free State of Ireland* (Dublin, n.d.).

16 *Irish Times,* May 17, 1926.

17 *Irish Independent,* June 24, 1929.

18 *Dail Debates,* 41, 1101, 1102.

19 *Constance Markiewicz,* p. 304.

20 *De Valera,* p. 123.

21 *Ibid.,* pp. 120–21.

22 "Eamon De Valera," 314.

23 "Principles and Propaganda," 197.

24 *De Valera,* pp. 123–24.

25 O'Sullivan, *Irish Free State,* pp. 385–88.*

26 *De Valera,* p. 147.

27 O'Faolain was not alone in his opinion of this document. During the Dail debate on the constitution, Dr. Rowlette pointed out that a constitution is essentially a legal document and should be declaratory of the structure of the state and, in particular, of the rights of the individual citizen. But this constitution was characterized more by directive than by declaratory phrases and had a distinctly homiletic tone. General principles were qualified to such an extent that their exact meaning was unclear, since the qualification almost contradicted the main statement (*Dail Debates,* 58, 386–87).

Donal O'Sullivan has also commented on the homiletic tone and has observed in addition that the constitution is unique among the constitutions of the world in at least three aspects. It does not designate the character of the state, whether monarchy or republic; it makes little reference to external affairs; and the language of the basic text (Irish) is one that the vast majority of members of Parliament, Bench and Bar, and of the population generally can neither read, write, speak, nor understand (*Irish Free State,* p. 492).

Padraic Colum voiced a critical comment on the evasiveness on fundamental issues, maintaining that "this deliberate veiling of essential situations, is bound to create a bad moral atmosphere in the country. The Irish people either see through it or make up their minds that they do not want to see through it, and in either case the result is morally bad: it makes for either cynicism or pretense" (*Irish Free State*, pp. 297–9).

28 *De Valera*, pp. 147–48.
29 *The Irish*, p. 120.*
30 *The Autobiography of Wolfe Tone*, p. 123.*
31 *De Valera*, p. 53.
32 *Ibid.*, p. 9.
33 *Ibid.*, p. 180.
34 "Principles and Propaganda," 202.
35 *Ibid.*, 203.
36 *The Irish*, pp. 168–69.
37 "Ireland After Yeats," *The Bell*, 18, 2 (Summer, 1953), 40.
38 "Principles and Propaganda," 204–5.

Chapter 4

1 *Constance Markievicz*, p. 74.
2 *De Valera*, p. 18.
3 *Ibid.*, pp. 23–24.
4 "Ireland After Yeats," 40.
5 "The Dilemma of Irish Letters," *The Month*, 2, 6 (December, 1949), 375.
6 *Ibid.*
7 Trilling, *The Liberal Imagination*, p. 207.*
8 *Ibid.*
9 "The Dilemma of Irish Letters," 371.
10 "The New Directions in Irish Literature," *Bookman*, 85, 5 (September, 1932), 447.
11 O'Faolain's attack on seventeenth- and eighteenth-century Irish culture as the decaying remnant of the former, aristocratic, more valuable heritage was justified. But his account of this culture was contradictory and inconsistent. Searching for evidence of the state of the national mind and not for literary virtues, he discovered a division in Irish life as revealed by the poets. They identified with the aristocratic past and thought solely in terms of their own class; they despised the people and fawned on the English conquerors. The twin themes of their poetry were the possibility of the return of the Stuarts and of the old patronage. As a result the people had little interest in the poetry. But having established this dichotomy, O'Faolain also praised O'Connell for liberating the people as much

from outdated loyalties to the aristocratic past as from unwilling loyalties forced on them by their English masters. He took the limited appeal of the poets and made it of national importance. But there is no real evidence that the people were hypnotized by the past and little justification for praising O'Connell as rejecting the Gaelic past as a necessary way of removing "the outer trappings of Gaeldom" (*King of the Beggars,* p. 29).

[12] Corkery, *Synge and Anglo-Irish Literature,* pp. 3–6.*

[13] Review of *Synge and Anglo-Irish Literature, Criterion,* 11, 42 (October, 1931), 141–42.

[14] "The Senate and Censorship," *The Bell,* 5, 4 (January, 1943), 249.

[15] "Emancipation of Irish Writers," *Yale Review,* 23 (Spring, 1934), 496.

[16] "Ireland After Yeats," 43.

[17] "Thoughts of a Juryman," *The Bell,* 9, 5 (February, 1945), 373.

[18] *The Irish,* p. 179.

[19] "Answer to a Criticism," *The Bell,* 1, 3 (December, 1940), 6.

[20] "To What Possible Future," *The Bell,* 4, 1 (April, 1942), 8.

[21] *Op. cit.,* 5.

[22] "Attitudes," *The Bell,* 2, 6 (September, 1941), 7.

[23] *Ibid.,* 8–9.

[24] "Standards and Tastes," *The Bell,* 2, 3 (June, 1941), 5.

[25] "From Bottom to Top," *The Bell,* 1, 6 (March, 1941), 2.

[26] "Signing Off," *The Bell,* 12, 1 (April, 1946), 2.

[27] "On Editing a Magazine," *The Bell,* 9, 2 (November, 1944), 100.

[28] "Silent Ireland," *The Bell,* 6, 6 (September, 1953), 458.

[29] "The Dilemma of Irish Letters," 377.

[30] "On Being an Irish Writer," *Spectator,* 191 (July 3, 1953), 25.

[31] "The Pleasures and Pains of Ireland," *The Bell,* 8, 5 (August, 1944), 370.

[32] "Why Don't We See It?" *The Bell,* 5, 3 (December, 1942), 162.

[33] "Gaelic—The Truth," *The Bell,* 5, 5 (February, 1943), 336.

[34] "Standards and Tastes," *The Bell,* 2, 3 June, 1941), 6.

[35] "Tradition and Creation," *The Bell,* 2, 1 (April, 1941), 2.

[36] *Ibid.,* 7.

[37] "The Gaelic and the Good," *The Bell,* 3, 2 (November, 1941), 101.

Chapter 5

[1] He is, in fact, not a prolific writer of short stories. The bulk of his work in this genre has appeared in six volumes: *Midsummer Night Madness* (1932), which contained seven stories; *A Purse of Coppers* (1937), which contained fourteen; *Teresa* (1947), which had thirteen; *The Man Who Invented Sin* (1948), an American edition of *Teresa,* with two new stories—"Up the Bare Stairs" and "The Fur Coat";

and *The Finest Stories of Sean O'Faolain* (1957), which was a selection of nineteen stories from the previous volumes with eight additional titles: "One True Friend," "The Judas Touch," "The End of the Record," "Lord and Master," "Persecution Mania," "An Enduring Friendship," "Childybawn," and "Lovers of the Lake." A British edition entitled *The Stories of Sean O'Faolain* appeared in 1958. His most recent collection is *I Remember! I Remember!* (1962). It has seven titles, two of which, "Love's Young Dream" and "No Country for Old Men," are excerpts from unpublished novels; four others are earlier stories: "The Sugawn Chair" (1947), "The Younger Generation" (1951, entitled "Eden"), "Angels and Ministers of Grace" (1956), and "Miracles Don't Happen Twice" (1954). Apart from these volumes there are a small number of stories to be found in Irish, English, and American magazines.

All quotations in Part II, unless otherwise stated, are from *The Finest Stories of Sean O'Faolain.**
² *Vive Moi!*, p. 225.
³ *Ibid.*, p. 226.

Chapter 8

¹ *The Short Story*, ix.
² "Proletarian Novel," *London Mercury*, 35 (April, 1937), 587.
³ *The Vanishing Hero, Studies in Novelists of the Twenties*, p. 195.*
⁴ *The Short Story*, pp. 159–160.

Chapter 9

¹ *Teresa and Other Stories*, pp. 146–47.*
² *Ibid.*, p. 147.
³ *Ibid.*, p. 160.
⁴ *The Irish*, p. 11.
⁵ *Ibid.*, p. 46. See also S. F. Kenney, *Sources for the Early History of Ireland*, p. 302.*

Chapter 12

¹ All quotations from this book are from the 1962 edition.*
² "On Writing: An Interview," by R. Davis, *Mademoiselle*, 56 (March, 1963), 213.
³ *Short Stories, A Study in Pleasure*, p. 18.*

Chapter 13

¹ All quotations from *A Nest of Simple Folk* are from the Viking Press edition.*

² All quotations from *Bird Alone* are from the Jonathan Cape edition.*
³ All quotations from *Come Back to Erin* are from the Viking Press edition.*
⁴ *King of the Beggars,* p. 133.
⁵ *The Finest Stories,* p. 251.
⁶ The sense of loss is a constant theme in this novel. Leo Donnell remembered his boyhood freedom when shut away in Portland jail. Bid Hussey's happy girlhood wilted into sorrow through anxiety and hard work in Cork.
⁷ *The Vanishing Hero,* pp. 219–20.
⁸ *Ibid.,* p. 221.
⁹ *Ibid.*
¹⁰ *James Joyce* (New York, 1962), p. 47.
¹¹ "Irish Literature Today," *Atlantic Monthly,* 176 (March, 1945), 70.

Chapter 14

¹ "Literary Provincialism," *Commonweal,* 17, 8 (December 21, 1932), 214.
² "Emancipation of Irish Writers," 492.
³ *Ibid.,* 497.
⁴ *Ibid.,* 501.
⁵ "Yeats and the Younger Generation," *Horizon,* 5, 25 (January, 1942), 50.
⁶ *The Vanishing Hero,* p. 14.
⁷ *Ibid.,* p. 17.
⁸ Frank O'Connor, "The Future of Irish Literature," *Horizon,* 5, 25 (January, 1942), 58.
⁹ "Literary Provincialism," 214–15.
¹⁰ *Op. cit.,* 61.
¹¹ "The Pleasures and Pains of Ireland," 371.
¹² "Plea for a New Type of Novel," *Virginia Quarterly Review,* 10 (April, 1934), 197.
¹³ "The Modern Novel, A Catholic Point of View," *Virginia Quarterly Review,* 11 (July, 1935), 340.
¹⁴ "It No Longer Matters, or The Death of the English Novel," *Criterion,* 15, LVIII (October, 1935), 50–52.
¹⁵ "The Modern Novel," 350.
¹⁶ "Proletarian Novel," 584.
¹⁷ "Yeats and the Younger Generation," 43.
¹⁸ "A.E. and W.B.," *Virginia Quarterly Review,* 15, 1 (January, 1939), 55.

Chapter 15

[1] *Vive Moi!,* p. 110.
[2] *Ibid.,* p. 111.
[3] *Ibid.,* p. 112.
[4] "Autobiographical Sketch," *Wilson Bulletin,* 8, 6 (March, 1934), 380.
[5] *Newman's Way,* p. 189.*
[6] *South to Sicily,* p. 34.*

Bibliography

Major Works

Lyrics and Satires from Tom Moore. Cuala Press, Dublin, 1929.
Midsummer Night Madness and other stories. With an introduction
by Edward Garnett. Jonathan Cape, Ltd., London, 1932.
The Life Story of Eamon De Valera. Talbot Press, Ltd., Dublin, 1933.
A Nest of Simple Folk. The Viking Press, Inc., New York, 1934.
Constance Markievicz, or The Average Revolutionary, A Biography.
Jonathan Cape, Ltd., London, 1934.
There's a Birdie in the Cage. Grayson and Grayson, London, 1935.
Bird Alone. Jonathan Cape, Ltd., London, 1936. Reprint: Millington
Press, London, 1974.
The Born Genius: A Short Story. Schuman's, Detroit, 1936.
A Purse of Coppers: Short Stories. Jonathan Cape, Ltd., London, 1937.
The Autobiography of Theobald Wolfe Tone. Thomas Nelson & Sons,
Ltd., London, 1937.
She Had to Do Something: A Comedy in Three Acts. Jonathan Cape,
Ltd., London, 1938.
*The Silver Branch: A Collection of the Best Old Irish Lyrics, Variously
Translated, Chosen by Sean O'Faolain*. Jonathan Cape, Ltd.,
London, 1938. Reprint: Books for Libraries, N.Y., 1968.

King of the Beggars, A Life of Daniel O'Connell, the *Irish Liberator.* in *A Study of the Rise of the Modern Irish Democracy* (1775–1847). The Viking Press, Inc., N.Y., 1938. Reprints: Allen Figgis, Dublin, 1972; Greenwood Press, N.Y., 1976; Poolbeg Press, Dublin, 1980.

De Valera. Penguin Books Limited, Harmondsworth, Middlesex, 1939.

Come Back to Erin. The Viking Press, Inc., New York, 1940.

An Irish Journey. Longmans, Green & Co., Ltd., London, 1940.

The Great O'Neill, A Biography of Hugh O'Neill, Earl of Tyrone. 1850–1616. Duell, Sloan & Pearce, New York, 1942.

The Story of Ireland. William Collins Sons & Co., London, 1943.

D 83222: I Did Penal Servitude. Preface by Sean O'Faolain. Metropolitan Press, Dublin, 1945.

Samuel Lover, *Adventures of Handy Andy.* Edited and introduced by Sean O'Faolain. Parkside Press, Dublin, 1945.

Teresa, and other stories. Jonathan Cape, Ltd., London, 1947.

The Irish. Penguin Books, West Drayton, Middlesex, 1947. *The Irish: A Character Study.* The Devin-Adair Co., New York, 1948. Reprint: Penguin, Harmondsworth, 1980.

The Short Story. William Collins Sons & Co., London, 1948.

The Man Who Invented Sin, and Other Stories. The Devin-Adair Co., New York, 1949.

A Summer in Italy. Eyre and Spottiswoode, Ltd., London, 1949.

Newman's Way, The Odyssey of John Henry Newman. Longmans, Green & Co., London, 1952.

South to Sicily. William Collins Sons & Co., London, 1953. *An Autumn in Italy.* The Devin-Adair Co., New York, 1953.

With the Gaels of Wexford. Introduction and compiled by Sean O'Faolain. Enniscorthy, 1955.

The Vanishing Hero, Studies in Novelists of the Twenties. Eyre and Spottiswoode Ltd., London, 1956. Reprint. Books for Libraries, N.Y. 1971.

The Finest Stories of Sean O'Faolain. Little, Brown and Company, Boston, 1957.

The Stories of Sean O'Faolain. Rupert Hart-Davis, Ltd., London, 1958.

John O'Donoghoe, *In A Quiet Land.* With a foreword by Sean O'Faolain. B. T. Batsford, Ltd., London, 1957.

Short Stories, A Study in Pleasure. Edited by Sean O'Faolain. Little, Brown and Company, Boston, 1961.

I Remember! I Remember! Little, Brown and Company, Boston, 1961.

Vive Moi! Little, Brown and Company, Boston, 1964.

The Heat of the Sun, Stories and Tales. Little, Brown and Company, Boston, 1966.

The Talking Trees. Atlantic Monthly Press, Boston, 1970; Jonathan Cape,

London, 1971.
Foreign Affairs. Constable, London, 1976; Little, Brown, Boston, 1976; Penguin, Harmondsworth, 1978.
Selected Stories. Constable, London, 1978; Little, Brown, Boston, 1978.
And Again? Constable, London, 1979.
Collected Stories, Constable, London, 3 vols., 1980-82.

Minor Works

"na tri oighreachta." Aistrithe O'n bhFraincis. *Father Matthew Record,* January, 1922.
"Prendergast," a short story in Irish. *Earna* (11, 5), 12–16, Meitheamh, 1924.
Uirscealta. "Maire." *Fainne an Lae,* Samhain 14, 1925.
"Deich mBliana d'Fhas i mBeatha Fhile," a study of Daibhidh Ua Bruadair's development between the ages of 40 and 50.
Earna (11, 7), 26–33, Feile Padraig, 1925; (8), 14–17, Nodlaig, 1925.
"The Best Irish Literature." *Irish Statesman* (4, 26), 816, September 5, 1925.
"Munster Fine Art Club." *Irish Statesman* (5, 9), 273, November 7, 1925; letter (5, 11), 333, November 21, 1925.
"A Plea for a New Irish Scholarship." *Irish Statesman* (5, 10), 296–97, November 14, 1925.
"Irish and Anglo-Irish Modes in Literature." *Irish Statesman* (5, 18), 558–59, January 9, 1926.
"Form in Poetry." *Irish Statesman* (5, 19), 591–92, January 16, 1926.
"In Lilliput." *Irish Statesman* (5, 22), 680–81, February 6, 1926.
"The New Education." *Cork Tribune* (1, 5), April 9, 1926; letter (1, 8), 16–17, April 30, 1926.
"Second Thoughts." *Irish Tribune* (1, 6), 7, April 16, 1926.
"The Gaeltacht Tradition." *Irish Statesman* (6, 7), 175–76, April 24, 1926.
"Calf Love." *Irish Tribune* (1, 10), 10–22, May 14, 1926.
"The Language Problem": 1. "Is Irish Worth Reviving?" *Irish Tribune* (1, 18), 20–21, July 9, 1926; 2. "Irish—An Empty Barrel?" (5, 19), 6–8, July 16, 1926; 3. "What a Bilingual Ireland Means. What Does an Irish-speaking Ireland Imply?" (1, 20), 9–10, July 23, 1926; 4. "Constructive" (1, 21), 13–15, July 30, 1926.
"The Spirit of the Nation." *Irish Tribune* (1, 20), 23, July 23, 1926.
"Under the Roof." *Dial* (81, 3), 220–23, September, 1926.
"The Bomb Shop." *Dial* (82, 3), 197–209, March, 1927.
"As Others See Ireland." *Irish Statesman* (8, 11) 256–57, May 21, 1927.
"Tristram" (E. A. Robinson), "The King's Henchmen" (Edna St. V. Millay). *Irish Statesman* (8, 26), 619–20, September 3, 1927.

"Fugue." *Hound and Horn* (2, 1), 7–28, September, 1928.

"Style and the Limitations of Speech." *Criterion* (8) 67–87, September, 1928.

"Cruelty and Beauty of Words." *Virginia Quarterly Review* (4), 208–25, April, 1928.

"Carol in Ireland." *Commonweal* (9), 261–62, January 2, 1929.

"Four Irish Generations." *Commonweal* (9, 26), 750–51, May 1, 1929.

"Almost Music." *Hound and Horn* (2, 2), 178–180, January-March, 1929.

"Young Man." *Living Age* (336), 195, May, 1929.

"Note on Masefield." *Dial* (86), 586–88, July, 1929.

"William Butler Yeats: Selected Poems, Lyrical and Narrative." *Criterion* (9, XXXVI), 523–28, April, 1930.

"Correspondence." *Criterion* (10, XXVIII), 147, October, 1930.

"New Irish Revolutionaries." *Commonweal* (15), 39–41, November 11, 1931; letter, 273, January 6, 1932.

"A.E: Enchantment, and Other Poems." *Criterion* (10, XLI), 748–50, July, 1931.

"Synge and Anglo-Irish Literature." *Criterion* (11, XLII), 140–42, October, 1931.

"Goldylocks and Curlypoll." *Spectator* (148), 620–21, April 30, 1932.

"A.E: Song and Its Fountain." *Criterion* (11, XLV), 725–27, July, 1932.

"Celts and Irishmen." *New Statesman and Nation* (4, 74), 93–94, July 23, 1932.

"De Valera, Rebel and Reformer?" *New Statesman and Nation* (4, 77), 173–74, August 13, 1932.

"New Directions in Irish Literature." *Bookman* (75), 446–48, September, 1932.

"Schwarzkopf and Godenhaaar." *Commonweal* (16, 23) 534–35, October 5, 1932.

"So this is the Pierian Spring?" *Spectator* (149), 477–78, October 15, 1932.

"Irish Year." *New Statesman and Nation* (6), 733–34, December 9, 1933.

"Literary Provincialism." *Commonweal* (17, 8), 214–15, December 21, 1932.

"An Irish Poet." *Commonweal* (17, 9), 251, December 28, 1932.

"Confessional." *New Statesman and Nation* (6), 104–05, July 22, 1933.

"Jubilee in the North Abbey." *Lovat Dicksons' Magazine*, 60–74, December, 1933.

"An Irish Letter." *Hound and Horn* (7, 2), 271–73, January-March, 1934; *New Statesman and Nation*, December 9, 1933.

"Letter from a Novelist to an Idealist." *Motley* (11, 7), 3-5, November,

1933.
"Autobiographical Sketch." *Wilson Bulletin* (8, 6), 380, March, 1934.
"Emancipation of Irish Writers." *Yale Review* (23), 485–503, Spring, 1934.
"An Irish Schooling." *Life and Letters* (10, 52), 27–32, April, 1934.
"Plea for a New Type of Novel." *Virginia Quarterly Review* (10), 189–99, April, 1934.
"A Born Genius." *Lovat Dickson's Magazine*, 468–98, April, 1934.
"Criticism by Forgetting." *Bookman* (86), 243–44; August, 1934.
"Sullivan's Trousers." *London Mercury* (31), 42–52, November, 1934.
"Irish Poetry Since the War." *London Mercury* (31), 545–52, April, 1935.
"*Give Us Back Bill Sykes.*" *Spectator* (154), 242–43, February 15, 1935.
"Novelists See Too Much." *Spectator* (154), 385–86, March 8, 1935.
"Poor Scholar." *Commonweal* (22, 5), 127–28, May 31, 1935.
"W. B. Yeats." *English Review* (9), 686–88, June, 1935.
"The Modern Novel: A Catholic Point of View." *Virginia Quarterly Review* (11), 339–51, July, 1935.
"Cost of Living in Ireland To-day." *New Statesman and Nation* (10), 156–57, August 3, 1935.
"A.E." *London Mercury* (32, 190), 361–64, August, 1935.
"Revamping Ireland." *Commonweal* (22, 18), 417–18, August 30, 1935.
"Meeting." *Living Age* (349), 66–69, September, 1935.
"Irish Letters: To-day and To-morrow." *Fortnightly Review* (138), 369–71, September, 1935.
"It No Longer Matters, or The Death of the English Novel." *Criterion* (15, LVIII), 49–56, October, 1935.
"The Case of Sean O'Casey." *Commonweal* (22, 24), 577–78, October 11, 1935.
"English as it is Spoken." *Commonweal* (22, 26), 633, October 25, 1935.
"New Ireland." *Yale Review* (25), 321–329, December, 1935.
"Pigeon-Holing the Modern Novel." *London Mercury* (33), 159–64, December, 1935.
"Christmas Rain." *Spectator* (104), 10–27, December 20, 1935.
"William Butler Yeats. Aetat 70." *Irish Times*, June 13, 1935.
"Re-Orientation of Irish Letters." *Irish Times*, September 21, 1935.
"Almost a Great Novelist." *Commonweal* (23, 2), 293–95, January 10, 1936.
"Roger Casement." *American Mercury* (37), 160–67, February, 1936.
"Daniel Corkery." *Dublin Magazine* (10, 2), 49–61, April-June, 1936; *Commonweal* (22), 35–37, November 6, 1936.
"In Defence of 'Oh Yeah!' " *Spectator* (157), 53–54, July 10, 1936.
"Gamut of Irish Fiction." *Saturday Review of Literature* (14), 19–20, August 1, 1936.

"Pater and Moore." *London Mercury* (34), 330–38, August, 1936.

"Is an Irish Culture Possible; James Devane." *Ireland To-day* (1), 21–31, 32, October, 1936.

"Charles Dickens and W. M. Thackeray," in *The English Novelists. A Survey of the Novel by Twenty Contemporary Novelists,* ed. Derek Verschoyle. Chatto and Windus, London, 1936.

"The Dangers of Censorship." *Ireland To-day* (1), 57–36, November, 1936.

"Stories of Three Decades: Thomas Mann." *Ireland To-day* (1), December, 1936.

"It is Raining Over Here." *Commonweal* (25, 9), 243, December 25, 1936.

"Chronos Ate His Children." *London Mercury* (35), 108–09, December, 1936.

"A Broken World." *London Mercury* (35) 123–32, December, 1936.

"The New Ireland. A Letter from any Irishman to any Englishman." *Yale Review* (25), 320–29, Winter, 1936.

"Proletarian Novel." *London Mercury* (35), 583–89, April, 1937.

"Holidays in Ireland." *Spectator* (158), 120, June 25, 1937.

"The Priests and the People." *Ireland To-day* (11), 31–38, July, 1937.

"Discord." *London Mercury* (36), 239–45, July, 1937.

'Don Quixote O'Flaherty." *London Mercury and Bookman* (37) 170–75, December, 1937.

"The Living Torch: A Memoir of A.E." *London Mercury and Bookman* (37), 217, December, 1937.

"O Yeah?" *Living Age* (384), 256–58, May, 1938.

"Abbey Festival." *New Statesman and Nation* (16), 281–82, August 20, 1938.

"O'Faolain Replies to Professor Tierney." *Leader* (76), 521–22, August 6, 1938; "The Gaelic Corpse." 565–67, August 20, 1938.

"A.E. and W.B." *Virginia Quarterly Review* (15, 1), 41–57, January, 1939.

"William Butler Yeats." *Spectator* (162), 183, February, 1939.

"W. B. Yeats." *New Statesman and Nation* (17), 209, February 11, 1939.

"Lords and Commons." *Spectator* (162), 801, May 12, 1939.

"Murderer." *Virginia Quarterly Review* (15, 3), 371–78, July, 1939.

"How the Irishman Talks." *Commonweal* (31, 7), 158–59, December 8, 1939.

"Provincialism and Literature" *Motley* (1, 3), 3-4, August, 1939.

"Warder." *Virginia Quarterly Review* (16, 4) 513–22, Autumn, 1940.

"Greatest of War Books." *Yale Review* (30), 141–49, September, 1940; "Greatest War Novel." *Bell* (5 ,4), 290–98, January, 1943.

"Fine Cottage Furniture." *Bell* (1, 3), 28–30, December, 1940.

"Jack B. Yeats." *Bell* (1, 4), 33–36, January, 1941.

"The Lonely Woman." *Yale Review* (31, 2), 269–78, December, 1941; *Bell* (17, 4), 205–12, July, 1952.

"Ah, Wisha! The Irish Novel." *Virginia Quarterly Review* (17), 265–74, Spring, 1941.

"Yeats and the Younger Generation." *Horizon* (5), 43–54, January, 1942.

"New Writers." *Bell* (3, 5), 370, February, 1942.

"Two Kinds of Novel." *Bell* (4, 1), 64–70, April, 1942.

"New Writers." *Bell* (4, 4), 253–54, July, 1942.

"Lady Lucifer." *Bell* (5, 1) 55–62, October, 1942.

"Twilight in Rome." *Bell* (5, 2), 127–34, November, 1942.

"Drama in Wexford." *Bell* (5, 5), 390–96, February, 1943.

"Antonio Fogazzaro." *Bell* (5, 6), 475–81, March, 1943.

"The Strange Case of Sean O'Casey." *Bell* (6, 2), 112–21, May, 1943.

"Case of the Young Irish Writer." *Commonweal* (38), 392, August 6, 1943.

"Personal Anthologies — 1." *Bell* (6, 6), 496–502, September, 1943; letter, *Bell* (7, 1), 76–77, October, 1943.

"The Land of the Great Image: Maurice Collis." *Bell* (7, 1), 78–80, October, 1943.

"Sense and Nonsense in Poetry." *Bell* (7, 2), 156–69, November, 1943.

"The Craft of the Short Story": 1. "When is a Story not a Story." *Bell* (7, 4), 337–44, January, 1944; 2. "Some Essential Comparisons." *Bell* (7, 5), 403–10, February, 1944; 3. "Significant Construction." *Bell* (7, 6), 529–36, March, 1944; 4. "Instead of Plot." *Bell* (8, 1), 46–54, April, 1944; 5. "The Problem of Style." *Bell* (8, 4), 306–14, July, 1944.

"Teresa." *Virginia Quarterly Review* (20, 2), 1944.

"The Greatest of These." *Bell* (7, 4), 360–62, January, 1944.

"Yesterday Morning: Lynn Doyle." *Bell* (7, 6), 543–45, March, 1944.

"Craft of the Short Story: Lowbrow." *Bell* (7, 6), 536–37, March, 1944.

"The Man Who Invented Sin." *Bell* (9, 8), 219–32, December, 1944.

"Passion." *Virginia Quarterly Review* (21, 2), 250–55, April, 1945.

"A Tale of a Town." *Bell* (10, 2), 106–21, May, 1945.

"*The Fourth Estate* — VI; Verdict on 'The Bell' by Vivian Mercier." *Bell* (10, 2), 156–67, May, 1945; (10,5), 431–37, August, 1945.

"The Trout." *Colliers* (15), 23, May 12, 1945; *Bell* (10, 6), 489–92, September, 1945.

"Shaw's Prefaces." *Bell* (12, 5), 425–32, August, 1946.

"Vive la France." *Irish Writing* (1, 1), 9–18, 1946.

"Innocence." *Yale Review* (36, 2) 257–61, December, 1946.

"The Silence of the Valley." *Virginia Quarterly Review* (23, 2), 209–30, April, 1947; *Bell* (12, 6), 466–89, September, 1946.

"Daudet's Wife." *New English Review* (15), December, 1947.

"The Sugawn Chair." *Bell* (15, 3), 22–25, December, 1947.

"Getting at Which Public?" *Virginia Quarterly Review* (24, 1), 90–95, January, 1948.

"Evening Star." *Irish Writing* (5), 9–20, July, 1948.

"Romance and the Devil." *New English Review* (1, 3), 193–96; November, 1948; *Atlantic* (183, 1), 73–75, January, 1949.

"Daniel O'Connell." *The Month* (2, 5), 340-43, November, 1949.

"The Bells that Nobody Heard." *Atlantic* (182, 6), 40–42, December, 1948.

"On Translating from the Irish." *Poetry Ireland* (4), 14–17, January, 1949.

"Secret of the Short Story." *United Nations World* (3), 37–38, March, 1949.

"End of the Record." *New Statesman and Nation* (38), 381–82, October, 8, 1949.

"Persecution Mania." *Kenyon Review* (11, 4), 588–94, Autumn, 1949.

"The Song of Salesman MacGinty." *Envoy* (1, 1), 20–26, December, 1949.

"The Dilemma of Irish Letters." *The Month* (2, 6), 366–79, December, 1949.

"The First Kiss." *Blarney Annual of Fact and Fancy* (2), 42–44, 1949–1950.

"The Unfallen: Donat O'Donnell." *Envoy* (1, 1), 44–50, December, 1949; reply by O'Faolain: (1, 2), 87–90, January, 1950; answer by O'Donnell (1, 3), 89–90, February, 1950.

"The City of Rome." *Commonweal* (11), 575–76, March 10, 1950.

"The Sighing Age." *Irish Writing* (12), 5–18, September, 1950.

"The Ould Jug." *Bell* (16, 2), 52–56, November, 1950.

"Religious Art." *Bell* (16, 4), 39–42, January, 1951.

"The Liberal Ethic." *Bell* (16, 5), 5–11, February, 1951.

"Autoantiamericanism." *Bell* (16, 6), 7–18, March, 1951; (17, 2), 8–28, May, 1951; (17, 3), June, 1951.

"The Death of Nationalism." *Bell* (17, 2), 44–53, May, 1951.

"From Italy." *Commonweal* (54), 139–141, May 18, 1961.

"The Dail and the Bishops." *Bell* (17, 3), 5–13, June, 1951.

"From Sicily." *Commonweal* (54), 546–47, September 14, 1951.

"The Bishop of Galway and the *Bell*." *Bell* (17, 6), 15–17, September, 1951.

"Eden." *Bell* (17, 9), 18–26, December, 1951.

"The Divided Generation." *Bell* (17, 11), 5–11, February, 1952.

"The New Criticism." *Bell* (18, 3), 133–42, June, 1952.

"Gamblers." *Virginia Quarterly Review* (28, 3), 417–34, July, 1952.

"Imaginary Conversation." *Bell* (17, 5), 261–73, October, 1952.

"Persecution Mania." *Bell* (18, 6), 325–30, November, 1952.

"Ireland After Yeats." *Books Abroad* (26), 325–33, Autumn, 1952; *Bell* (18, 2), 37–48, Summer, 1953.

"Enduring Friendship." *Commonweal* (57), 355–57, January 9, 1953.

"On a Recent Incident at the International Affairs Association." *Bell* (18, 9), 517–27, February, 1953.

"Golden Hill Towns of Italy." *Commonweal* (57), 571–73, March 13, 1953.

"Love Among the Irish." *Life* (34), 140–47, March 16, 1953; *Readers' Digest* (63), 53–57, November, 1953.

"On Being an Irish Writer." *Spectator* (191), 25–26, July 3, 1953; *Commonweal* (58), 339–41, July 10, 1953.

"Visit to Padre Pio." *Commonweal* (58), 507–09, August 28, 1953.

"The Irish and the Latins." *Bell* (19, 1), 145–50, December, 1953.

"The Irish; Thoughts on St. Patrick's Day." *The New York Times Magazine*, March 14, 1954.

"Miracles Don't Happen Twice." *Irish Writing* (3, 28), 18–21, September, 1954.

"Childybawn." *Bell* (19, 10), 11–20, November, 1954.

"Italy; Her Wonderful People." *Holiday* (17), 36–43, April, 1955.

"For the Child and for the Wise Man." *The New York Times Magazine*, March 27, 1955.

"Venice." *Holiday* (18), 42–47, October, 1955.

"Sei romanzieri in cerca di uneroe." *Quaderni AC1*, Torino, 39–65, 1955.

"Doomed Daredevils of the I.R.A. Warm Up Their Forty Year's War." *Life* (39), 139, November 7, 1955.

"St. Patrick's Day; Thoughts about Ireland." *The New York Times Magazine*, March 11, 1956.

"Angels and Ministers of Grace." *Irish Writing* (4, 34), 8–19, Spring, 1956.

"Sicily." *Holiday* (19), 48–51, May, 1956.

"Las Vegas." *Holiday* (20), 56–61, September, 1956.

"Naples." *Holiday* (20), 98–104, October, 1956.

"Looking Back at Writing." *Atlantic* (198), 75–76, December, 1956.

"End of the Record." *Atlantic* (198), 53–55, December, 1956.

"Philadelphia Tradition." *Holiday* (21), 50–67, May, 1957.

"Liberal Tory?" *Spectator* (199), 21, July 5, 1957.

"World of Los Angeles." *Holiday* (22), 50–63, October, 1957.

Comments on "The Worm as Hero: Brian T. Cleeve." *Studies*, 29–31.

"Ireland." *Holiday* (23), 54, June, 1958.

"Texas." *Holiday* (24), 34–49, October, 1958.

"Flavour of Boston." *Holiday* (24), 92–101, December, 1958.

"Love's Young Dream." *Saturday Evening Post* (232), 40–41, October

3, 1959.

"Touch of Autumn in the Air." *Atlantic Monthly* (204), 76–79, November, 1959.

"Lovely Lakes of Italy." *Holiday* (25), 90–97, March, 1960.

"Pontificial Splendour." *Holiday* (27), 82–91, April, 1960.

"New Spirit of St. Louis." *Holiday* (27), 80–85, May, 1960.

"Convention" in S. Barnet, M. Berman and W. Burto (eds.) *The Study of Literature; a handbook of critical essays and terms.* Little, Brown, Boston, 1960, 117-36.

"Design in Ireland: a symposium of comments." *Forgnán, Journal of the Building Centre* (1, 3), 6-12, March, 1962.

"Is Architecture a Was?" *Forgnán, Journal of the Building Centre* (1, 5), 7-11, May, 1962.

"A Clean, Well-lighted Place" in R. P. Weeks (ed.) *Hemingway: a collection of critical essays.* Prentice-Hall, 1962.

"On Writing: An Interview," by R. Diers. *Mademoiselle* (56), 151, March, 1963.

"Irish Families." *Nation* (196), 269–71, March 30, 1963.

"Fair Dublin." *Holiday* (33), 72, April, 1963.

"One Man, One Boat, One Girl." *Saturday Evening Post* (236), 48–49, October 19, 1963.

"Too Beautiful, Too Good." *Ladies Home Journal* (80), 84–87, October, 1963.

"Convention"; excerpt from *The Short Story* in H. S. Summers (ed.) *Discussions of the Short Story.* Heath, 1963.

"Southern Italy." *Holiday* (36), 38–46, September, 1964.

"Writer in Search of Himself," excerpt from *Vive Moi! Atlantic Monthly* (214), 104–108, October, 1964.

"Miracle of Lourdes." *Holiday* (36), 66–7, November, 1964.

"Vive Moi!" excerpt from the book of the same title. *Atlantic Monthly* (213), 81, January, 1964.

"The Meaning of Place" in Francis Brown (ed.) *The New York Times Book Review. Opinions and Perspectives.* Houghton, 1964.

"Faulkner's Stylistic Failings"; excerpts from *The Vanishing Hero* in F. L. Utley, L. Z. Bloom and A. F. Kinney (eds.) *Bear, Man and God: seven approaches to William Faulkner's The Bear.* Random House, 1964.

"Don Juan in Dublin." *Saturday Evening Post* (238), 48–51, January 19, 1965.

"Three Shapes of Love." *Atlantic Monthly* (215), 124–28, March, 1965.

"In Search of Sardinia." *Holiday* (39), 52–3+, January, 1966.

"Operation Rosebud." *Redbook* (127), 58–60, August, 1966.

"Jungle of Love." *Saturday Evening Post* (239), 54–63, August 13, 1966.

"About Individual Works: AE and WB" in M. Cowley (ed.) "Yeats and

O'Faolain. *Think Back On Us . . . A contemporary chronicle of the 1930s.* Southern Illinois University Press, 1967.

"Smithsonian: biographer to the world." *Holiday* (42), 44-9, August, 1967.

"Fool of a Man." story. *Saturday Evening Post* (241), 60-65, September 7, 1968.

"This is Your Life: Louisa May Alcott." *Holiday* (44), 18, November, 1968.

"Turin." *Holiday* (43), 58-65, February, 1968.

"Vatican City: Where the decisions are made." *Holiday* (44), 68-71, December, 1968.

"What a Stunning Night!" story. *Saturday Evening Post,* (242), 46-7, December 28, 1968.

"Kitchen." story. *Atlantic Monthly* (223), 42-5, June, 1969.

"Planets of the Years." story. *Ladies Home Journal* (86), 102-3, September, 1969.

"Florentine Hill Towns: suburbs Tuscan style." *Holiday* (46), 42-3, September, 1969.

"And Svengali was a Reviewer." in E. F. Brown (ed.) *The Best of "Speaking of Books" from The New York Times Book Review.* Holt, 1969.

"Portrait of the Artist as an Old Man." *Listener* (87), 605-8, May 11, 1972.

"Being an Irish Writer." *Commonweal* (99), 193-5, November 16, 1973 (reprint from July 10, 1953).

"Liberty." story. *Atlantic Monthly* (235), 73-7, April, 1975. *Irish Press,* April 3, 1976.

"Curtain Raisers." *Irish Press,* February 7, 1976; review of Terence De Vere White, *Big Fleas and Little Fleas.*

Irish Press, March 13, 1976, review of Michael McLaverty, *The Road to the Shore.*

Irish Press, March 25, 1976; review of Gillman Noonan, *A Sexual Relationship and other stories.*

"In Search of Truth." *Irish Press,* April 16, 1976; review of Conor Cruise O'Brien, *Writers and Politics.*

"Irish or 'Irish'?" *Irish Press,* May 23, 1976; review of David Marcus (ed.), *Best Irish Short Stories.*

"Dire Innocence." *Irish Press,* June 26, 1976; review of William Trevor, *The Children of Dynmouth.*

"Sex and Sensibility." *Irish Press,* July 17, 1976; review of John Broderick, *The Pride of Summer.*

"More for the Procession." *Irish Press,* August 14, 1976; review of Patrick Boyle, *A View from Calvary and other stories* and of Desmond Hogan, *The Ikon Maker.*

"The O'Flaherty." *Irish Press,* September 16, 1976; review of Liam O'Flaherty, *The Pedlar's Revenge.*

"What is the Stars?" *Irish Press*, November 25, 1976; review of John Banville, *Doctor Copernicus.*

"For to End yet Again." *Irish Press*, December 10, 1976; review of Samuel Beckett.

"A World of Fitzies." *Times Literary Supplement* (3920), April 29, 1977.

"Sean O'Faolain on Frank O'Connor". *Irish Press*, May 26, 1977; review of Maurice Wohlgelernter, *Frank O'Connor; an Introduction.*

"Valedictory." *Irish Press*, January 6, 1977; his farewell as resident reviewer for 1976.

"How Not to Write an Irish Short Story." *Irish Press*, April 29, 1978.

Sunday Press, December 23, 1979; review of his favourite reading of 1979.

"The Burning Deck." *Irish Press*, January 10, 1980; review of Michael O'Beirne, *Mister: A Dublin Childhood.*

"A Present from Clonmacnoise." story. *Irish Press*, May 10, 1980.

"From Huesca with Love and Kisses." story. *Irish Press*, November 4, 1982.

"What it means to be Irish." *Sunday Independent*, March 18, 1984.

Editorials in The Bell

"This is Your Magazine" (1, 1), October, 1940.

"For the Future" (1, 2), November, 1940.

"Answer to a Criticism" (1, 3), December, 1940.

"On Conversation" (1, 4), January, 1941.

"A Challenge" (1, 5), February, 1941.

"From Bottom to Top" (1, 6), March, 1941.

"1916–1941: Tradition and Creation" (2, 1), April, 1941.

"Provincialism" (2, 2), May, 1941.

"Standards and Taste" (2, 3), June, 1941.

"Ulster" (2, 4), July, 1941.

"Our Nasty Novelists" (2, 5), August, 1941.

"Attitudes" (2, 6), September, 1941.

"Beginnings and Blind Alleys" (3, 1), October, 1941.

"The Gaelic and the Good" (3, 2), November, 1941.

"Dare we Suppress that Irish Voice?" (3, 3), December, 1941.

"F. R. Higgins" (3, 4), January, 1942.

"Fifty Years of Irish Literature" (3, 5), February, 1942.

"Books in the Country" (3, 6), March, 1942.

"To What Possible Future. . . ?" (4, 1), April, 1942.

"The Gaelic League" (4, 2), May, 1942.

"The Mart of Ideas" (4, 3), June, 1942.

"An Ulster Issue" (4, 4), July, 1942.

"New Wine in Old Bottles" (4, 6), September, 1942.

"Third Year (5, 1), October, 1942.
"That Typical Irishman" (5, 2), November, 1942.
"Why don't We See It?" (5, 3), December, 1942.
"The Senate and Censorship" (5, 4), January, 1942.
"Gaelic—The Truth" (5, 5), February, 1943.
"Ireland and the Modern World" (5, 6), March, 1943.
"On State Control" (6, 1), April, 1943.
"Books and a Live People" (6, 2), May, 1943.
"The Stuffed Shirts" (6, 3), June, 1943.
"Shadow and Substance" (6, 4), July, 1943.
"Silent Ireland" (6, 6), September, 1943.
"The Plain People of Ireland" (7, 1), October, 1943.
"The State and Its Writers" (7, 2), November, 1943.
"Past Tense" (7, 3), December, 1943.
"One World" (7, 4), January, 1944.
"One World" (7, 5), February, 1944.
"One World" (7, 6), March, 1944.
"The University Question" (8, 1), April, 1944.
"One World" (8, 2), May, 1944.
"Toryism in Trinity" (8, 3), June, 1944.
"One World" (8, 4), July, 1944.
"The Pleasures and Pains of Ireland" (8, 5), August, 1944.
"One World" (8, 6), September, 1944.
"One World" (9, 1), October, 1944.
"On Editing a Magazine" (9, 2), November, 1944.
"The Gaelic Cult" (9, 3), December, 1944.
"One World" (9, 4), January, 1945.
"Thoughts of a Juryman" (9, 5), February, 1945.
"One World" (9, 6), March, 1945.
"Eamon De Valera" (10, 1), April, 1945; reply by M. J. MacManus, June, 1945.
"The Next Geneva" (10, 2), 1945.
"Principles and Propaganda" (10, 3), June, 1945 (reply to M. J. MacManus).
"One World" (10, 4), July, 1945.
"Romance and Realism" (10, 5), August, 1945.
"All Things Considered" (1) (11, 2), November, 1945.
"All Things Considered" (2) (11, 3), December, 1945.
"All Things Considered" (3) (11, 4), January, 1946.
"Signing Off" (12, 1), April, 1946.

Works Consulted

Bagwell, Richard. *Ireland Under the Tudors.* 3 vols. Longmans, Green

& Co., Ltd., London, 1890.

Bates, H. E. *The Modern Short Story, a Critical Survey*. Thomas Nelson & Sons, Ltd., London, 1941.

Beckett, J. C. *A Short History of Ireland*. Hutchinson University Library, London, 1952.

Blanshard, Paul. *The Irish and Catholic Power, An American Interpretation*. The Beacon Press, Boston, 1953.

Boyd, Ernest. *Ireland's Literary Renaissance* Rev. ed. Alfred A. Knopf, London, 1922.

Bromage, Mary. *DeValera and the March of a Nation*. Hutchinson & Co., London, 1956.

Burleigh, John H. S. *The City of God, A Study of St. Augustine's Philosophy*. James Nisbet & Co., Ltd., London, 1949.

Clarke, Austin. *Poetry in Modern Ireland*. Sign of the Three Candles, Dublin, 1951.

Clarke, Thomas J. *Glimpses of an Irish Felon's Prison Life*. Introduction by P. S. O'Hegarty. Maunsal & Roberts, Ltd., Dublin, 1922.

Commission of Inquiry into Banking, Currency and Credit, 1938. The Stationery Office, Dublin, 1939.

Coonan, Thomas, L. *The Irish Catholic Confederacy and the Puritan Revolution*. Clonmore & Reynolds, Ltd., Dublin, 1954.

Corkery, Daniel. *Synge and Anglo-Irish Literature*. Cork University Press, 1931.

The Hidden Ireland: A Study of Gaelic Munster in the Eighteenth Century, M. H. Gill & Son, Ltd., Dublin, 1925.

Cross, Eric. *The Tailor and Ansty*. Chapman & Hall, Ltd., 1942.

Curtis, Edmund. *A History of Ireland*. Methuen & Co., Ltd., London.

Dail Eireann, Parliamentary Debates, Official Report.

Dillon, Myles. *Early Irish Society*. Sign of the Three Candles, Dublin, 1954.

Edwards, R. Dudley, and T. Desmond Williams. *The Great Famine, Studies in Irish History, 1845–1852*. Browne & Nolan, Ltd., Dublin, 1956.

Ehler, Sidney Z., and John B. Morrall. *Church and State Through the Centuries*. The Newman Press, Westminster, Maryland, 1954.

Ehler, Sidney Z. *Twenty Centuries of Church and State*. The Newman Press, Westminster, Maryland, 1957.

Falls, Cyril. *Elizabeth's Irish Wars*. Methuen & Co., Ltd., London, 1950.

Flanagan, Thomas. *The Irish Novelists 1800–1850*. Columbia University Press, New York, 1959.

Gibbon, Monk. *The Living Torch*. With an introductory essay. Macmillan, London, 1937.

Graham, J. K. "An Historical Study of the Career of Hugh O'Neill." (Unpublished dissertation, Queen's University, Belfast).

Gwynn, Denis. *Daniel O'Connell, The Irish Liberator*. Hutchinson &
    Co., London, 1929.
_____. *O'Connell. Davia and the Colleges Bill*. Cork University Press,
    1948.
_____. *DeValera*. Jarrolds Publishers Ltd., London, 1933.
Harrold, Charles F. *John Henry Newman, An Expository and Critical
    Study of His Mind, Thought and Art*. Longmans, Green & Co.,
Heller, Erich. *The Ironic German, A Study of Thomas Mann*. Secker
    and Warburg, Ltd., London, 1958.
Henry, Paul, S.J. *Saint Augustine on Personality*. The Macmillan Co.,
    New York, 1960.
Holt, Edgar. *Protest in Arms, The Irish Troubles 1916–1923*. Putnam
    & Company, Ltd., London, 1960.
Howarth, Herbert. *The Irish Writers 1880–1940; Literature Under
    Parnell's Star*. Rockliff Publishing Company, London, 1958.
Inglis, Brian. *The Story of Ireland*. Faber and Faber, Ltd., London,
    1951.
Irwin, Clarke H. *A History of Presbyterianism in Dublin and the South
    and West of Ireland*. Hodder and Stoughton, Ltd., London, 1890.
Jones, Frederick M. *Mountjoy 1563–1606: The Last Elizabethan Dep-
    uty*. Clonmore and Reynolds, Ltd., Dublin, 1958.
Kenney, J. F. *Sources for the Early History of Ireland*. 2 vols. Columbia
    University Press, New York, 1929.
Killen, Rev. W. D. *History of Congregations of the Presbyterian
    Church in Ireland and Biographical Notices of Eminent Presby-
    terian Ministers and Laymen*. With introduction and notes by
    the Rev. W. D. Killen, D.D. James Clerland, Belfast, 1886.
Kermode, Frank. *The Romantic Image*. Routledge & Kegan Paul, Ltd.,
    London, 1957.
Macardle, Dorothy. *The Irish Republic, A Documented Chronicle of
    the Anglo-Irish Conflict and the Partitioning of Ireland of the
    Period 1916–1932*. With a preface by Eamon De Valera. Victor
    Gollancz, Ltd., London, 1937.
McDowell, R. B. *Public Opinion and Government Policy in Ireland,
    1801–1846*. Faber and Faber, Ltd., London, 1952.
MacNeill, Eoin. *Phases of Irish History*. M. H. Gill & Son, Ltd., Dub-
    lin, 1920.
_____. *Early Irish Laws and Institutions*. Burns Oates & Washbourne,
    Ltd., Dublin, 1935.
Mansergh, Nicholas. *Ireland in the Age of Revolution and Reform*.
    George Allen and Unwin, Ltd., London, 1940.
Mathews, David. *The Celtic Peoples and Renaissance Europe. A Study
    of Celtic & Spanish Influences on Elizabethan History*. Sheed &
Ward, Ltd., London, 1953.

Maxwell, Constantia. *Country and Town in Ireland Under the Georges.* Dundalgan Press, Dundalk, 1949.

Moody, T. W. *Thomas Davis 1814–1845, A Critical Address.* Hodges, Figgis & Co., Ltd., Dublin, 1945.

Murphy, Gerard, ed. *Duanaire Finn, The Book of the Lays of Fionn. Part III.* Introduction, notes, appendices and glossary by G. Murphy. Irish Texts Society, Educational Company of Ireland, Dublin, 1953.

——. *The Ossianic Lore and Romantic Tales of Medieval Ireland.* Sign of the Three Candles, Dublin, 1955.

Neider, Charles, ed. *The Stature of Thomas Mann.* New Directions Pub. Corp., New York, 1947.

O'Brien, Conor Cruise, ed. *The Shaping of Modern Ireland.* Routledge & Kegan Paul, Ltd., London, 1960.

O'Brien, R. Barry, ed. *Two Centuries of Irish History 1691–1870.* Kegan Paul, Trench, Trubner & Co., Ltd., 1907.

O'Clery, Lughaidh. *The Life of Hugh Roe O'Donnell, Prince of Tirconnell (1596–1602).* Translation by Denis Murphy, S.J. Sealy, Bryers & Walker, Dublin, 1893.

O'Connor, Frank. *An Only Child.* Macmillan & Co., Ltd., London, 1961.

O'Hegarty, P. S. *The Victory of Sinn Fein.* Talbot Press, Ltd., Dublin, 1924.

O'Rahilly, Thomas F. *Early Irish History and Mythology.* Institute for Advanced Studies, Dublin, 1946.

O'Sullivan, Donal. *The Irish Free State and Its Senate.* Faber and Faber, Ltd., London, 1940.

Pender, Seamus, ed. *Feilscribhinn Torna.* Clo Ollscoile Chorcai, 1949.

Reynolds, James A. *The Catholic Emancipation Crisis in Ireland, 1823–1829.* Yale University Press, New Haven, Connecticut, 1954.

Ryan, Desmond. *Unique Dictator, A Study of Eamon de Valera.*

Tierney, Michael, ed. *Daniel O'Connell, Nine Centenary Essays.* Browne & Nolan, Ltd., Dublin, 1949.

Trilling, Lionel. *The Liberal Imagination, Essays on Literature and Society.* Doubleday and Co., New York, 1954.

Trilling, Lionel. *The Opposing Self, Nine Essays in Criticism.* Secker and Warburg, Ltd., London, 1955.

White, Terence de Vere. *The Road of Excess.* Browne & Nolan, Ltd., Dublin, 1945.

Witherow, Thomas. *Historical and Literary Movements of Presbyterianism in Ireland, (1731–1800).* William Mullan & Sons, London, 1880.

Woodward, E. L. *The Age of Reform.* Clarendon Press, Oxford, 1938.

Criticism

Achilles, Jochen. "Sean O'Faolain: 'Unholy Living and Half Dying' and James Joyce 'Grace'. Ein Vergleich." in *Die englische und amerikanische Kurzgeschichte,* ed. Hans Bungert, Ars Interpretandi, Darmstadt, 1982.

Bonaccorso, Richard. "Sean O'Faolain's Foreign Affairs." *Eire-Ireland* (16, 2), 134-144, Summer, 1981.

Braybrooke, Neville. "Sean O'Faolain: A Study." *Dublin Magazine* (31, 2), 22–27, April–June, 1955.

Butler, Hubert. "*The Bell*: An Anglo-Irish View." *Irish University Review* (6, 1), 66-72, Spring, 1976.

Cowley, Malcolm. "Yeats and O'Faolain." *New Republic* (126), 49–50, February 15, 1939.

Craig, Patricia. "The Temperate Observer." *Times Literary Supplement,* November 7, 1980.

Craig, Patricia. "Aspects of Irishness." *Times Literary Supplement,* November 20, 1981.

Curtis, Edmund. "The Great O'Neill." *Bell* (6, 1), 66–68, April, 1943.

Dillon, Eilis. Sean O'Faolain and the Young Writer." *Irish University Review* (6, 1), 36-44, Spring, 1976.

Dillon-Malone, Aubrey. "Younger Every Day." *Books Ireland,* 192-3, November, 1978; review of *And Again?*

Doyle, Paul. *Sean O'Faolain.* Twayne Publishers, N.Y., 1968.

Doyle, Paul. "Chekhov in Erin: the short stories of Sean O'Faolain." *Dublin Review* (513), 263-8, January, 1968.

Duffy, Joseph. "A Broken World: The Finest Short Stories of Sean O'Faolain." *Irish University Review* (6, 1), 30-36, Spring, 1976.

Foley, Dermot. "Monotonously Rings the Little Bell." *Irish University Review* (6, 1), 54-62, Spring, 1976.

Hanley, Katherine. "The Short Stories of Sean O'Faolain: Theory and Practice." *Eire* (6, 3), 3-11, Fall, 1971.

Harmon, Maurice. "Sean O'Faolain: 'I Have Nobody to Vote For'." *Studies* (56), 51-60, Spring, 1967.

Harmon, Maurice (ed.). "Sean O'Faolain Special Issue." *Irish University Review* (6, 1), Spring, 1976.

Harmon, Maurice. "Sean O'Faolain." *Ireland Today,* (995), 12-16, February, 1983.

Harrod, L. V. "The Ruined Temples of Sean O'Faolain." *Eire-Ireland* (IX, I), 115-119, Spring, 1974.

Harries, Christopher. "The Hawk in Its Flight: Sean O'Faolain and the Stuffed Shirts (*The Bell*)." *Cork Review* (2, 3), 16-17, 1981.

Hopkins, Robert H. "The Pastoral Mode of Sean O'Faolain's 'The Silence of the Valley'." *Studies in Short Fiction,* (1), 93-98, Winter, 1964.

Hyman, S. E. "O'Faolain's Wonderful Fish." in *Standards: a chronicle of books for our time*, 53-56, Horizon Books, 1966.

Irish Times February 22, 1980. "Sean O'Faolain at 80."

Jenkins, Hilary. "Newman's Way and O'Faolain's Way." *Irish University Review* (6, 1), 87-94, Spring, 1976.

Kelleher, John V. "Irish Literature Today." *Atlantic Monthly* (176), March, 1945.

_____. "Sean O'Faolain." *Atlantic Monthly* (199), 67–69, May, 1957.

_____. "Matthew Arnold and the Celtic Revival" in *Perspectives of Criticism*. Harvard University Press, Cambridge, Mass., 1950.

Kiely, Benedict. "The World of Sean O'Faolain." *Irish Times*, November 22, 1980; review of *Collected Stories*.

Kosok, Heinz. "Sean O'Faolain: The Man Who Invented Sin." in *Die Englische Kurzgeschichte*, eds. Karl Heinz and Gerhard Hoffman, Bagel, Dusseldorf, 1973.

Lewis, Peter, "Ana, Anador and all." *Times Literary Supplement*, February 15, 1980; review of *And Again?*

Levander, Marianne. "Sean O'Faolain, Nationalism and the Gaelic League." *Moderna Sprak* (LXXII, 3), 257-60, 1978.

Levander, Marianne. "Sean O'Faolain and Nationalism." in *Studies in Anglo-Irish Literature* ed. Heinz Kosok, 306-313, Bouvier, Bonn, 1982.

Lyons, F. S. L. "Sean O'Faolain as Biographer." *Irish University Review* (6, 1), 95-109, Spring, 1976.

Lynch, Patrick. "O'Faolain's Way." *Bell* (18, 10), 628–31, March, 1953.

McCartney, Donal. "Sean O'Faolain: 'A Nationalist Right Enough'." *Irish University Review*, (6, 1), 73-86, Spring, 1976.

Macauley, Robie. "Sean O'Faolain, Ireland's Youngest Writer." *Irish University Review*, (6, 1), 110-117, Spring, 1976.

McMahon, Sean. "O My Youth, O My Country." *Eire* (6, 3), 145-56, Fall, 1971.

Mercier, Vivian. "The Professionalism of Sean O'Faolain." *Irish University Review* (6, 1), 45-53, Spring, 1976.

Le Moigne, Guy. "Sean O'Faolain's Short Stories." in *The Irish Short Story* ed. by P. Rafroidi and T. Brown, 205-26, Lille, 1979.

Moynahan, Julian, "God Smiles, the Priest Beams and the Novelist Groans." *Irish University Review*, (6, 1), 19-29, Spring, 1976.

Mutran, Munira H. review of *And Again? Irish University Review* (10, 1), 177-79, Spring, 1980.

Mutran, Munira H. "Some Considerations on *And Again?*" *Revista Lingua e Literatura* (9), 307-311, 1980.

O'Brien, Felim. "Daniel O'Connell: A Centenary Evaluation." *Studies* (36, 143), 257–70, September, 1947.

O'Donnell, Donat. "The Parnellism of Sean O'Faolain." *Renascence*, 3–14, Autumn, 1950. (Reprinted in *Maria Cross*, Oxford University Press, New York, 1952).

O'Donnell, Peadar. "The Irish Press and Sean O'Faolain." *Bell* (18, 2), 5–7, Summer, 1953.

O'Faolain, Julia. "Sean at Eighty." *London Magazine* (20), 18-28, June, 1980.

Rippier, Joseph Storey. *The Short Stories of Sean O'Faolain; a study in descriptive techniques.* Colin Smythe, Gerrards Cross, Bucks., 1976.

Sampson, Denis. " 'Admiring the Scenery': Sean O'Faolain's Fable of the Artist." *The Canadian Journal of Irish Studies* (111,1), 72-79, June, 1977.

Sealy, Douglas. "Dr. Faustus Irish Style." *Hibernia,* October 4, 1978.

Tierney, Michael. "The Great O'Neill." *Studies* (32, 125), 125–127, Spring, 1943.

_____. "O'Connell and Irish Democracy." *Leader* (86, 21), 492–503, July 30, 1938. "Sean O'Faolain Replies to Professor Tierney." (86, 22), 521–22, August 6, 1938. "Professor Tierney Replies to Sean O'Faolain." (86, 23), 538–39, August 13, 1938.

_____. "The Gaelic Corpse." (86, 24), 565–67, August 20, 1938. "The Corpse That Came Alive." (86, 25), 595–96, August 27, 1938.

_____. "Politics and Culture: Daniel O'Connell and the Gaelic Past." *Studies* (27), 353–80, September, 1938.

Vere White, Terence de "Terence de Vere White talks to Sean O'Faolain." *Irish Times,* April 10, 1976.

Comments by D. A. Binchy, Gerard Murphy, Fr. John Ryan, and Sean O'Faolain.

Irish Independent.

Irish Times.

Index

Abbey Theater, 44, 46, 164, 190
"Admiring the Scenery," 79, 82, 83, 85-87, 92
A.E. (George Russell), 53-55
And Again? 179-185
Angela (in "Childybawn"), 92, 113, 114
At Swim Two Birds 181
Aunt Nell (in *Come Back to Erin*), 144, 160, 171
Aunt Virginia (in *Bird Alone*), 142, 143, 177
Autobiography of Theobald Wolfe Tone, The 40

Bacon, 22, 39
Bagenal, Mabel, 25
Ballantyne, R. M., 190
Balzac, 47
"Before the Day Star", 186
Bell, The, 16, 18, 51-55, 87, 183, 185
Berenson, 191
Bergin, Kitty (in "A Touch of Autumn in the Air"), 132-134
Bernie (in "The Patriot"), 66-68, 71
Binchy, Daniel A., 17

Bird Alone, 29, 139, 141-143, 148-153, 156-160, 166, 169, 172, 174, 176-178, 194
Blake, Michael, 14
Bloom (in *Ulysses*), 171
"Born Genius, A," 79, 82, 83
Boswell, 52
Bowen, Elizabeth, 168
Bradley, Edward (in "The Patriot"), 66-68,71
Brand, 161
"Broken World, A," 11, 71-79, 81, 83, 91, 93, 95, 110
Browne, Noel 15, 16, 201-03
Browne, Sir Thomas, 86

Calvert, Mrs. (in "One True Friend"), 110
Canon, the (in "Sinners"), 79, 83-85
Canty, Mrs. (in "Unholy Living and Half Dying"), 112, 115
Cardew, Jacky (in "Unholy Living and Half Dying"), 112-115, 197
Carleton, William, 28
Cashen, Daniel (in "A Touch of Autumn in the Air"), 132-134
Catholic Church, xii, xiv, 6, 7, 11-17, 39,

233

42, 48-51, 54, 167, 172, 187, 192, 193, 200-03

Celtic Dagda, 102

Censorship, 48-50, 167

"Childybawn," 92, 112, 113

Chekhov, 88, 90, 170

Civil War, xii, 32, 38, 45, 64, 65, 96, 153, 165, 170, 183

Clarke, Austin, 49

Clarke, Tom, 141

Coeur Simple, Un, 169

Coleridge 181

Colum, Padraic, 55, 164

Come Back to Erin, 30, 139, 152-154, 160-163, 177

Conolly, James, 42, 43, 45, 193

Conrad, 132

Constance Markievicz, 44, 140, 193

Constitution of 1937, 35, 39, 40, 42

Cooke, Henry, 14

Corkery, Daniel, 48, 49, 52, 169

Costello, Mr., 16, 17, 201, 203

Cotter, Sarah (in "I Remember, I Remember"), 134-136

Crone, Corney (in *Bird Alone*), 29, 30, 141-144, 148-152, 154-160, 163, 166, 167, 170, 172-174, 176, 177, 194

Crone, Philip (in *Bird Alone*), 141-144, 148, 149, 176, 177, 194

Dante, 125, 158

Davis, 14

"Dead Cert, The" 187

Dedalus, Stephen, 156, 158, 171

De Valera, Eamon, 4, 12, 32-45, 48, 80, 140, 152, 154, 183

Diarmaid and Grainne, 126

"Discord," 80, 83, 85-88, 92

"Dividends," 188

Donnell, Leo (in *A Nest of Simple Folk*), 140, 141, 143-145, 147, 148, 155, 167, 174-176, 192-94

Dostoevsky, 170

Dubliners, 164, 169, 171

Dunne, Larry (in "The End of a Good Man"), 92

Easter Rising of 1916, x-xii, 141, 192

Edgeworth, Maria, 28

Electoral Amendment Bill, 36

"End of a Good Man, The," 92

Exiles, 161

"Faithless Wife, The" 186

Falling Rocks, Narrowing Road, Cul-de-Sac, Stop" 186, 188

Famine, The, 30, 144, 145

Father Peter (in "Discord"), 80, 85, 86, 88

Faulkner, William, 168

Faust, 30, 78, 142, 151

"Feed My Lambs" 186

Fenians, 141, 142, 148, 149, 162, 172, 191, 194

Finest Stories of Sean O'Faolain, The, 62, 66

Flannery, Robert (in "The Lovers of the Lake"), 115-128, 197

Flaubert, 81, 169, 172

Foreign Affairs, 185

"Fugue," 65, 66, 68, 70, 71, 191.

"Fur Coat, The," 91

Garnett, Edward, xv, 47, 48

Goethe, 181

Gogarty, St. John, 44

Goldberg, S. L., 159

Gould, Eileen, xi, xiii, xiv

Grattan, 13, 15

Gray, 86

Great O'Neill, The, 19-31, 173, 194

Greene, Graham, 168

Hanafan (in "Admiring the Scenery"), 79, 82, 86, 87, 94

Hannafey, Bea (in *Come Back to Erin*), 160, 162, 163

Hannafey, Frankie (in *Come Back to Erin*), 30, 31, 143, 144, 152-155, 160-163, 167, 171, 174, 178

Heat of the Sun, The, 62, 136, 197-99, 185

Hemingway, Ernest, 168

Henty, G. A., 190

Hidden Ireland, The, 48

Hogan, Josephine (in *Come Back to Erin*), 153

Holiday, 196

Hugo, Victor 181

Hussey, Denis (in *A Nest of Simple Folk*), x, 140, 141, 143-148, 152, 154-157, 160, 166, 174-176, 192

Huxley, Aldous, 168

"Hymeneal", 186

Ibsen, 161

"In the Bosom of the County", 186, 187

'I Remember! I Remember!', 134-136

Irish, The, 41, 101

Irish Journey, An, 45

Irish Statesman, The, 53, 55

James, Henry, 46, 47
Jenny (in "The Lovers of the Lake"), 115-128
John Bull's Other Island, 190
Joyce, James, 44, 46, 54, 57, 155-159, 164, 165, 168, 169, 171, 173, 174

Kafka, 169
Kelleher, John V., 4, 162
King of the Beggars, a Life of Daniel O'Connell, the Irish Liberator, 3-18, 28, 29, 34, 49, 140, 173
Kittredge, George Lyman, xiv

Lady Gregory, 54, 170
"Lady Lucifer,"a 94, 95, 100
Lake, The, 164
Laws of Life, 50
Lenihan, Pat (in "A Born Genius"), 79, 82
Leonard (in *Come Back to Erin*), 153, 162
Lever, Charles, 28
"Liars", 186
Liberal Imagination, The, 47
Literary Revival, 45, 164, 165, 169
Lombard, Bishop, 31
"Lonely Woman, The," 109
"Lovers of the Lake, The," 92, 108, 115-129, 197

MacCumhaill, Finn, 102
MacManus, M. J., 4
Magee, 10
"Man Who Invented Sin, The," 62, 80, 95-100, 111
Mann, 169
Markievicz, Constance, 37, 45
Mary (in "I Remember! I Remember!"), 134-136
Maupassant, 87
Maynooth, 16
Midsummer Night Madness, xv, 47, 48, 61, 64-68, 79, 83, 165, 192
Moore, George, 44, 54, 164, 165, 169, 171, 173
Moore, Mrs. (in "One True Friend"), 109-112
Mother and Child Scheme, 15-17, 200-03
"Mother Matilda's Book," 80
Murphy, Gerard 17
Murray, T. C., 164
"My Son Austin," 83

Neider, Charles, 28
Newman, Cardinal, 17, 196

Nest of Gentle Folks, A, 169, 170
Nest of Simple Folk, A, x, 139-141, 145-148, 169, 170, 174, 192
New Ireland, 12, 15, 32, 52, 98, 145, 167, 194
Norah (in "The Patriot"), 66-68

Oath of Allegiance, 33, 35, 36, 38
O'Brien, Flann, 181
O'Connell, Daniel, 3-15, 17-20, 24-32, 34, 38, 39, 43, 51, 55, 56, 144, 192, 195
O'Connor, Frank, 49, 52, 55, 57, 165, 169, 170
O'Flaherty, Liam, 49, 52, 165, 169, 171
"Old Master, The," 79, 82, 90
O'Leary, John, 43, 141
"One Man, One Boat, One Girl", 188
"One Night in Turin," 130
"One True Friend", 92, 109-112
O'Neill, Hugh, 4, 19-32, 51, 55, 56, 144, 195, 196
O'Sullilvan, John Aloysius (in "The Old Master"), 79, 82, 90
O'Sullivan, Seumas, 55
"Our Fearful Innocence", 187

Parnell, 43, 141, 143, 148, 149, 158, 172, 194
"Patriot, The," 65-68, 70, 71, 88, 110, 192
Patriots, 190
"Planets of the Years", 186, 188
Poe, 181
Portrait of the Artist as a Young Man, A, 155, 159, 171
Provost, 181
Priest, the (in "A Broken World"), 71-79, 81, 95
Proust, 169
Purse of Coppers, A, 11, 61, 62, 69-80, 82, 83, 87, 88, 92-95, 139, 156, 160, 194, 195

Raleigh, 22
Republicans, xii, xiii, 32, 33, 35, 36, 38, 40, 65, 152, 160, 162
Rilke, 169
Robinson, F. N., xiv
Robinson, Lennox, 164, 180, 190, 191
Roche, Kennedy F., 13

Samhain, 53
Sartre, 185
Shaw, George Bernard, 48, 190
Sherlock, Elsie (in *Bird Alone*), 148-151, 172, 173, 177

Short Story, The, 87, 88, 90-92

Short Stories, A Study in Pleasure, 129

Sidney, Sir Henry, 22

"Silence of the Valley, The," 92, 100-106, 119

"Sinners," 79, 83-85, 90, 92

"Something, Everything, Anything, Nothing", 186

South to Sicily, 197

Spillane, Benjy (in "Childybawn"), 92, 113, 114, 197

Sportsman's Notebook, A, 169, 170

Stella (in *Bird Alone*), 157, 158, 177

Stendhal, 140, 185

Stephens, James, 44, 54, 55, 141

Stevenson, R. L., 190

St. John (in *Come Back to Erin*) 153, 161, 178

Study of the Rise of Modern Irish Democracy, 1775-1847, A, 3

Sunday Chronicle, The, 33

"O'Sullivan's Trousers," 80

Sutherland, Halliday, 50

Synge, 54, 171

Synge and Anglo-Irish Literature, 49

"Talking Trees, The", 185, 186, 187

Teresa, 62, 89, 90, 92, 178

"Teresa," 89, 90, 92

Tinsley, Arthur (in *Bird Alone*), 142

Tolstoy, 170

Tone, Theobald Wolfe, 10, 13, 32, 40, 43

"Touch of Autumn in the Air, A," 131, 132

Trilling, Lionel, 47

"Trout, The," 91

Turgenev, 169-171

Ulysses, 159

"Unholy Living and Half Dying," 112

Untilled Field, The, 164, 169

Valery, 169

Vanishing Hero, The, 156, 168

Vive Moi!, viii, 62

Waugh, Evelyn, 168

Woolf, Virginia, 168

Yale Review, 12, 34, 166

Yeats, 4, 24, 44, 46, 53, 54, 141, 164, 166, 169, 170, 171, 173, 174

Younger, Robert (in *And Again?*), 179-185

Zola, 171